EMSI.

Rick Bretton

SHANE COMES HOME

ALSO BY RINKER BUCK

Flight of Passage: A Memoir
First Job: A Memoir of Growing Up at Work

WILLIAM MORROW
An Imprint of HarperCollins*Publishers*

SHANE COMES HOME

Rinker Buck

PHOTOGRAPH CREDITS: pages 54, 69, 137, 210: Steven G. Smith/Corbis; 162: Jonna Walker; 238: Steven G. Smith

HarperCollins books may be purchased for educational, business, or sales promotional use. For information please write: Special Markets Department, HarperCollins Publishers Inc., 10 East 53rd Street, New York, NY 10022.

FIRST EDITION

Designed by Renato Stanisic
Illustration of Childers house by Sara Buck

Printed on acid-free paper

Library of Congress Cataloging-in-Publication Data has been applied for.

ISBN 0-06-059325-3

05   06   07   08   09   DIX/RRD   10   9   8   7   6   5   4   3   2   1

This book is respectfully dedicated to the exceptional marine depicted in its pages, First Lieutenant Therrel Shane Childers. All of us have a Shane or two in our lives, but I doubt that the world will ever again see another quite like this one.

SEMPER FIDELIS, SHANE CHILDERS

The Marines' Hymn

From the halls of Montezuma
To the shores of Tripoli,
We fight our country's battles
In the air, on land, and sea.
First to fight for right and freedom,
And to keep our honor clean,
We are proud to claim the title
Of United States Marines.

Our flag's unfurl'd to every breeze
From dawn to setting sun;
We have fought in every clime and place
Where we could take a gun.
In the snow of far-off northern lands
And in sunny tropic scenes,
You will find us always on the job–
The United States Marines.

Here's health to you and to our Corps
Which we are proud to serve;
In many a strife we've fought for life
And never lost our nerve.
If the Army and the Navy
Ever look on Heaven's scenes,
They will find the streets are guarded
By United States Marines.

CONTENTS

A CALL IN THE MORNING

A t 4:30 in the morning on Friday, March 21, 2003, while Americans on the East Coast were waking up to the first news reports about the invasion of Iraq, the commander of a small United States Marine Corps reserve detachment in Billings, Montana, was awakened by an urgent phone call. Later, Captain Kevin Hutchison would recall that he had slept poorly the night before, and not simply because his house was under renovation and he'd spent the night on a spare combat mattress on the hardwood sill of his bedroom bay window. He was also depressed. No marine enjoys being left behind while his fellow officers are fighting overseas, and Hutchison had spent Thursday night watching *Nightline* and CNN, fitfully dozing off to the images of military convoys massing at the border of Iraq. As the cameras panned south, the long formations of tanks, Humvees, and light armored vehicles thinning off into the sands reminded him of his own humiliating distance from the war. But now the vast terrain between the deserts of Iraq and the Montana high country were about to be joined.

Hutchison was an unusual marine. A suave, worldly Californian–

bookish and sensitive, almost to a fault–he had nevertheless succeeded brilliantly in the man's-man world of the marine officer corps.
At thirty-three, he was one of the marine's most highly rated and
youngest captains. Qualified with "expert" rankings in underwater
demolition, parachute jumping, reconnaissance, and mountain and
river warfare, Hutchison had led rifle platoons in Okinawa and Greece
and, because of his fluency in Spanish, drawn several plum assignments in Latin America during the late 1990s. In Peru, where he had
spent eighteen months training counter-drug police, he had acquired a
stunning Peruvian girlfriend and spent long romantic weekends with
her camping out in an elevated, Tarzan-style "jungle-hut" that he had
built from driftwood along the broad, sandy banks of a river outside
Lima. Blond, rail-thin, as charmingly earnest as he was tough, Hutchison epitomized the sort of glamorous image promoted by those
catchy marine recruitment spots–"The Few. The Proud"–broadcast
during the halftimes of weekend NFL games.

Over the past year, however, Hutchison's dream existence as a
globe-trotting marine had come to a dispiriting end. As part of a routine noncombat rotation used to season young officers, he had been
assigned to lead the small training battalion in Billings that handled
all marine affairs across a broad expanse of the west, a five-state area
running from the Dakotas to Idaho. Now his days were filled with
the humdrum details of running a military command in backwater
Montana–whipping out-of-shape weekend warrior reservists through
training exercises, fielding requests to provide marine details for
Memorial Day parades or the openings of new car lots, providing
color guards and gun salutes for the funerals of Greatest Generation
World War II marines who, with lugubrious regularity, were dying off
as the new century progressed.

Indeed, by late March that year, Hutchison's mood had reached
a typically conflicted state. He had just returned from a seven-week
Winter Mountain Leaders Course at a marine camp in the Sierra

Nevada mountains near Lake Tahoe, California. The grueling regimen of forced marches on cross-country skis, winter camping in the peaks, and precision night reconnaissance had left Hutchison feeling strangely refreshed, even euphoric about his marine career. But when he returned to his office inside a modern, low-rise armory on the outskirts of Billings, a mountain of paperwork and personnel hassles had accumulated on his desk. It was grim, getting back to staff work.

Then there was Iraq, of course. Hutchison had his own views about the Bush Doctrine of preemptive strikes against perceived enemies like Saddam Hussein, but he was too discreet an officer to express many reservations to his fellow marines. The disquiet he felt was more personal than that. Most of his closet friends in the marines had been deployed to Iraq, and now they were massed along the berms of northern Kuwait in their speedy, light armored vehicles, waiting to head north through the sands for Nasiriya, Najaf, and Baghdad. For Hutchison, being left behind in Billings didn't raise issues of machismo or bravery—he had always disliked the false manhood bravado affected by many marines, just as he distrusted the ritualized patriotism of politicians who invoked the flag while placing soldiers in harm's way. He was tormented, instead, by an intellectual riddle, typical for the highly educated and motivated warrior class of officers attracted to the all-volunteer American military after the draft was abolished in 1973.

He had spent the last nine years, the best of his life, becoming one of the most highly trained military officers of his generation. But he had always been insatiably curious about one thing. Did all this preparation and sacrifice—the constant moves and reassignments, year after year of physical conditioning, the parachute jumps, underwater dives, mountain rescues in the snow, the endless training classes—really amount to anything? In the real-time exhaustion and confusion of war, could he lead men under fire? The question had nagged him for years, and returned as an unresolved agony as the long buildup for Iraq had begun the summer before. By then, he had grown to love the American west, especially his weekend training forays across the mountains and high rolling plains of Montana and Wyoming, but, still, he felt trapped in Billings. Through the fiat of assignment, the only war he would probably have a chance to fight in, his first real opportunity to prove himself and answer the riddle, had passed him by.

That despairing thought still troubled him, early that Friday morning, as Hutchison fitfully endured his half-sleep on the sill of his bedroom bay window.

But now in the gray vagueness of dawn, the ringing phone was calling him to other service. Outside the lawns were silvery with frost, and tiny orbs of pink and cobalt light, thrown down as the sun rose against the rimrock plateaus surrounding Billings, danced in the sky. The air was still and cold—the kind of glorious western morning that Hutchison normally enjoyed. Shaking off his incomplete sleep, he stepped across the newly refinished hardwood floors of his bedroom and picked up the phone. He immediately recognized the voice of his gruff but personable second-in-command, First Sergeant Barry Morgan.

"Sir. Sorry to wake you so early, but . . ."

"That's all right Barry. It must be important. What's up?"

"Sir, shit. Shit, shit, shit. We've got a CACO. There's a young marine from Powell, Wyoming, who's been killed in Iraq already. Sir, all we know is that he was a platoon leader from First Battalion. He took it in the gut while taking a pumping station in the Rumaila oil field. Second Lieutenant Therrel Shane Childers."

"Ah, fuck, Barry. Fuck."

"Fuck is right, sir. It's a CACO from Iraq and we've got it."

Hutchison tensed in his chest and his arms, swirled by contradictory emotions. CACO is a military acronym for Casualty Assistance Calls Officer, and Hutchison was familiar with the elaborate procedures for notifying the parents of a deceased marine, and knew that the Marine Corps was meticulous to the point of obsession about proper military burials and caring for families of their own. The previous summer, he and Morgan had handled the case of a young marine recruit from Deer Lodge, Montana, who had died during swimming training at a marine base in Corpus Christi, Texas. The experience of dealing with a grieving, single mother had been emotionally draining, and a CACO case also tended to overwhelm the meager resources of a small command like Billings. Seven months after they had buried the young marine who died in Texas, they were still filling out paperwork and hassling with the Casualty Assistance Branch at Marine Corps headquarters in Quantico, Virginia.

Hutchison was overcome by another feeling. A skeptical intellectual who enjoyed spoofing everything, including the bureaucratic foibles and platitudes of the Marine Corps, he could nevertheless turn instantly somber and impassioned—corny, even—when it came to duty, honor, service for a fellow marine and his family. These values meant everything to him. Welling up, almost as if he could cry, Hutchison blurted out the first thing that came to mind, even though it meant exposing his emotions to the infinitely more grounded and realistic First Sergeant Morgan.

"Oh Christ, Barry. Why couldn't this have been me? I could have been over there and taken this bullet. I *wanted* to be over there. I don't want to tell this guy's parents. Why couldn't it have been me?"

"Sir, I know. I know. It should have been *me*. But godammit, it wasn't and now we've got a CACO on our hands and we've got to do it. And, sir, there's another thing."

"What's that?" Hutchison said.

"Sir, Quantico is already all over us on this thing," Morgan said. "Second Lieutenant Childers will be identified as the first killed in action in Iraq. The press is already calling. We've got to do a next-of-kin notification fast, and we've got to do it right. We *can't* fuck up. Can't."

What his sergeant said shook Hutchison into action. But first he was momentarily distracted by a queer brain meld, a play of light against his memories of the night before. Glancing outside, Hutchison could see that the light thrown down by the rimrock plateaus had grown to slender pastel ribbons, pale blues and reds bleached onto a wispy cirrus sky. A light mist was rising from the condensing frost on the lawns. The watercolor sky and the ghostly tendrils of mist carried him back to his fitful thoughts of the night before, then back to the present. Iraq. Desert sky. Montana high country. The first CACO of the war, way out here. What were the chances of that?

But the changing light had also forced him through to a hard thought, as strong as a spiritual agenda.

Fuck it, captain. Get a grip. You'll never lead men in combat. You'll never know. But you will know if you get this right. There's a family down in Powell. Waiting. Your command will be watching. They'll see how you react.

"All right, first sergeant," Hutchison said. "I'm leaving for the office right away, and you should too. I want the entire staff in for this. Wake them all up."

Hutchison crisply instructed Morgan to break out all their CACO manuals, and the Marine CACO training video, which the entire command would watch. Any important work that they had that day should be rerouted to the junior sergeants, and he wanted Morgan to dig up everything he could on Lieutenant Childers and his family. If the small Billings battalion didn't have all the paperwork they needed to apply for benefits and assistance for the family, he should have it faxed from Marine Corps headquarters at Quantico. Hutchison wanted a government vehicle gassed, cash, maps, phone numbers, and anything else they needed for the drive to Powell.

"Where the hell is Powell anyway, Barry?"

"Fuck if I know, sir. But I will by the time you reach the office."

"I want to be on the road by seven thirty," Hutchison said.

"Done," Morgan said.

Hutchison quickly showered and shaved and dressed in his usual street clothes of crisp blue jeans and a polo shirt—at smaller commands like Billings, marines changed into their uniforms at the office—and decided to skip his morning ritual of brewing gourmet coffee so that he could race into the office. When he stepped outside, however, his car wouldn't start. On a captain's salary, with a major home renovation underway, the only vehicle Hutchison could afford was an eight-hundred-dollar battered Toyota diesel pickup, which earned him a lot of ribbing around the Billings command when the other marines learned that Hutchison called his wheels "Sugar." But now, cranking the starter over and over again in the cold morning air, coaxing and cursing so much that his breath froze the inside of the windshield, he couldn't get Sugar going.

"Ah, fuck, Sugar. C'mon. Not today. I've got a CACO."

Hutchison gave Sugar a ten-minute rest and stepped back inside to brew coffee after all. When he walked back outside, the diesel fired on his first try.

"Okay, bitch. Sorry, sorry," Hutchison said, patting the steering wheel. "Now, just get me to the armory."

And so, jittery about the day he faced, his mind racing with the multitude of tasks to be performed before he left for Powell, Hutchison slipped out of his driveway and headed north along the quiet residential streets of the university district in Billings. As he merged into the light morning traffic downtown, no one watching him pass could have guessed the importance or drama of his mission that day, the awful news that he carried for a family down over the snowy rim of the Bighorns. He was just another driver in a faded pickup with Montana plates, spewing a sooty contrail of diesel exhaust as he stopped for the lights. At the interstate, Hutchison turned right and climbed the ramp. Then the freshly assigned CACO, the first of America's new war, disappeared toward work under a red Montana sky.

* * *

Hutchison was momentarily relieved when he reached the ground-floor suite of offices of the Marine Corps Company B, Fourth Reconnaissance Battalion at the armory in suburban Billings. A dozen enlisted men were scurrying around in response to the orders that First Sergeant Morgan had issued when he reached the armory fifteen minutes earlier. A young private was chasing between the fax machine and the copier, assembling in neat piles the enormous load of paperwork–forms for death benefits, forms for cancellation of bank accounts, forms for confirmation of awards, more than thirty in all–required to process a CACO case. The battalion mechanic was outside, washing and gassing one of the unit's Chevy Suburbans. Another private sat staring intently at his computer and manning the phones, compiling into a loose-leaf notebook MapQuest directions to Powell, lists of phone numbers, and a log of calls that had already arrived from the Casualty Assistance branch in Virginia. No one was saying very much and the usual Friday morning banter and the throwing around of full bags of doughnuts had been abandoned. Morgan had obviously taken command of all the details and whipped the unit into shape. This would free Hutchison to concentrate on the two matters he knew would be most important all day–reporting "up" to Marine Corps headquarters in Virginia, and steeling himself emotionally to confront the Childers family down in Wyoming.

Information, too, would be vital. From his earlier CACO work, Hutchison was aware that families were often desperate for precise information–how their son had died, whether he'd suffered or lingered long in a field hospital–that served as a kind of shock relief in the hours after they learned of the death. But he knew he would be able to provide the Childers family with very little detail about how their son had died, beyond the routine information that he'd been shot while leading his platoon at the Rumaila oil field. An autopsy would not be performed until Childers's body reached the joint-services mortuary at Dover Air Force Base in Delaware, which could probably take over a week. A full battlefield report, which wouldn't even be written until Childers' unit finished its long march north to Baghdad, or perhaps even until they returned to the United States, was probably months away.

But Hutchison knew that he could probably comfort the family with other knowledge. He wanted to arrive at the house with as complete a picture of Lieutenant Childers as he could obtain, appearing before the family not as a stranger, an anonymous bearer of devastating news, but instead as a marine officer who was considerate enough to have familiarized himself with their son's record and accomplishments in the service. Marines are fortunate in this respect. Detailed, computerized profiles of every marine in service–their Basic Individual Record and Basic Training Record–are available to officers on a marine personnel website. Childers' records had already been printed up by the time Hutchison arrived at the armory. After verifying all their other forms against a CACO manual checklist, Hutchison and Morgan sat at a table together and read up on Childers.

They quickly realized that Childers had been an exemplary, even remarkable, marine. After enlisting in the U.S. Marines fresh out of high school in Gulfport, Mississippi, in 1990, Childers had scored high marks at boot camp in Parris Island, South Carolina, and then at a Light Armored Driver's course in California. Eight months after enlisting, Childers had briefly served in combat during the Persian Gulf War. After seasoning in a combat platoon at Camp Lejeune, North Carolina, Childers had been selected for a particularly coveted duty, marine security guard service at foreign embassies, and eventually had been stationed at embassies and consulates in Geneva; Paris; and Nairobi, Kenya. In a variety of disciplines–platoon tactics, light armored reconnaissance, guard command, and especially physical fitness–Childers had consistently achieved the highest training and personal evaluations, and scored average in only one area, marksmanship.

But one achievement stood out. Childers was what the marines called a prior enlist, one of a handful of grunts picked every year for promotion from the enlisted to commissioned officer ranks. After returning from a Western Pacific cruise in 1998, he had used the Marine Enlisted Commissioning Education Program to enroll at the prestigious military academy, The Citadel, in Charleston, South Carolina, where he graduated with honors after just three years and was commissioned as a second lieutenant. After basic officers' training and infantry-tactics school, he was assigned to the Fifth Marine Division at Camp Pendleton just north of San Diego. Within a year, Childers had already achieved every young marine officer's dream—leading a rifle platoon in combat. He'd spent exactly twelve hours doing that before he was shot in Iraq.

The butterflies in Hutchison's stomach returned and his arms felt weak. He couldn't remember the last time he confronted a Basic Individual Record this strong. The subtle social connotations of a basic record, the character and personal choices implied by the raw test scores and the climb through the ranks, fascinated him, and he was particularly drawn to Childers' prior enlist status. Was he one of those soldiers, like so many Hutchison had met, who had discovered himself in the military and become the first in his family to finish college? Hutchison loved that aspect of the military, how it acted as a social safety net, catapulting so many toward their first real shot at success in the civilian world. But maybe Childers had left home early for some other reason, only to be nagged later by his relatives to follow the family tradition toward a college degree. Which was it? Hutchison didn't know, but in life—as with his death as the first killed in action in Iraq—Childers seemed to possess almost totemic significance as a model marine.

When Morgan looked up from the records, rubbing his hand through the stubble of his hair, Hutchison knew exactly what he was going to say. Fleetingly he recalled a distant curriculum point from

basic officers' school, which was that a command was probably working well when an officer and his noncom could always read each
other's thoughts. Morgan, a former drill sergeant, was so obsessive
about guns that he was already teaching his two-year-old son how to
break apart a rifle. Hutchison loved to needle his first sergeant about
that, goading him about being such a hardass, overparenting his
young son. He was pretty sure Morgan would focus on this one, relatively minor, weakness in Childers' record.

"God, captain, this guy's a real star," Morgan said. "The only thing
he couldn't do was shoot."

"Marksmanship isn't everything, sergeant. Childers has an ex-
traordinary record."

"I know, sir, I know. I don't want to face this family."

"No," Hutchison said. "This isn't going to be easy."

Before they left, Hutchison and Morgan stepped into their offices
to change into the dress blue uniforms required for a next-of-kin notification. They emerged a few minutes later in their pressed woolen
dress blue slacks and spit-polished oxfords, with their white caps
tucked under their arms. Because they didn't want their dress-blue
tunics to wrinkle during the hour-and-a-half drive to Wyoming, they
carried these thrown over their shoulders on dry-cleaning hangers,
with the clear plastic covering drooping down below their waists. Or-
dering their eleven-member command to assemble near the door,
Hutchison and Morgan stood facing their men in crisp white T-shirts.

Hutchison was feeling tremendous pressure, and he was still
battling emotionally to keep this from his men. Speedy next-of-kin notification was particularly important in this case not only because
Lieutenant Childers' status as the first killed-in-action was almost
certain to draw intense media attention. Under marine regulations,
CACO officers are officially designated as the personal representative
of the commandant of the Marine Corps, and he knew he would be
evaluated carefully for his performance. From Quantico, faxes and

phone messages were already backed up, demanding to know if Hutchison and Morgan had left for Wyoming yet.

But Hutchison felt stubborn about it. He wasn't going to be rushed.

"Men," he began, "there's a colonel back in Quantico who's called three times already demanding that we do this in a hurry. Some of you have talked to him already. But we're not going to do that. We're going to do this *right*. You got that? *Right*. Whatever this family needs in the next two weeks? Two months? Years? I don't care. That's what we're going to do for them. Short of war, this is the most important duty you'll ever face, and don't any of you forget it."

A chorus of "Yes, sir," echoed off the walls as Hutchison and Morgan briskly saluted and marched out through the door.

As they walked side-by-side toward their Chevrolet Suburban in the armory garage, the dry-cleaning plastic covering their tunics gently lifted above their backs, catching the first light from the prairie streaming in through the large overhead doors.

Hutchison and Morgan drove west on Interstate 90 for several miles, turning south for the Wyoming line at Laurel. They were businesslike and glum as they passed down through the badland country of Rockvale and Edgar, quietly reviewing their CACO files, rehearsing what they'd say to the Childers family. Marine regulations stipulated that CACO officers calling on a family should always begin, "We regret to inform you," but Hutchison and Morgan had already concluded that this was drivel out of a Hollywood script. They'd say whatever the hell came to their hearts first, depending on what they found there, who the Childers were. The important thing, they agreed, was to let the family know that they felt this loss too, that they were going to be there for the Childers for as long as they were needed.

After Bridger the sun finally poked through and the countryside changed, gradually giving way to the irrigated wheat fields and extensive ranch lands along the Clark's Fork of the Yellowstone River. The snowy crests of several discrete mountain ranges–the Pryors directly to the east, the Beartooths and Yellowstone Park to the south and west, and the massive, dreamy folds of the Bighorns dominating the horizon farther south–changed from gray to lavender and then hard blue as the sun rose against the Continental Divide. The two marines were more talkative now, even laughing, relieving their anxiety by falling back on the gently mocking humor that had always marked their relationship. Hutchison enjoyed chiding Morgan about his gun collection and the big, chrome-encrusted Harley-Davidson Classic Road King that took up a whole bay in his garage. Morgan considered his commanding officer a hopeless "wienie" for owning a Vespa motor scooter and for reading too many books.

Hutchison particularly loved one aspect of the American West. The big, soulful landscapes, with the aperture of light changing around every river bend or mountain pass, could profoundly alter and elevate his mood. As they approached Powell from the north, they crossed a long alkali plain surrounded by a massive, U-shaped formation called the Polecat Bench. Even in a speeding SUV, this stretch of high desert took more than thirty minutes to cross. The unforgiving terrain and the crepuscular shafts of light thrown down through holes in the overcast made Hutchison feel moody, almost manic. Since arriving in Montana the summer before he'd spent a great deal of his free time touring the neighboring Indian reservations, all the battlefields and western museums, and his tables and shelves at home overflowed with books about General Custer and Lewis and Clark, Chief Joseph, Red Cloud, and Crazy Horse. Driving anywhere on the high plains, even on a mission like this, reminded him of the long continuum of history way out here. To him, the vast mosaic of badlands and wheat fields, encompassed by the snowy Bighorns, conveyed both the limitless opportunity and the despair of a hard western land.

Powell, a farm-and-ranch town of five thousand just east of Cody, was surprisingly tidy and prosperous—not at all the shuttered and derelict downtown that Hutchison had come to expect after several months of traveling the agricultural West. The main commercial thoroughfare running off Route 14A, North Bent Street, was wide and long in the old western style, with thriving hardware, book, and furniture stores, two barbershops, even a pharmacy with an old-fashioned soda fountain stand. A mural painted on a building near a pedestrian mall advertised that the town was named after the famed western explorer and irrigation-system developer, John Wesley Powell. Hutchison also saw a small Homesteader Museum on the edge of town, near a restored railroad siding, and made a mental note to check it out.

Hutchison and Morgan lost almost an hour meandering around the lonely section roads west of town, trying to find the Childers place by consulting their maps. The mixed-use agricultural area was dotted with small cattle-raising operations, horse farms, and the occasional luxury vacation house. In other spots, concrete irrigation canals feeding immense barley and sugar-beet fields interrupted the grid pattern of the roads, resulting in frequent, unmarked dead ends. The CACO detail finally gave up and wandered back into town to ask for directions at the police station and the post office. For two reconnaissance officers who were supposed to know their way around, this proved embarrassing, but it was also quite tricky. The CACO rulebook stipulated that they remain inconspicuous and not inform anyone of their reason for being in town until they had made the next-of-kin notification directly to the family. It was almost 10 A.M. by the time they located the small, ramshackle Childers ranch three miles from town, just over the first rise on Road 12.

Pulling past the driveway, they parked down the hill, beside a small irrigation sluice roaring with the spring overflow from the nearby Shoshone River. Retrieving their tunics and caps from the car, they dressed and then gave each other a last-minute inspection.

"Ah, shit, sir," Morgan said. "Here goes nothing. I don't think I can stand the hurt we're about to bring to these people."

"Barry, I know, I know. Let's just be as personal as we can. They've got to know that we'll take care of them."

"Sir. Yes."

And so, their wheels turning up a gentle plume of dust, unaware of the high drama still left in their day, or the remarkable family saga they were about to confront, they drove up the rise and turned in for the house.

A Rumor in Town

The Childers house was a modest wood-frame structure with eaves facing east and west and simple, shed-roof additions slapped onto either side. The rubble from an unfinished foundation project was piled in front of the kitchen window and mounds of rusted farm machinery, lumber, and irrigation pipe were haphazardly scattered around the yard, almost as if God's Little Acre of Appalachia had been transported whole to northern Wyoming. Out back, a dozen swayback jackasses, mules, and horses browsed among the hay piles of a dusty corral.

"Oh Christ, sir," Morgan said. "Look at this place. Now we've got to go in there and tell them that the star of the family is dead."

"Yes," Hutchison said thoughtfully. "This marine has got to be a huge deal for this family."

"Huge," Morgan said. "Huge."

For Hutchison, that moment seemed to reprise nine years of social conditioning in the marines. His own upbringing had been privileged. Hutchison's father was the CEO of a successful industrial waste company in California, and he had been raised in a spacious, meticulously decorated contemporary perched on the cliffs of Palos Verdes south of Los Angeles, with spectacular views down to the surf at Haggerty's Reef and west over the Pacific Ocean. Every Christmas his family vacationed along Mexico's west coast and he often spent Thanksgiving and Easter at his father's hunting camp in Arizona. But most of the officers and enlisted men he met in the marines had been raised on military bases, or in the trailer parks or gritty blue-collar neighborhoods of the South and Midwest. With such different backgrounds and none of the advantages that he enjoyed, how had so many of them succeeded? This was another riddle of military life that endlessly fascinated Hutchison and the experience humbled him every time.

At the door of the house, a small decal with the Marine Corps insignia was affixed to the pane of glass just above the handle. PROUD FAMILY OF A UNITED STATES MARINE. But when they rang the doorbell and then knocked more loudly on the door, no one seemed to be home.

Exasperated, feeling slightly creepy about it, the two marines circuited the house, knocking on every door, as if they were staking out a stranger's house, or poking through a ghost town. The Childers place amazed them. Beside the house, an antique wooden sleigh was parked at an angle on the lawn, as if it had just been unhitched, and old iron-wheeled sickle-bar cutters, harrows, and tractor implements climbed the side hill. In the jumble of barns and sheds out back, every doorway was filled to the rafters with blacksmithing and welding equipment, harness and antique cavalry saddles, a collection of one-horse plows and piles of chains, come-alongs, acid-stained batteries, and tools. This could have been the storage annex of the Smithsonian Institution, or maybe the restoration shop of a prairie museum somewhere, and they were enormously intrigued about the Childerses now, and frustrated that no one was around. Their CACO manuals, which seemed to have provided for every conceivable contingency, made no provision for this, the most obvious of possibilities: that no one was home. The intense emotions that had built from dawn, and which should have climaxed here, were now deflated.

Hutchison and Morgan drove back out to the section road and stopped at the closest house, a gray clapboard ranch just across the road. Lance Hoffman, the son of the owners, answered the door, and couldn't have been more helpful. He didn't seem to know much about the Childerses–the first indication Hutchison would have about how private they were–but by calling his mother at work Hoffman was able to learn that they were probably traveling. Mrs. Hoffman had seen the pickup truck of another neighbor two miles down the road, John Van Valin, driving in every morning and evening, probably to feed the horses. John and Deb Van Valin, Mrs. Hoffman said, were close friends of the Childerses.

So the two marines piled back into their government Suburban, chased down the valley to the Van Valins, found no one at home there either, and then drove back to the Hoffmans to use the phone. While Morgan disappeared with Lance Hoffman to swap hunting tales and tour the house–the walls of the living room and den were covered with the stuffed heads and racks of elk, antelope, and Bighorn sheep–Hutchison started dialing around Powell to find the Van Valins, whom he hoped could lead him to the Childerses.

By now, Hutchison was beginning to realize just how delicate, even precarious, his situation was. On the second day of a war, two marines in dress blues and a big, shiny government Suburban had been poking around a small town in Wyoming for two hours, asking at the police station, knocking on doors, circuiting the desolate section roads of a community where the neighbors could usually tell who was driving by just by the signature of their pickup's dust cloud. Half the town must know about their arrival by now, but the CACO rules forbade them to reveal their mission to anyone except the immediate next of kin. Meanwhile, an annoyed colonel from Marine Corps headquarters in Virginia had already called Hutchison on his cell phone twice, asking whether the family had been notified yet. It was already past noon on the east coast and the newspapers and major television networks were hounding the Pentagon for identification of the young marine shot at the Rumaila oil field, fixating, as Hutchison had suspected they would, on Childers' status as the first killed in action in Iraq.

"Captain, we'll give you every resource you need," the colonel from Quantico had told him over the phone. "You have the complete support of headquarters and the Fifth Marine Division, if you need it." Translation? "Hutchison, don't fuck up." But that's exactly what the day was shaping up to be–a classic, CACO fuckup that Hutchison had vowed to avoid.

When he finally tracked Deb Van Valin down at work, Hutchison thought she was very helpful, but also quite shaky, as if she'd already heard that a marine detail was poking around Powell and had reason to be worried.

"Captain, just tell me, all right? Why are you here?"

"Ah, ma'am, I can't tell you that right away. I'm sorry. But can we meet with you? We need your help."

"Okay, captain. I know the rules. Meet me back at my house. I'm leaving right now."

The Van Valin house stands on land with a broad, picturesque vista down the Powell Valley. While he waited for Deb Van Valin to arrive, Hutchison leaned against the fender of the Suburban, taking in the view. The morning clouds had finally broken up, revealing the immense, moody folds of the Bighorns to the east. This was altogether too beautiful a place, Hutchison thought, too beautiful a day, to be deciding what he could or couldn't tell this woman about his mission.

Deb Van Valin is angular and trim, with a few wisps of gray in her brown hair, warm but very direct. As soon as she invited the two marines into her house, Hutchison could understand why she had seemed so concerned. On the living room wall there was a recent photograph of a young marine noncom. He was Deb's son, Sergeant Travis Dusenberry, a helicopter crew chief who had been briefly deployed over the winter in Afghanistan. He was now stationed at Quantico, Virginia, and assigned to the crew of Marine One, the aviation detail that operates the shiny olive-drab helicopters that whisk the president, his staff, and the press on White House trips.

Deb looked directly at Hutchison's face across the kitchen floor.

Hutchison was filled with such utter sympathy for her at that moment, and anger at himself, that he was practically speechless. All he could do was shake his head and repeat, "No. No-no-no." *Christ, I practically killed this poor woman here, racing all the way out from Powell in her car. I should have told her on the phone. How many other marine mothers, or marine wives, were there in Powell? They must all know by now. Forget the CACO rules.* He knew that he could trust Deb because she was the mother of a marine and would probably understand the next-of-kin notification rules. But, mostly, he just wanted to take her out of her misery and tell her everything, then get her to help him find the Childerses.

Finally Hutchison said. "We have to find Joseph and Judy Childers. Their son has been killed in Iraq."

Deb slowly lowered herself to a chair at the kitchen table and placed her face in her hands. Her shoulders began to shake as she cried. She blinked back tears as she looked back up to face Hutchison.

"Just tell me that it's not Shane Childers. Captain, please say that. It's not Shane, right?"

"Second Lieutenant Therrel Shane Childers. Deb, we really are so sorry."

"Oh my God. Shane. Shane, Shane. Oh, poor Judy and Joe. And

my John. John is like a father to this boy. He'll be so upset. Oh, captain, you just can't know what this means. Who this boy was. Shane. You just thought that nothing could ever hurt Shane Childers."

Deb cried some more and then, for a while, she cycled back and forth between the two marines in her life right now. Hutchison decided to let her vent. He'd already lost too much time trying to locate the Childerses, but he just didn't have the meanness inside him, the practicality, to force her to focus right away. Besides, psychologically, he found what she was going through to be very interesting. It was almost as if she had intense, motherly feelings for two sons in the marines. But before she could break through to the terrible news about one, Shane, she had to expunge the trauma of racing home over the section roads of Powell, thinking that it was about the other, Travis.

"Okay, so, it's a small community, right, and everyone in town knows why you're here," Deb told them. "We all thought it was about Travis–I mean, helicopters crash all the time. And, you know, the whole time Travis was in Afghanistan we never heard a word or even knew where he was, whether it was just that the marines kept him that busy, or he wasn't allowed to tell us. And now. I can't imagine what these mothers are going through. How they wait. This war in Iraq just seems so much more violent already."

Deb was still overwrought about Shane, but she seemed to calm down once she began to tell them about the Childerses. The Van Valins had first met Joe and Judy twelve years ago, shortly after the Childerses had moved from Mississippi to Wyoming when Joe Childers retired from a twenty-two-year career in the Navy Seabees. John also raised mules, and he'd become curious about the Childerses after seeing mules in their fields, and dropped in one afternoon to introduce himself and check out the new neighbor's jacks.

Joe was colorful and abrupt, Deb said, a nonstop talker and raconteur. The family had followed him around the world on his various

Seabee billets–Midway Island, Puerto Rico, the Middle East, and even Iran–and led a very interesting life. Even while working full-time for the navy, Joe had spent most of his weekend and evening time as a blacksmith and farrier, and he told wonderful stories about his horse-shoeing junkets on several continents. John Van Valin soon fell under Joe's spell, and before long they were spending their weekends together, ranging out across the Wyoming countryside to take in the farm sales and mule auctions. Joe had joined a local trail-riding group, the Shoshone Back Country Horsemen, and John often tagged along on their outings and packing expeditions up into the mountains. The innumerable farm-equipment breakdowns over at the Childerses were legendary, a running joke between the two families.

Deb assured Hutchison and Morgan that, despite the circumstances, they were going to love the Childerses. Judy was a lot more understated than Joe, the one who kept the household running and everyone grounded, while Joe was off on another one of his adventures.

But, God, Shane. This was going to be such upsetting news for everybody. Shane wasn't just the hope of the Childers family. He was this whirlwind of energy and talk, very grounded but also hilariously madcap in his own way. When he was visiting Wyoming and went to one of the Shoshone Back Country Horsemen barbecues, or just met people around town, all of the mothers would talk about him afterward. "Hey, what happened here. We got robbed. How come none of us got a son like Shane?"

Shane was Joe and Judy's second child and oldest son, and he had enlisted in the marines the same year the Childerses had moved to Wyoming, 1990. Deb had met him the following year, when he was just eighteen, a raw recruit returning from the Persian Gulf War, and watched him grow over the years as he passed through Wyoming in between his marine assignments. Shane was particularly fastidious about his body, his physical conditioning. In the mornings, when

Shane was home, Deb would see him on her way out to work, pedaling furiously on his mountain bike as he began a twenty-five-mile circuit out over the mountains. Home by noon, Shane once helped John carpet a friend's house, and then Joe would chase them down by phone because his baler had broken down while he was haying one of his fields. That night, driving back in from work and some food shopping, Deb would see them all together out on the corner of the Childers place, while Shane helped Joe break apart and fix the New Holland baler. Everyone could see that there was a lot of Joe in Shane—all that chronic Childers intensity, the racing from event to event, interest to interest, from dawn to dusk. But Shane was different too, more organized and thorough. Even Joe said that Shane always got his projects done.

Deb had always felt that Shane was irresistible in another way. He had taken the opportunities for travel and adventure much further than the average marine, and was always bubbling over with new curiosities and passions, and told such interesting stories, when he raced through Wyoming between assignments. When he was stationed in Europe, he toured art museums, learned to sail on Lake Geneva, and climbed the Alps. In California, he surfed and climbed Mount Shasta. Shane spoke with particular affection and awe about Mount Kilimanjaro in Tanzania, a peak he'd climbed several times. In the late 1990s, he had entered The Citadel in South Carolina and become intensely involved in his college courses. After that, everyone had noticed a big change and thought that Shane was beginning to round a new corner. Now all that manic energy was poured into books, and an intense enthusiasm for people. At the Shoshone Horsemen barbecues, when he was home, Shane would meet someone new and get involved in long, windy conversations about French literature, the Battle of Shiloh or changing careers—whatever interested him at the moment, or had just come up in conversation with his new friend. Then he'd chase across the driveway to his pickup truck, swing open the door of his cab, and pull out a particular book from the pile behind the seat. "Okay, this is a novel, but it's really a great self-improvement book too, see? You've got to read it. And I *will* be e-mailing you about this."

Shane Childers, Deb said, was lovably, irresistibly, intense.

Deb said one other thing about Shane. "Okay, so sorry, captain, but you know marines. Too many of them have this kick-butt, macho attitude about everything, always bragging about their accomplishments, and that even includes my son. But Shane wasn't like that at all. He was definitely all marine, and totally believed in the mission, but also very polite, considerate, a total gentleman. You should just know that, captain."

Hutchison waited patiently for Deb to talk herself out, his mind occasionally distracted by other thoughts. He was very close to his own mother and older sister, and spoke with each of them by phone several times a week. What if he had taken this bullet in Iraq, and the CACO detail had just arrived at his house in California? Would they treat his mother and sister, or their friends, the same way? And Shane Childers. He was beginning to feel very drawn to Childers' story. He could tell from what Deb said that he would have liked Childers quite a lot, and this reminded him of his own loneliness sometimes, the lack of intellectual companionship, of officers who shared his interests, in the Marine Corps. The day so far seemed such a jumble, impossibly tragic and dreamy at once. He was supposed to be on a CACO call, but his mind kept wandering off like that—Powell to Palos Verdes, Iraq to the Bighorn country, with the snowy bosom of mountains outside the Van Valin kitchen window throwing long lavender shadows on the browsing cattle below.

This was one thing about Hutchison that royally pissed off Morgan. Hutch. Captain Hutch. Always nice to everybody, always ready with some engaging thought. Morgan did consider Hutchison an outstanding head of command. He liked working with him, and particularly appreciated how graciously Hutchison responded to a ribbing. Still, all of these commissioned officers were the same–college-educated and thus dumb as shit. This pimply-faced, dogmeat enlistee is having girlfriend problems, so Hutch spends hours with him, dispensing worldly advice. This trailer-trash grunt doesn't know his ass from a munitions dump about obtaining a mortgage, so Hutch takes an afternoon to brief him on interest rates. Now, when they desperately need to locate the Childers family to make a next-of-kin notification, the captain was letting this neighbor down the road moan on and on about her feelings. Christ. If the fucking guy wanted to be a psychiatrist, why the hell didn't he go to medical school instead of joining the marines?

"Ah, sir," Morgan said from across the kitchen floor, shifting on his feet. "Would you mind if we maybe got down to . . ."

Deb Van Valin held up her hand.

"No, that's okay, sergeant," she said. "You're right. I can help you find Joe and Judy Childers. They're in Texas."

The Childerses had spent that week at Fort Hood, Texas, the sprawling military base just north of Killeen that houses the U.S. Army's Fourth Infantry Division. Joe and Judy's daughter, Sandra, was married to Richard Brown, a Powell resident who had originally served in the air force and then worked at several jobs around Wyoming before deciding to reenlist in the military, this time the army. He now worked as a sergeant for the 297th Transportation Company at Fort Hood. For several months, the Childerses had known that they faced a kind of double jeopardy as a military family. Since the previous fall, it had been abundantly clear that Shane's unit, with the First Battalion of the Fifth Marine Division, would be one of the first fighting forces sent into Iraq. They had trained intensively since the summer at Camp Pendleton, California, and then worked on specialized assault tactics at the marines' combined arms warfare center in Twentynine Palms. Then, over the winter, Richard had gradually realized that his army unit would be sent too, as part of the large convoy force that would be shuttling between Kuwait and Iraq, ferrying munitions and supplies north. In early March, Sandra let her parents know that Richard's unit would be deploying by the end of the month. Joe had already asked for a week off from his job as a mechanic at a large oil and gas service company outside Powell, and Judy had booked a flight for Dallas and reserved a rental car.

Joe had looked forward to the trip. More than thirty years ago, as a much younger man, he had shipped out for two tours in Vietnam, but his parents still had school-age children at home, and were too tied up with work on their small West Virginia farm, to see him off for war. Now he could be there for Sandra during the chaos and high emotions of her husband's deployment, something he'd always vowed to do if any of his children joined or married into the service.

And they'd been having a good time so far. Sandra was still fixing up the interior of her small, detached house in a subdivision on the base, and Judy had kept her busy with those projects. Joe had particularly enjoyed his tour of the vast Fort Hood motor-pool parking lots and bays, crouching on one knee as he inspected the big convoy trucks, drawling away in his soft, West Virginia accent about this hydraulic line or that suspension system, all the elaborate trailer hitches. Just the sight of a diesel-fired auxiliary power unit, or a bumper-mounted winch, set Joe off, and Richard's friends in the motor pool had enjoyed listening to Joe's yarns about Vietnam or horseshoeing forays across several continents. Richard was still laughing about it when he got home.

"Hey, Sandy, Judy, everyone in the unit loves Joe. They want to kidnap him and bring him with us to Kuwait."

That week, Joe, Judy, Sandy, and her two children had all driven together for six hours west across Texas to visit Judy's sister and brother-in-law in Lubbock. The visit had gone well, but it was a confusing time. Sandy had already said good-bye to Richard, because she expected his unit to be deployed before she returned, but then he had called Lubbock Thursday night to report that the 297th wasn't leaving until the weekend. When they returned to Fort Hood on Friday, Sandy would have to say hello and good-bye to Richard all over again–the standard, hurry-up-and-wait emotional torture experienced by military families during major deployments. On the radio as they drove to Lubbock, and then on the evening television news at their in-law's house, the drumbeat for war was building. President George W. Bush's final ultimatum for Saddam Hussein to give up his weapons of mass destruction, or to leave Iraq, expired on Thursday night, and then the "shock and awe" bombardment of Iraqi cities had begun. Shane's unit would be going over the berm into Iraq any hour now. Then Richard would deploy. It was a double-whammy of butterflies and last-minute changes of plans as the Childerses waited for the war to commence.

On Friday morning, Joe and Judy woke at 6 A.M. and she immediately turned on the television. All the morning news shows were carrying the same reports.

"Oh, Joe, look," Judy said. "The ground war has begun."

"Yeah, well, here we go then," Joe said. "I just sure hope that they can manage this thing to minimize the casualties. That's what I hope."

Most of the television cameramen and reporters embedded with the army and marines seemed to be with units that were swinging west and then north for Nasiriya and Najaf in central Iraq, deliberately avoiding the first few engagements in the south, about which little was known so far. But there were scattered reports of fighting at several key objectives in southern Iraq as British units advanced toward Basra and the Shatt al Arab waterway, and a few U.S. Marine assault platoons pushed due north toward oil field installations that Pentagon planners were determined to secure before the Iraqis set them on fire as they retreated. Most of the network and cable news reports also included one other piece of information. A marine officer had been killed while his unit was attacking a pumping station at the Rumaila oil field, barely twenty miles inside Iraq. His identification was being withheld pending notification of next of kin.

Joe and Judy both thought the same thing but decided not to talk about it.

It made no sense to worry right then whether or not the marine officer who had been killed was Shane. From his Vietnam experience, Joe knew that Shane was in danger—marine platoon leaders, because they were trained to lead from the front, had exceptionally high casualty rates. But Joe had also served his first tour in Vietnam during the explosive, violent Tet Offensive in 1968, and he knew that there was an incredible randomness to war casualties. Even if he did know where Shane's unit was, that didn't mean that his son was engaged or even hurt—there would have been dozens of other marine officers in the same area. Besides, the Childerses were familiar with the precise military procedures for notifying families of soldiers who had been killed. Probably by the time they returned to Fort Hood that afternoon, they'd learn that the marine officer had been identified and that there was no longer any reason to worry about Shane.

But all across Texas that day, as they drove through the dry and scrubby Brazos River country and then pushed east through Sweetwater and Abilene, the radio reports were the same. The marine officer killed at Rumaila still hadn't been identified. They tried to force themselves not to worry. Once his grandchildren settled down in the backseat and the car was quiet, Joe had a lot of time to daydream and think while he enjoyed the Texas ranchland and the occasional irrigated farm belts they passed through.

At Christmas, Shane had visited Wyoming for almost a week, just before he raced off in his red pickup to join some friends in Oregon for a predeployment skiing trip. He'd devoted the vacation to his usual frantic curriculum—rising early to make his morning run along the icy roads around Powell, noodling around with his laptop and e-mailing friends across the country from the dining room table, then making a stab at his father's foundation project out front until the frost line stopped him. A decent snow had fallen on the eastern face of the Rockies that week. One afternoon, Shane decided to hitch up his father's team of matched Belgian draft horses, Amigo and April, and take them out for a sleigh ride. He found the team in the corral out back, curried and harnessed them in the barn, then drove them out on foot to the large, crazyass assemblage of antique farm machinery and vehicles—almost forty in all—that Joe kept out back.

Joe's box sleigh has two fixed sets of runners under the rear flatbed, with a steerable bob, mounted on a fifth wheel, up front—an enormously fun rig. Shane had a ball out there, urging on the big prancing horses while the harness jingled, the hooves pounded the prairie snow, turning up fluffy rooster tails from the rusty front runners every time he pulled the team around through a tight turn. After careening around the hayfields for a while, he headed out back for the steeper, winding terrain up against the Polecat Bench. Shane loved it back there, all that Wyoming vastness, the views of the snowy Pryors and the Bighorns, the slight quiver of weightlessness as he stood up from the seat and pushed the horses hard uphill and then went for some air as he cleared the top of a gulch.

Red-faced and cheery in his cowboy hat, his eyes glistening from the prairie wind, Shane was just pulling in with the team when his father returned from work. Together they unhitched the team and left the sleigh there beside the house, and then Shane drove Amigo and April back to the barn.

Joe joined his son in the barn a few minutes later. This was Joe's favorite time of the day, doing his barn chores before he returned to the house for dinner, and he considered it a rare treat to share some time there with Shane while he was home on vacation. The smells and sounds of the barn—the briny harness coming off the team, decaying manure, the other horses whinnying as they came in to feed—reminded Joe of their old times together back in Mississippi, when Shane was still a teenager. The snowy Polecat Bench was sunset pink out through the open barn door and the steam rising off the backs of the Belgians clouded up at the low rafters, obscuring the light of the single electric bulb.

Being a military man himself, and impressed with Shane's marine credentials, Joe knew that this was no time to deliver the standard fatherly lecture: Son, don't be a hero over there, don't try to win the war yourself. The conversation just naturally took a different turn. Shane was ebullient that week, better than Joe had ever seen him. He'd taken over his unit, Alpha Company of the Second Platoon, from a freaking Harvard graduate no less, trained the men hard, even moving several soldiers around to new positions and responsibilities to better reflect their abilities. At both Pendleton and Twentynine Palms, Alpha Company had received top performance reviews, one reason that Shane suspected that they'd be assigned very near the front. He liked his commanding officer and was confident that those feelings were reciprocated. Shane was upbeat about deploying for Kuwait, which would probably be in early February, and was both excited and quietly confident about leading a company in combat once they were sent into Iraq.

Shane seemed to be changing, or at least considering change, in other ways. One day he would insist that he'd remain in the marines for another eight years and climb up to captain or colonel or whatever rank he'd achieve, and then be in a position to collect a full twenty-year military pension. The next day he'd jump to pure Childers-quality dreams—as soon as Iraq was over, he was coming back to Wyoming to buy a farm. At The Citadel Shane had majored in French and become fluent, and now he also talked a lot about going back to graduate school and becoming a United Nations interpreter, or a State Department employee. "Oh, hell, Dad, maybe I'll just do both–teach French somewhere *and* buy a farm." Shane was the first member of the family to graduate from college, and Joe wasn't sure what all this meant, but it was probably a good sign that his son was considering so many possibilities about his future. Part of it was just a consequence of his frantic schedule. After The Citadel, Shane had chased all over the country for the marines–first basic school for officers, then infantry tactics school, then Pendleton and Twentynine Palms. Now he had a war to fight. There hadn't been much time for him to figure out a clear plan.

As he drove back across Texas toward Fort Hood that Friday, Joe's thoughts returned to that conversation. Shane had seemed so confident and well when he was home for Christmas. He had trained very hard and obviously had gained the respect of his commanders. Nobody could devote that much time and energy to becoming a good soldier just to get killed on the first day of a war. He just wasn't worried about it as he drove along the interstate toward Waco and then Killeen.

Besides, he and Shane had a pact. Shane and his younger brother, Sam, had not had much opportunity to spend time together since they'd left home. While Shane was globe-trotting with the marines, Sam was in the navy for eight years and then had settled in Illinois. But now Sam had a son, Aksel, who was very bright and doing well in school, and he loved horses and the outdoors. Joe dreamed of getting the three generations together for a packing trip up into the mountains, and had spoken about it with Shane that night in the barn.

"Say, Shane, I've kind of been thinking about taking that sorrel mule there and training it for pack work, you know? And the foxtrotter filly is ready to break, too. How 'bout next summer, as soon as you're back from Iraq, you, me, Sam, and Aksel will go packing? We'll do Jack Creek again."

Jack Creek, in the high, timber-spruce country, down near the

Shoshone National Forest in northern Wyoming, was a favorite spot where Joe and Shane had packed in with mules during earlier summers.

"Hey, Dad, Jack Creek. It's a great plan. We'll get little Aksel up there."

Shane was excited about the trip and mentioned it several more times during his Christmas visit. One day just before Shane left for Oregon, he and Joe drove into Cody to pick out a new buckstitch-canvas tent at an outfitters' store.

"Hey, Dad," Shane said as they stepped back into their pickup in the parking lot. "As soon as I get back from Iraq? That buckstitch is headed for Jack Creek."

So it was settled. When Shane got back from the war, the men of the family would be saddling up and then packing in to Jack Creek.

When they arrived back at Ford Hood, the marine officer who had been killed at Rumaila was still not identified, but they were all too busy to focus on that. Sandy had to get her children settled in the house, Judy was planning to run up to the base to cash traveler's checks, and Richard was running in and out, deranged by last-minute deployment chores for his unit. Before dinner, his first sergeant had called and asked Richard if he had time to run over to the Fort Hood hospital, where a member of the 297th who was off on maternity leave had just delivered her baby. Her husband had deployed with another unit and everyone thought it was a good idea to visit to make sure that she was all right. Joe volunteered to make the hospital run with his son-in-law as soon as they finished dinner.

At dinner, Richard seemed distracted and was acting somewhat strangely. He kept getting cell phone calls, ducking out of the room to talk with someone, and then he would log on to his computer to send e-mails, returning to the table looking upset. But the rest of the family barely noticed. Richard was appreciated in his unit for being generous with his time, and the first sergeant often called during dinner to assign him extra errands or evening work. In the craziness of a major army base deploying for war, it wasn't unusual for a departing soldier to have a bad case of the jitters.

Back in Wyoming, the rest of the day was hell for Captain Hutchison, an afternoon that contributed new meaning the old military acronym, snafu, situation normal all fucked up. From Deb Van Valin, he was able to obtain the phone number but not the address of Richard and Sandy Brown at Fort Hood, but this information was virtually worthless because the CACO rules explicitly required that a next-of-kin notification be made by a personal visit by at least two marine officers. Obviously, Quantico would have to reassign the initial CACO call to a detail from central Texas—assuming that one could be quickly assembled—and then Hutchison would take over once the Childers family returned to Wyoming. Before he called Marine Corps headquarters in Virginia to relay this news, Hutchison made several cell phone calls to track down the Browns' address. When this was passed to Quantico, he was told to stand by and remain within cell phone range in Powell, because the family might need him for something there once they were notified of their son's death.

Marines thrive on action, organization, a certainty of purpose—placing a call, moving a platoon around, or reorganizing a training program, relying on the comforting and usually reliable equation that a specific input applied to a problem makes something specific happen. But nothing was happening now. There weren't any good inputs to expend. Hutchison didn't dare dial Sandy Brown's number at Fort Hood because that would violate the CACO rules about personal notification, and might run the risk of inadvertently tipping off the family or a friend before a marine detail arrived for the Childerses. Casualty Assistance at Quantico required at least two or three hours to assemble a call team from Texas. From far-off Wyoming, and an increasingly frantic headquarters in Virginia, the United States Marine Corps was now conducting a national wild goose chase for the parents of the first killed-in-action in Iraq, but no one in charge had any way of knowing that they were somewhere on the interstate highway system between Lubbock and Killeen.

Frustrated and glum, Hutchison and Morgan drove into Powell to see if they could find a place still open for lunch. Their opportunities for relieving the tension of the day with humor—Morgan deriding his captain for reading too many books, Hutchison chiding his first sergeant for owning too many guns—seemed exhausted, and so they rode in silence past sugar-beet and barley fields spotted with mud where the last of the winter snow was melting. In town, they chose a Mexican restaurant across the street from the post office because its location seemed to offer the best cell phone reception.

The next-of-kin notification of the Childers family was now being supervised by a full colonel out of Quantico, a development that made Hutchison feel uneasy because the duty he had not been able to perform on the ground in Wyoming was now being assumed by a higher chain of command. Every forty-five minutes, if Quantico didn't call him to update events, he called there. From these increasingly tense exchanges, Hutchison was able to learn that the marines were experiencing difficulties assembling a CACO detail in Texas. National newspapers and the television networks were still clambering for an identity on the first killed in action, which they desperately wanted before their evening news deadlines, and many reporters were beginning to voice suspicion that the marines were deliberately withholding information. During one of his calls to Quantico, Hutchison confessed his frustrations to the colonel and said that he felt personally responsible for the delay in notifying the Childerses.

"Nonsense, captain, and I want you to keep your morale up out there," the colonel replied. "You continue to have the full support, and all of the resources, of headquarters staff and the Fifth Division."

Translation?

"Ah, shit, Barry," Hutchison said, flipping shut his cell phone after the call. "We've fucked up. It's a CACO meltdown. I just feel terrible for this family."

Morgan felt bad about it as well, but he thought that Hutchison was placing too much blame on himself.

"Oh Christ, captain," Morgan said. "Here we go now. This isn't your fault! Okay? Jedd Clampett back there at the ranch decided to go to Texas this week and wasn't around when we made the CACO call. That doesn't make it your fault."

"Yeah, but I feel that it's my fault. I feel terrible for the family."

"Well fuck your freaking feelings then, godamnit, sir," Morgan said. "Fuck your fault. You're just acting like a commissioned asshole here and blaming yourself for something that couldn't be prevented."

It didn't get much worse than this, an officer and his first sergeant exchanging expletives over a CACO snafu, but then it really did get much worse. After returning to the ranch country west of Powell and positioning themselves on a rise near the Childers place where cell phone reception was good, Hutchison received an unexpected, frantic call from Texas.

It was Richard Brown, calling from outside his house at Fort Hood. He had just heard the news from his mother, who had provided Hutchison's cell phone number because the captain had left it with her in case she needed to call.

Sobbing convulsively, Brown identified himself as First Lieutenant Shane Childers' brother-in-law and said he knew that Shane was dead. The news that a marine CACO detail was in town had spread like wildfire around Powell, Richard told them, and the traffic going by the Childers ranch had led the local rumor mill to conclude that the marine killed at Rumaila was Shane.

Between crying jags, Richard assured them that he understood and would respect the CACO rules. He would just have to wait until

the marine detail from Texas arrived, but what was he going to do? He
was so upset. Joe and Judy Childers had just returned from Lubbock
and were sitting inside right now, waiting for dinner, but Richard was
in agony imagining how they were going to react to the news about
Shane. And there were so many other worries and complications for
the family.

"I mean, captain . . . what am I supposed to do here?" Richard said.
"I feel so torn. My unit is literally deploying for Kuwait any hour now
and I can't abandon them. But what about Shane? Shouldn't I be at his
funeral? Support my family? Captain, I am just so torn. What do I *do*
now?"

Rallying the resolve to say the right thing to Richard was difficult
for Hutchison. He sympathized deeply with Brown's anguish. Technically, because they worked in different services, Hutchison couldn't
issue any orders to Brown. But by unofficial tradition, just between two
military men, Hutchison outranked Brown. And, from the scowl he
could see on Morgan's face across the front seat of the Suburban, he
wasn't looking forward to his reaction either once this phone call was
over.

"All right, sergeant," Hutchison began. "First of all, we completely
understand what you're going through. It sounds like First Lieutenant
Childers was a hell of a guy. But . . ."

"Okay, sir, I know, I know. . . . It's Shane though. I mean, Christ,
Shane. You don't know what he meant to people, so many people."

"Sergeant, now look. I can't give you an order."

"Sir, thanks. I know that. But . . . what am I supposed to *do*?"

"Sergeant! You've got to get a grip now, you've got to remember
your obligations to the service and your family. You *can't* let anyone
know until there's been a proper CACO notification. After that, we're
all going to need your help. Understand?"

"Sir, yes. But it's *Shane*. He's dead. God. It's Shane."

When Hutchison suggested that Brown contact his unit chaplain and his first sergeant, Brown said that he had already done that. They were telling him the same thing. Get a grip, wait for the CACO detail, and they'd all worry tomorrow or the next day about whether he should ship with his unit or obtain emergency leave to attend the funeral in Wyoming. (A few days later, Brown would receive permission from his commanding officer to attend the funeral.) Just when Hutchison thought he had Brown calmed down, the sergeant wanted to say one more thing.

"Okay, sir, I just want you to know this. I didn't see Shane at all after he finished up at The Citadel and got commissioned. We've both been too busy getting ready for Iraq. But it was a big deal for this family, a real big deal, Shane getting his college degree and then getting his commission. So, we had a pact. The whole family was in on it. The next time I saw Shane? Me, the noncommissioned officer, would salute him, the first commissioned officer in the family. I was really looking forward to it, giving Shane my first salute, you know? Now what do I do? Is this all that's left? I get to salute Shane in his coffin? Oh God. Shane. I get to salute him in his coffin."

By now, Hutchison felt drugged, but strangely calm inside, as if the adrenaline flow of the afternoon had acted as a narcotic dispensing inner confidence and peace. Whatever came first to his mind now, he felt, whatever he said, would probably be right.

"Sergeant, I want to work with you on this," Hutchison said. "I promise to remain in touch, all right? But maybe giving that first salute to Lieutenant Childers would be the highest honor you could bestow."

"Yeah, yeah, captain. I'm going to salute Shane."

Richard Brown finally seemed to calm down and then hung up. Hutchison was obligated to call Quantico and tell Casualty Assistance that a family member now knew that Lieutenant Childers was dead, which caused a lot of concern because they all realized that the news could leak to the press before Joe and Judy Childers had been notified in person. And Richard Brown called several times, sometimes in control, sometimes in a panic, which required a lot of grief management via cell phone. By the late afternoon, Hutchison was able to reassure him that a new detail had been assembled and was on the road from Waco. When the replacement CACO team hadn't arrived by dinnertime, Richard called again, this time volunteering to search the base at Fort Hood, just in case the marines were lost. Once more Hutchison mustered his negotiating skills and talked Brown out of that.

First Sergeant Morgan, listening to the cell phone traffic from his side of the Surburban, was a model of charity about all this.

"Oh Christ. What a mess. Sir, just tell that army guy down there to get back into the house, and shut the fuck up until the marines arrive."

"Barry. I *am* doing my best here, all right? I'm doing my best."

"Sir, I'm not mad at you."

"You're mad at him."

"Exactly! Army. They always fuck it up for the marines."

As Hutchison and Morgan waited on the rise for new orders, their legs propped up on the dashboard, the sun became a pale half-disk against the Beartooths and then fell away.

Hutchison didn't learn that the CACO call had begun in Texas until nearly 8 P.M. that night, and by that time he and Morgan had been released by Quantico and made the drive back to Billings over the black-on-black Pryors. Reaching home, he felt jittery and exhausted. Quantico didn't know whether the Childerses would return immediately to Wyoming or wait a few days in Texas, which kept him in limbo for the weekend while he waited to pick up the normal CACO routine of caring for the family. And, given the unsatisfactory turn of the day's events, he felt even more nervous than before about meeting the Childerses.

It was just about the lowest point in his marine career, in fact; a sad denouement to the depression he'd felt all year about being left behind during the combat in Iraq. His house felt empty and lonely. He had not moved in a stick of furniture during the renovations, and a filmy coat of sawdust left behind by the floor sanders covered the stacks of books and paintings leaning against the walls, offending his sense of orderliness. He missed his old girlfriend from Peru—at this point, any girlfriend would do—and he had few friends outside the marines in Billings. To top it all off, Richard Brown called one last time from Texas, a real mess this time, and he had to devote another twenty minutes to grief counseling with him.

From the hardwood sill of his bedroom bay window, he could hear the wind outside, howling down from the rimrock plateaus. For some reason, the drive back and forth over the Pryors kept returning as he tried to fall asleep.

Drifting off, Hutchison made a mental note to call Richard Brown in Texas first thing in the morning. He wanted the sergeant to know that he cared. There was something else about it. Despite the sadness of the circumstances, the two weeks of sleeplessness and hell they were all going to endure, he was pleased by the image of Lieutenant Childers receiving his brother-in-law's first salute.

Next of Kin

The marine detail arrived at the Browns' house, pulling up in a van. It was just after dinner and the rest of the family had settled down on the living-room couch. Sandy was showing everyone a collection of jewelry that she kept in a special box because Shane, Joe, and Judy had given the pieces to her over the years. They all felt tired and road-weary from the long drive across Texas that day.

When Richard stepped outside to greet the CACO team, the accumulated tensions–the waiting and waiting, not being able to share with anyone that his brother-in-law was dead–overwhelmed him once more. He stood out by the curb, shaking hands with the CACO detail, gasping in deep breaths and desperately attempting to compose himself and stand straight without doubling over in tears. When he turned back for the house, the three-man detail, a chaplain, a first sergeant, and a major named David Blassingame, followed him single file up the cement walk.

Richard led the marine detail into the living room and then stood slightly away, revealing three sets of crisply pressed, telltale dress blue slacks with red stripes down their sides.

A three-man marine detail in dress blues doesn't show up on an army base for any other reason. They all knew, right then. It's Shane. This explained why Richard had looked so awful all afternoon. Dropping the pieces of jewelry to the coffee table, they fell silent and looked up.

"Sandy! What was I supposed to do? I couldn't tell you, couldn't. I felt so torn," Richard said.

The first sergeant and the chaplain stood side by side in a kind of respectful, parade rest position, with their hands clasped behind their backs. Major Blassingame stood in front, nervously examining a faxed piece of paper that he pulled out of his uniform pocket.

Good, Joe Childers thought, he's going to do this straight from the book. That was Joe's first reaction—relief—because he felt sorry for the major, who looked so uncomfortable. Delivering the news right out of the CACO manual would make it easier on an officer who obviously had been dragged into this at the last minute and had no idea how the family would react.

But, God, Shane, what happened here? Shane, what happened? Fighting his emotions, Joe decided to just sit there respectfully and let the major do it in his own way. Perhaps this was the last thing he could do for his son—showing these visiting marines just what kind of family Shane had.

"On behalf of the commandant of the United States Marine Corps, I regret to inform you that your son, Second Lieutenant Therrel Shane Childers, was killed in action on March 21 . . ."

If they heard anything after that, none of them remembered it. Joe immediately welled up and unashamedly began to cry, Sandy wailed beside him, and Judy sat stoically at her end of the couch, reaching behind Sandy to touch Joe's shoulder in support. Before they could say anything the chaplain stepped around the major, placed his arm around Joe's shoulder and suggested that they pray. The Childers family had never been particularly religious and prayer right then wouldn't have occurred to them, but they were all too dazed to do anything else except follow along. As the chaplain began his prayer, Richard began to sob uncontrollably and his eight-year-old daughter, Autumn, called out.

"Sandy, Dad, wait a minute!" Autumn cried. "What's happening? I don't understand. Is this about Shane? Is Shane hurt?"

On Tuesday morning, before they left for Lubbock, Sandy had woken up overwhelmed by the sudden fear that Shane would be killed in Iraq. She hadn't dared express this to her parents and upset them and, besides, crazy premonitions were a big part of being a military sibling or wife. Maybe she was really just worrying in advance about Richard's deployment, through Shane. She had brooded about it all afternoon in the car and finally talked herself out of worrying about it. Why trouble yourself with something that wasn't even going to happen, or was months away? But now, here they were already, the marines. So soon and it's Shane.

But now Sandy had to worry about her stepdaughter. In 1995, when she and Richard began dating, the Childerses had immediately accepted his daughter from an earlier marriage, and Autumn's puppy-love for Shane had become a constant and touching source of humor for everyone in the family. When the Browns visited Wyoming and Shane was there, Autumn followed him around all day, moon-faced and in awe of her stepuncle, chattering at his heel as he moved from the barn to the corral to the fields. Shane made her laugh, he taught her how to hold newborn kittens and coil a lasso, he listened and he never talked down to her. They all loved the way Autumn would burst through the kitchen door exclaiming about Shane. "Mom, guess what Shane did? He fell off the mule and squished his cowboy hat." A few times, when he rushed through Wyoming between assignments, Shane's schedule was so tight that he flew in and out by airliner. Au-

tumn loved riding into the Cody airport to see him off, and always insisted upon standing by the big glass windows and watching until his
plane disappeared over the Bighorns.

Now Autumn was disconsolate and confused. Sandy knew that
she had to get Autumn out of there and comfort her alone. She
stepped up to lead her stepdaughter off to her bedroom.

Major Blassingame would be among the first to notice a curious
but touching division of emotion in the Childers marriage. It was almost as if they had been working for years on redefining traditional ex-
pectations of gender. Joe was voluble and completely unashamed
about his grief. "All right, major, just let me bawl my head off for a couple of minutes here and then maybe we can talk." Judy, meanwhile, sat
stolidly on the couch, biting her lip occasionally but maintaining control. She was naturally hospitable and insisted that the major and his
detail relax. She was practical and take-charge, an experienced military wife comfortable with assuming authority over details while her
adventuring husband was away. She wanted to know how the detail
had first heard about Shane, how the marines had managed to track
the family down in Texas, whom they should contact when they arrived back home.

Once he had calmed down, Joe seemed most comfortable telling
stories, investing his unexpected visitors with his fabulous gift for talk.
"Oh, my Shane, you know?" Joe told the marine detail. "Not many
fathers get a son like this." He could go on forever, with elaborate digressions, even digressions within digressions. Shane home for Christmas, jingling across the fields with the Belgians and sleigh, Shane
climbing Kilimanjaro or the Alps, Shane filling the barn with cartons
of "borrowed" military-issue Meals Ready to Eat, so they had enough
stores for their next packing trip up to Jack Creek. Joe's memory for
dates was precise, and the word he used most often to describe his son
was "intense."

Major Blassingame and his detail stayed at the Browns for another two hours, mostly listening to Joe's stories, eventually moving to the kitchen table. When he had arrived for his visit in Texas, Joe had tacked a snapshot that he carried in his wallet, of Shane in his dress-blue marine uniform, onto the edge of Sandra's portrait gallery in the living room. When they all moved into the kitchen, Joe had taken down the picture and carried it in for Major Blassingame. The major brightened up as soon as he saw the photograph, astounded by the coincidence.

"Oh my God, I know this marine," Blassingame said. "He was one of my students at Miramar."

It was true. Over the summer of 1998, just before matriculating at The Citadel, Shane had attended a marine college-prep course at Miramar Naval Air Station in San Diego, where Blassingame was one of his instructors.

"Well, Joe, you're certainly right about his intensity," Blassingame said. "Shane was the kind of student you would assign ten problems in the textbook and the next morning he would come back having solved thirty of them in the rest of the chapter. I never forgot him."

The Childerses were exultant about this. Shane's friends in the service, and even a few of his professors at The Citadel, had always depicted him as a marine's marine, the kind of soldier whom all the enlisted men and officers boasted about and who was well known throughout the network of marine bases across the country. Now his status as a Corps legend even seemed confirmed by the major who had come to notify them of his death.

Joe, in particular, seemed reluctant to let the CACO team leave, as if telling one more story about Shane, sharing one more yarn about his navy Seabee years would prevent the Childers family from being left alone with their terrible news. But Blassingame was eventually able to ease himself away by giving them Captain Hutchison's name and explaining that the Billings command would assume responsibility for the family as soon as they returned home.

As soon as the marines left, Richard got on the phone and changed the reservations for his in-laws' return flight from Monday to the next day. Earlier, on the couch in the living room and then in Sandy's kitchen, as Joe's stories had droned on, Judy was overwhelmed by a strong sensation, a sudden desire for escape. She just wanted to be *home*, now. Major Blassingame had told them that it might be a week, or even longer, before Shane's body was returned. During their long wait, Judy knew, they would be inundated by relatives and friends pressing in on their lives, an enormous intrusion on the quiet ranch life that she and Joe enjoyed. Now she just wanted to be surrounded by the familiar mix of possessions and appliances of her own home–her photo albums, a phone message machine that she knew how to work, Joe's work jackets and boots stored by the door. It was the most powerful of instincts, she thought–*Shane's dead, let's get home.*

Judy would later say that she thought Joe slept about twenty minutes that night, but that she slept a little more. At 4 A.M., realizing that neither of them was going to sleep any more, they rose and prepared to leave for the airport, lingering at the front door to hug Sandy and Richard before they left. There were a few times along the highway to Dallas that they actually felt unified with something to discuss–the anticipated arrival of relatives for Shane's funeral, whether or not Sandy and Richard would be able to get up to Wyoming–but mostly Shane's death seemed to have placed them in two different worlds, two sides of the car with a wall between them. Every forty or fifty miles, a sudden wave of uncontrollable emotions flowed over Joe and he started to cry. Judy was quiet, weeping a few times, but she didn't break down like Joe.

That was the oddest part about it, Joe thought. The terrible helplessness of losing Shane never hit them the same way at the same time.

*   *   *

As soon as he woke on Saturday morning, Captain Hutchison decided to honor his personal pledge of the night before and call Richard Brown in Texas. Richard seemed much better now, less consumed by the shattering emotions caused by his brother-in-law's death than the dilemma of whether to ship with his unit to Kuwait. Richard also told Hutchison that Joe and Judy Childers had changed their travel plans and were returning to Wyoming right away. Before they left the Browns in Texas, Joe and Judy had insisted that they didn't need a marine detail to meet them in Billings and were confident that they could get back to Wyoming alone. They just wanted to get home.

Richard had told Hutchison, however, that everyone in the family was worried about calls from reporters now that the next of kin notification had been made and the Pentagon had released Shane's identity to the media. After he hung up with Richard, Hutchison turned on his radio and heard several news broadcasts identifying Shane Childers, though it would take several hours for the media to track down the Childers family in Wyoming. This aroused Hutchison's protective instincts, and he decided that he and Morgan would meet the family's late-afternoon flight into Billings. He spent the rest of the day nervously anticipating the mission—at this point, he didn't even know what the Childerses looked like, and he suspected that they might feel as frustrated and exhausted as he did about the difficulty in locating them the day before.

But these doubts were dispelled as soon as they reached the airport baggage area just before sunset. Near the baggage carousels, a couple obviously in distress and comforting each other stood apart from the rest of the crowd. Joe Childers looked surprisingly youthful and broad-shouldered, and he was wearing cowboy boots, jeans, and a western-cut shirt with a bright red navy cap bearing the insignia of the USS *Tortuga,* a gift Shane had given him after one of his Pacific expeditions. As soon as Childers saw the marines in their dress blues, he smiled and walked right over.

"Hi. I guess you folks are looking for me. I'm Joe Childers."

Hutchison extended his hand, introduced himself and Morgan, and told Joe how sorry he was to learn the news about his son. Hutchison could see that Joe was bravely struggling to contain his emotions, and was impressed with how utterly candid and unashamed he was about that.

"I'm not afraid to tell you that I'm having a rough time with this, captain," Joe said. "Shane was quite a son to lose. But look, we better get back over to Judy."

Judy seemed to be in better shape. Her eyes were milky and she was bravely forcing a smile when they walked over but she was obviously more reserved and calm than Joe. There was an awkward moment or two while Hutchison decided whether or not to embrace her—ah, hell, yes, I should—but she was gracious about that and gave both Hutchison and Morgan long bear hugs. Hutchison's first instinct was to focus his attention on the dead marine's mother, saying all the obvious things and pouring on all the solicitous charm he could muster to console her. But when he began to speak and called her "Mrs. Childers," Judy smiled again and held up her hand.

"Captain, number one, you just call me Judy and I'll call you Kevin, all right? We're pretty informal about that. Number two, I'm handling this a lot better than Joe. He's the one we should be worried about."

They all fell into an easy rapport together after that. Joe was obviously pleased to have the undivided attention of a big, beefy platoon sergeant like Morgan, and began regaling him with his Seabee tales. Hutchison spoke with Judy, compensating for her initial reticence by telling her about himself. A couple of times, when Joe broke down, Hutchison reached over and gently held his arm while continuing to speak with Judy, and Joe gratefully clutched him back. Hutchison liked the Childerses' directness, how a sudden thought or emotion didn't just sit there, unexpressed. When he was done describing his marine career, Judy said, "Well, I'm already not believing this. You remind me so much of Shane."

Hutchison was particularly impressed with Morgan that afternoon and quickly realized that he had to check himself, resist his urge to command. When the baggage carousel started running and the Childerses briefly stepped out of earshot to look for their luggage, Hutchison spoke up.

"First sergeant, I think the best thing we can do for this couple now is just listen. You know? Just listen."

"Sir, I *am* listening. Christ, I've already been from Puerto Rico to Nam with this guy. All right?"

All of them were also aware of another, quiet dynamic that had taken over in the baggage terminal as soon as Hutchison and Morgan had arrived in their dress blues. They were standing together in a small knot—two uniformed marines with a man in a bright red navy cap who was occasionally crying, and a wife trying to buck him up. When they saw the Childerses and the marines together, the other airline passengers waiting for their baggage, and their friends and relatives who had arrived to meet them, stood in small groups against the walls, saying nothing, abandoning the usual gaiety and bustle of a baggage terminal. A number of the men took off their cowboy hats and held them against their chests and stood politely, staring straight ahead. The building was as hushed as a church. They knew, they all knew what this meant, even the ones who hadn't heard that the first casualty of Iraq was from nearby Wyoming. There was nothing embarrassing or uncomfortable about it. What the Childerses and their CACO detail felt from that silent airport crowd was respect.

At one point, after Judy had decided to rest on a bench near the wall, a Crow Indian woman quietly walked over, sat down beside Judy and patted her on the back. She told Judy that she was sorry for the family's loss. Hutchison thanked her and spoke with her for a while about the Crow reservation, which he liked to visit when he was out seeing the Custer Battlefield along the Little Bighorn River nearby.

Hutchison's initial feelings of respect and even deep affection for Joe and Judy were cemented once they had finally collected their luggage and they all headed out for the Childerses' car in the airport parking lot. It was a tan, 1986 Ford LTD with high mileage, and it wouldn't start. But this didn't seem to faze the Childerses at all, and there was no trace of embarrassment or the need to explain as Joe stepped to the back of the car and opened the trunk, which was full of farm equipment, tools, and spare parts.

"Ah, dang it all anyway," Joe said. "It's the electrical system again."

Once he had the front hood raised, Judy joined him at the engine and seemed even more adroit than Joe at monkeying around with the alternator and the battery connections until the engine turned over. The engine raced as they all said good-bye in the parking lot.

"Joe, are you sure that we can't run you back down to Powell?" Hutchison asked. "We don't mind at all."

"Nah, that's okay, cap'n," Joe said. "After all this, you know? Judy and I would just like to spend tomorrow alone. Get settled."

Hutchison said fine and handed Joe his business card with all his phone numbers, and urged him to call if he needed anything. Joe seemed to brighten as he read the business card and looked up with a playful smirk on his face.

"Recon, hunh? Marine recon. It says here that you guys are Company B, Reconnaissance Batallion."

"That's right, Joe," Hutchison said.

"Well good," Joe said. "Recon. I heard from the major down in Texas that you boys got lost trying to locate my ranch."

"It's not an easy place to find, Joe," Morgan said.

"All right, all right," Joe said. "How 'bout you guys showing up at eleven on Monday? That'll give marine recon plenty of daylight to find me."

Hutchison and Morgan were still laughing about it in their government Suburban as they followed the Childerses' taillights down the long, winding access road that descended the rimrock plateau.

"God, I love these people already," Hutchison said. "I just love them."

"Fine, sir, fine," Morgan said. "I love them too. But this Joe Childers is sure one piece of work."

At a discreet distance, so that the Childerses wouldn't consider them too intrusive, they followed the taillights of the Fairmont through downtown and didn't peal off until Joe and Judy made the turnoff for the interstate.

The drive that night down through the black, moody Pryors was difficult, especially for Joe. It had never bothered him much that he presented such a divided personality to the world. Sure, he was manly enough and always had a dozen projects going on at once–the farm machinery repairs, laying new irrigation pipe, shoeing a nasty mule or Percheron that nobody else wanted to touch–but he was always quite open, too, about his emotions, how he was by far the more demonstrative and vulnerable partner in his marriage with Judy. He was sometimes emotionally needy, but he'd always felt that he could control that by expressing himself, reaching out to someone, telling another one of his favorite stories about himself. But this was different now–Joe felt that he had no control whatsoever. The slightest thing, the smallest reminder, set off palpitations of regret and then convulsions of tears for Shane, which arrived in waves that seemed determined by an unseen force.

When Shane was home for Christmas, he was excited about his

pending skiing trip to Oregon with friends, which would be his last stretch of free time away from the marines before he was deployed to Iraq. One day, Shane decided to drive an hour north to the Red Lodge Mountain Ski Area in southern Montana to make some practice runs before he left for Oregon. Shane was elated when Joe decided to go along too.

They ended up sharing a wonderful day together–the best of his visit, they both thought. All the way up through the snowy badlands, before they turned in for Red Lodge at the Belfry cutoff, Shane and Joe jawed away in the pickup. They talked about Shane's plans after the war, or how his younger brother Sam was doing back in Illinois, Joe's various schemes for improving his ranch and catching up on the home repairs Judy was bugging him about. Shane was excited because he had arranged beforehand to rent telemark skis that day, and would be practicing the knee-bending turns required to use them, in preparation for his ski trip after Christmas. When they reached the ski area and Shane clomped off in his ski boots for the chairlifts, Joe stayed behind in the lodge. He chatted up all the waitresses in the cafeteria, discussed horses with another nonskier whom he met, and struck up a conversation with a group of ski instructors and learned all about what they did. Joe liked the atmosphere around the ski lodge–everyone seemed so buoyant and relaxed, devoted simply to having fun. This was one thing that Joe just loved about being with Shane. In so many ways, his world wasn't Joe's world any longer, but Joe always felt that he'd learned something new, met such interesting people, when he tagged along and peeped into Shane's life.

At nightfall, Shane returned to the lodge, cheery and red-faced from his runs, looking handsome and tall in his nylon jumpsuit and boots. He was energized from spending the afternoon on the slopes, excited about how quickly he had picked up making telemark turns. Joe could always tell when Shane had enjoyed a particularly good day and was bursting with manic joy about one of his interests. Every other

word became "freaking." All the way home in the pickup, he evangelized Joe about skiing, yapping away about all the freaking expensive
equipment you need, this freaking mountain and its freaking powder
in freaking Colorado, the girls on their freaking snowboards, and
Dad-you-know-I-really-mean-it-even-you-could-take-it-up, freaking
skiing.

Now Joe and Judy were on a lonely highway, passing the sign for
the Red Lodge Mountain Ski Area just above the Belfry cutoff. God,
this is so hard, Joe thought, blinking his eyelids to adjust for the mois-
ture so he could remain focused on the road. We drove through here
together, just three months ago. There's still snow beside the road.

It would be worse when he got home, Joe knew. There were reminders of Shane everywhere–the patches on the roof where he'd replaced shingles on his visit home last summer, the foundation trench
dug over Thanksgiving, all the cartons of Meals Ready to Eat stashed
out in the barn. Joe was worried about his reaction to that and mentioned this to Judy.

Judy knew that impatience never worked with Joe. She just had to
let him vent and then make suggestions that wouldn't work. But, she
told him, maybe anticipating a reaction just made it worse when you
actually had one. Why not concentrate instead on all of the practical
things they had to do–reserve motel rooms for family and friends, plan
the funeral, ask the marines for help getting all Shane's things back
from Camp Pendleton in California. In that sense, the long drive
through the badlands between Belfry and Powell was a telescoped version of their marriage. While Joe got dreamy and emotional, working
through his pain by telling a story, Judy knuckled down and faced the
details.

There was one last moment, a touching scene that Joe and Judy
knew they would never forget, after they had negotiated the back
roads of Powell and approached their ranch from the north. When
John Van Valin came over to feed the horses that day, he had run an

electrical cord out from Joe's shop, rigged a spotlight on a patio chair, and then trained it on the flagpole in front of the Childers house. Normally their place couldn't be seen from the road at night. But now, as they cleared the rise on Road 12, a soft beam of light illuminated the clapboard front of the house and, alone against the black prairie was an American flag at half-mast for Shane.

Joe just felt at peace about that, gently sad and pleased at once. They were home and the flag was lit for Shane.

"That was nice of John," Joe said to Judy, turning in for the drive. "It's typical of him to think of something like that."

At the last bend in the driveway the car's headlights swiveled southeast and reflected brightly off the splashboard of Joe's sleigh, still parked on the corner of the lawn where Shane had left it at Christmas. Oh Lord, Shane. Shane, what happened over there? You were so happy that day when you came in with the horses.

So he was crying again, but it didn't matter now because he was home and no one was around to see him. In the morning, he would have to figure out what to do with the sleigh. Maybe they'd be lucky this week and have one last snow so that he could hitch up the team and drive the sleigh out back. This week, as the house began to fill up with family and friends, no one else would notice or care about an extra sleigh hanging around the Childers front yard. But to Joe it was just too painful a reminder of Shane.

HOME ALONE

T he full day of travel that Joe and Judy spent returning to Wyoming on Saturday turned out to be a blessing in disguise, inadvertent relief from the deluge of national media. Through the Pentagon press office, the Marine Corps Casualty Assistance Branch in Quantico had finally released Shane's name at 9 P.M. on Friday and by noon the next day the parking lot of the big Blairs supermarket up on Route 14A in Powell, the first commercial stop on the road in from Cody, was jammed with film trucks and newspaper reporters. The supermarket's overwhelmed checkout-lane staff, appalled at the intrusion upon a grieving family's privacy, quickly huddled among themselves and refused to provide directions to the Childers ranch.

But because they were either on a plane or changing flights through Denver all day, Joe and Judy were mercifully unaware of the intense first-day rush of media interest until they arrived home Saturday night. In the kitchen, Judy found so many messages from the press on their phone machine that the tape had run out, and a camera crew from ABC's *Good Morning America* had left an interview request on a Post-it note attached to the front door.

Joe woke Sunday morning feeling tired and physically exhausted after a sleepless night, engulfed by sadness that he was facing another day without Shane. But he knew that he'd feel overwhelmed if he sat around all day in the house answering phone calls, brooding about his son, so he spent most of Sunday deliberately distracting himself with chores around the ranch. Talking to himself, occasionally blurring up and leaning against his workbench for support when he ran into another reminder of Shane, he moseyed around in the barn with his horses and mules, and then cleaned out and plugged in an extra refrigerator so there would be enough soda and cold drinks for the large numbers of family and friends expected to arrive during the week. Then, driving out the rutted lane along the perimeter of his property, he loaded his Toyota pickup with hay and fed his cattle. The brisk Wyoming wind burned his cheeks and, after a week of inactivity in Texas, Joe's muscles ached from heaving the heavy bales. But he felt sheltered and even momentarily buoyant out among the browsing steers and his piles of farm machinery, with the open views north and south to the mountains. Losing himself among the familiar confines of his own land seemed the only comfort left for him now.

Joe would later realize that his search for privacy that day taught him a few useful lessons about the national media. Reporters kept calling all day Sunday, and he and Judy eventually decided that, if they wanted to get anything done, they could pick up the phone only when they happened to be passing by in the kitchen. Joe ended up liking the reporters he spoke with—they all seemed unfailingly polite and expressed sincere condolences about Shane—but most of them just wanted a quick hit on their assigned story *that day*. If Joe and Judy simply ignored them for lack of time, or passed them onto someone else, most of the news outlets had no problem meeting their deadline needs and moving on.

By the end of the day, Joe had already heard from Shane's younger brother Sam, in La Salle, Illinois. Sam had heard from his parents about Shane's death late Friday night, and by 6 A.M. the next morning the phone was already ringing constantly as reporters called for interviews. So many television crews had called him—or just showed up at his house—that he literally had a traffic jam of satellite transmission trucks outside his door. Sam had always felt overshadowed by Shane and asserted himself less readily, especially around strangers, but now he had surprised even himself. Sam insisted that the television networks set up just one camera and group of lights in his living room, shooting all of their footage off the same equipment. It was very heady stuff at first, a shock course in media attention—at one point Sam was scheduled for a live interview with NBC anchor Tom Brokaw on Saturday morning, but this was later rescheduled to Sunday with another correspondent.

Meanwhile, down in Texas, Richard Brown faced the same onslaught of press calls. Although crazed by the details of preparing to deploy with his unit, Richard managed to find time to speak with reporters from the *Washington Post, Los Angeles Times,* and *Good Morning America.* Richard was particularly impressed with the way that the major network anchors, from distant studios in Washington and New York, could pick up on nuances of the family's story and go well beyond the obvious element of Shane being the first killed in Iraq. He found the experience curiously satisfying, even therapeutic, a welcome relief from the awful pressure of trying to decide whether or not to travel back to Wyoming with Sandra. It was almost as if the reporters' questions affirmed his own instincts about what was important in his personal story and were helping him work out what to do.

Joe was annoyed by one seemingly unimportant but highly visible aspect of the media coverage over the weekend. As soon as Shane's identity was released by the Pentagon, the wire services and the television stations ran to the only source for a picture that they could reach overnight—an old yearbook from Harrison Central High School in

Gulfport, Mississippi, dating back to the late 1980s. That was the first image of Shane that winged its way across the country as a digital photo file, appearing in countless newspapers and cable news reports. There wasn't anything really that wrong with the picture, but Shane's hair was long and his cheeks and chin were still boyish and unformed, not at all the image of the chiseled and determined marine officer he would become. Joe didn't really blame the media for the use of that dated photograph, and he couldn't quite put his finger on what riled him so about it. But he couldn't chase away the annoyance. Why couldn't they have waited for the family or the marines to provide a formal portrait of Shane with a proper haircut, all his medals on his chest, the tunic of his dress blues riding up to a crisp line around his neck? It seemed like such a trivial detail. Shane was dead, Joe's world had stopped, and now he was obsessing about a dated high school photograph that the press could hardly have avoided anyway. How could he get all tangled up inside about something like that?

A few reporters did get through, however, on Sunday and Monday. Correspondents for the *New York Times,* the Billings *Gazette,* and the Associated Press called out to the house first and then drove over. Both afternoons were unseasonably warm, and the wind had dropped, so Joe sat out on the ramshackle patio in front of the house, jawing away in his West Virginia drawl. He talked about Shane's rise in the marines, how prepared he had seemed just before he left for Iraq, and his eyes welled up with tears as he pointed out the sleigh in the yard and described how Shane had hooked up his team over the winter. The reporters all seemed entranced by Joe's Seabee career and wondered if his status as a Vietnam veteran made him question the rationale for the Iraq War. But Joe was steadfast about that. Despite the loss of his son, he had no reservations about the war and expressed strong support for the Bush administration's decision to topple Saddam Hussein.

To illustrate the story, the *Times* assigned a local freelance photographer, Stephen Smith, who had just moved to Cody after a successful stint with the *Rocky Mountain News* in Denver. Smith is a strong portraitist and, the following month, would win a Pulitzer Prize for photographs he took during the Colorado wildfires the summer before. In the photograph Smith took, Joe stood on the edge of the patio in his denim work shirt and navy ball cap, with the barbecue grill and the flag flying at half-mast etched hard against the Wyoming prairie behind him. The photographer from the Billings *Gazette* caught Joe in a similar pose. In both photographs Joe stared straight into the lens with a grim but satisfied "so, there" look on his face. Against his chest he held the formal Marine Corps portrait of Shane. In his dress blues, Shane was very military in bearing, and from the way Joe was holding the photo his son appeared to be gazing out over the sleigh and the fields to the southern rim of the Pryors.

Many strangers who reached out to the Childerses in the days after Shane was killed were impressed with the strength and resolve they displayed in public, a stoicism they ascribed to the unwavering patriotism of a couple who had been steeped in military values for most of their lives. But the Childerses' equanimity in the face of a crisis did not surprise their closest friends. Their thirty-four-year marriage had been forged during the crucible of Vietnam and afterward survived both economic hardship and some of the most tumultuous events of their times.

Joe was only eighteen in 1967 when he left his family's small subsistence farm along the dark, mountainous end of Smith Creek Hollow in Salt Rock, West Virginia. His father, Wilton Childers, made a more or less reliable living working factory jobs in nearby Huntington, but could never escape the lure of planting cash crops and fattening cattle on his rocky acres climbing both sides of the hollow. The extended

Childers family in the area were devout Southern Baptists, teetotalers and stubbornly resistant about leaving the West Virginia hill country, values and traditions that Joe would mostly leave behind. But he did inherit from his father both a penchant for grand story-telling and the lovable impracticality of part-time farming. More than thirty years after his son had left the hollow and made a name for himself at military postings around the world, Wilton Childers still loved to tell a favorite story about Joe. When he was just nine or ten, Joe had secretly saved his school lunch money to buy a goat, had it freshened, and then sold the milk to buy more goats. He soon enjoyed a thriving business derived from his small herd. Rising early to perform his own chores before work, Wilton could hear his son down in the barn, whistling amid the clatter of buckets and goats bleating. Then he watched from a window while Joe left the yard pulling a wagon, disappearing into the mists down the hollow to make his milk rounds.

Lovely and remote as they were, however, the West Virginia hollows could not escape the impact of the distant conflict in Vietnam. Like most West Virginia boys who displayed no interest in college, Joe knew by the time he finished high school that he faced a stark decision: either enlist in the branch of military service of his choice, or face being drafted by the army for the front lines of Vietnam. Joe would later describe his decision as less a matter of avoiding combat than the first of many romantic choices he would make about how he wanted to lead his life. Around his father's farm, he had always loved big, ambitious building projects–jacking up a whole barn from the sills to restore a foundation, laying new bridge timbers across the creeks to improve the roads–and by the time he was a teenager he was already a talented mechanic. While other boys fell for the lore of armored tanks or fighting ships, Joe loved the idea of traveling the world with the navy Seabees, the engineering battalions that built bridges, docks, and airport hangars for large military operations and bases. He was delighted, eight months after high school, when he was accepted for navy boot camp and then assigned to a steel-building unit of the Seabees.

Joe's two tours in Vietnam, in 1967 and 1968, were harrowing enough, but he was never in any real danger. During his first tour he was based at Quang Tri, where his unit was occasionally shelled or strafed with small arms fire while building airfields and railroad bridges, and his second tour in 1968 was conducted during the explosive fury of the Viet Cong's Tet Offensive, though generally his unit was involved in major construction projects far away from the major fire fights. Joe would later seem almost defiantly unreflective about Vietnam, not at all troubled by the post-traumatic stress or humiliation over the political divisions at home endured by so many returning Vietnam veterans. But this was mostly because the antiwar protests—largely an urban and college campus phenomenon—seemed so far away. In between his two hitches, Joe had returned to West Virginia to relax and work on his father's farm, or to share his new tales of Asia with the neighbors. Around Salt Rock, the military was respected and no one questioned his service in Vietnam.

Joe cut an antic figure among his fellow Seabees in Vietnam. He was a monster for work who could fix almost anything, was considered a genius at extricating heavy equipment from rice paddies, and never stopped talking. Joe regaled his friends with tales of the bizarre mishaps on his father's West Virginia farm—this draft horse that kicked him all the way across a stall, that mule that ran away with the plow—and then he'd drone on and on about his extravagant dreams of owning a draft horse farm some day. There were elaborate asides, and Joe's listeners soon learned that the only way to end a Childers tale was to stand up and walk away. Mail calls at the end of the month, when everyone's magazines arrived, were another Childers legend. While everyone else looked forward to receiving their *Playboy* or *Newsweek*, Joe was probably the only serviceman in Vietnam to receive both *The American Horseman* and *Dairy Goat Journal*. The Seabees in his unit howled with delight and chided him mercilessly when the magazines arrived, but Joe didn't care. Stretching out on the tarmac or against a pile of I-beams, he devoured his farm journals cover to cover, jawing away to anyone who wandered over about the latest in creamery barns or Tennessee Walkers.

Joe and Judy met at a USO party in Oxnard, California, near the Point Mugu Naval Air Station, just before Joe shipped out for his second tour of Vietnam. They corresponded regularly all through 1969, were engaged halfway through Joe's tour, and married within three days of his return. After a brief visit home to West Virginia to meet Joe's family, they were stationed back in Oxnard for several months before Joe was assigned to finish out his Seabee tour on Midway Island in the Pacific. The variety of their junkets around the world would be expressed by the birthplaces of their three children. Sandra, the oldest, was born on Midway in 1970, Shane was born in West Virginia in 1972, and Sam arrived during Joe's tour of service at Roosevelt Roads, Puerto Rico.

Judy knew that she had married an armful, an energetic dreamer and doer who always had a dozen outdoor projects going at once. But she was the first to tell Joe's Seabee pals that she was no cupcake herself. Naturally matriarchal and take-charge, she would prove adroit over the years at managing her rambunctious brood during Joe's frequent absences with the navy. From the start, however, they shared a love of adventure and a strong sense that they were running away from the same thing. Judy liked to say, "We never looked back and jumped right into life."

Joe would fail at an initial attempt to escape the economic orbit of the navy, but in a way that would establish his colorful reputation and career. After returning from Midway in November 1970, Joe used the GI Bill to enroll in a horseshoeing school in Porterville, California, north of Bakersfield. Joe loved the course and enjoyed slowly feeling more competent at clipping and filing down hooves, forging and fitting the red-hot shoes, and then driving home the nails at just the right angle so that they could be clipped off and rasped against the hoof, all the while entertaining his fellow students and teachers with his glorious talk. The family's needs were simple, and after Joe's savings from the navy ran out, they subsisted on state unemployment insurance. Judy and Sandra lived in a converted motel out near the edge of town and soon fell into the relaxed pace of a tourist town that called itself "The Gateway to the Sequoias." In early 1972, after he heard that a lot of quarter horses were being imported into West Virginia and that the trade was taking off, Joe moved the family back to West Virginia to follow his dream of building up enough of a stake as a blacksmith to buy a farm.

Joe loved the rural smithy's life, an occupation that fit his talkaholic, makeshift style. Outfitting a pickup with a portable forge, anvil, and tools, he ranged out over the hollows as far as Kentucky and Ohio, picking up jobs by word of mouth and often leaving before light in the morning to make his distant appointments. He roamed all the local auctions and horse sales in three states, lingering afterward to swap tales and learn about new breeds. But it was a tough, economically unstable life, especially after Shane was born in June that year and Judy began to complain about the loneliness and isolation of living in a house two hollows over from her in-laws in Salt Rock. Over that summer, when jobs opened up at feed stores or a railroad car foundry, Joe worked a regular day job and then struggled to meet his blacksmithing obligations at night. But these were the "stagflation" years of the Nixon economy and companies always seemed to be hiring just before they changed their minds and announced layoffs. Regular work got in the way of lining up horseshoeing jobs, and horseshoeing got in the way of regular work. In fact, even though few people saw it clearly at the time, West Virginia was in the midst of a massive deindustrialization, as basic industries like steel and transportation foundries either died or moved overseas. Joe was just skidding from job to job, a dreamy blacksmith in a nascent Rust Belt.

So two days after Christmas 1972, he reenlisted in the navy Seabees. But Joe's youthful economic defeat laid the foundations for a future that was both secure and alluring. Their first assignment was a Seabee unit in Roosevelt Roads, Puerto Rico, and Joe was overjoyed to learn that the navy's generous freight allowances for traveling families permitted him to ship all his blacksmithing tools. For Judy, the navy housing compound at the edge of the base in Roosevelt Roads seemed like a tropical paradise after the dark, rainy hollows of West Virginia, and she soon fell into a comfortable routine with the other navy wives, taking Sandy and Shane to the base swimming pool and playgrounds. Raising Shane was not at all like the experience Judy had with Sandra. By the time he was walking later that spring, Shane was ferociously energetic–the family pediatrician would eventually conclude that he was hyperactive. So Judy loved having the long Puerto Rican beaches and a fenced-in backyard where she could turn him loose. Scrambling up tree trunks or digging holes in the wet sand, Shane would literally run himself dry, collapsing into a deep sleep right where he sat, the beginning of a lifelong trait. His energy was a lot like his father's–boundless and spread across a half-dozen madcap diversions all day.

Joe was infinitely happy in Puerto Rico and kept up his own frantic pace. By day he roamed the navy base with his crew, entertaining everyone with his tall tales while he repaired hangar doors or built ports, and by night he roamed the fringes of the base and even a few of the neighboring farms, shoeing horses. There were more than one hundred pleasure horses on the main Roosevelt Roads base, and several dozen more at a smaller navy facility on the island, and he loved the schedule–finishing up with his Seabee crew by late afternoon, wolfing down an early dinner with the family, and then shoeing and talking, shoeing and talking while the sun slowly fell over the green

Puerto Rican hills. As Shane got older, Joe often brought him along, teaching him how to hold a pile of nails or hand over his hoof clippers, and then draping a blanket over a bale of hay when he fell asleep.

Joe had his own rationale about his horseshoeing rounds. In West Virginia, most of the fathers he knew were essentially absentee parents because they held down an extra job or two, an admirable display of the work ethic. He and Judy also felt strongly that at least one parent, preferably the mother, should be home with the children all day, but meanwhile they needed a second income to save for a farm back in the United States. Horseshoeing was the family's second job. But it also appeased Joe's enormous energy and wanderlust, his joy at discovering a new audience for his tales as he bent over a hoof and shoe pounding in the nails.

Roosevelt Roads set Joe on his course. Evenings and weekends he gypsied around in his truck, pulling on a big leather apron as he sized up each new job. He was a horseman and a smithy now, well known on a sprawling navy base. And it was at Roosevelt Roads that Joe Childers established his personal best. One weekend in the spring of 1973, with just a ten-hour break for dinner and some sleep, he completed hoof trims or full shoeing jobs on a grand total of twenty-one horses.

All day Sunday, when he wasn't interrupting his rounds on the ranch to meet with reporters, Joe was surprised by the number of markers of Shane lying around, reminders that he hadn't even noticed before. The Buena Vista saddle Shane had used when he was helping Joe break his foxtrotter filly was sitting on a pile of tack near the barn entrance, and a stainless steel coffee cup Shane had brought back from one of his Pacific cruises, engraved with the initials USMC, was gathering dust on a piece of two-by-four framing near the horse stalls. Joe picked up the coffee cup, cleaned off the dust and the cobwebs with his handkerchief, and then leaned against a pile of mule saddles and cried. There wasn't anything he could do except surrender to these "moments" for Shane and reflect on the memories they evoked. Often, when Shane was home, they would sit out in the barn together in the evening, sipping coffee and chatting, trying to decide which horse they should break first for the big trek up to Jack Creek, or discussing the next step in Shane's marine career.

All weekend Joe was rushed with gratitude about something else. On his last day home at Christmas, before he stepped into his red pickup and raced off for Oregon, Shane had stood up from the dining-room table, hugged Joe and Judy good-bye, and then deliberately tried to leave in a hurry, hoping to avoid a painfully drawn-out departure. But Joe wouldn't let Shane leave before he said one last thing. Now those words returned again and again as a mantra, and over the next several days Joe would repeat them when friends asked him about Shane's last visit home.

I loved him, and I told him that I loved him. I was proud of him and I told him that too. Now I've lost him and I'm sad. No shame in that, Joe Childers. Every time I saw him, every time he left, I told him that I loved him, that I was proud of him. Sorry folks if you remember another Joe Childers but that's what I said every time and now I'm okay with my tears.

There were a few happy, distracting moments on Sunday, too. Just before lunch, as Joe came in from feeding the cattle, a delegation from the Shoshone Back Country Horsemen pulled up the drive in their pickups. Joe was overjoyed to see them and blurred up again as he paused for long hugs with his friends. In their pickup cabs the wives all had tins of baked meals and desserts on their laps, so that Judy wouldn't have to worry about cooking. The pickup beds were filled with haphazard piles of equipment–folding tables and chairs, gas generators, extra garbage pails–which the Horsemen figured Joe might need to accommodate guests.

For a while, Joe enjoyed feeling useful, even festive about the arrival of so many friends. The house overflowing with guests reminded him of his boyhood in West Virginia, when the small farms along the hollow would fill up with visitors because someone had died. Funerals were social occasions, a time to visit and tell stories. Stepping inside, Joe checked that someone had made coffee and then ran out to the refrigerator in the barn a few times for cold drinks for their guests. Back in the house, Joe heard Judy repeating something she had said to Captain Hutchison and Sergeant Morgan the day before.

"Oh, I'm okay for now," she said. "Joe's the one we have to worry about. He's really taking Shane's death hard."

Joe wasn't sure that this was really accurate–maybe Judy holding so much in wasn't a good sign. But as a couple they had settled down to a kind of unspoken agreement about the matter. Joe was bawling his head off in front of friends and Judy was preserving her reputation as the rock of the marriage. So what? Whatever it took. Shane's death seemed so irretrievably unfair and *final* right now that he was willing to face almost anything just to get through each day.

It was blustery and gray when Joe joined the men out by the open shed doors of his shop. They could see the long, bluish ravines of the Pryors and the Bighorns, and the half-mast flag for Shane snapped in the gusts. Joe and his friends talked about mule-breeding and the weather, all the packing trips they were dreaming of this year once the snow melted off the peaks. When Joe told them that he was actually enjoying being alone on his first day home, his friends stepped inside for their wives and discreetly moved toward their pickups.

Over the winter, Joe had purchased two new Levi's jean jackets, one for himself and one for Shane. One of the wives of the Shoshone Back Country Horsemen was a talented seamstress who had promised to stitch the lettering and logo of the group on the back of the jackets, the kind of goofy, all-American gift that Shane loved. Joe hadn't heard from her after he'd given her the jackets, but she was among those who visited on Sunday and he asked her about it.

"Say, did you ever manage to get that logo stitched on the jackets?"

"Oh gosh, Joe," she said. "I'm sorry. The jackets are done. I'll get them back over here pronto. I promise."

"No rush, dear, no rush," Joe said. "Either way. It's just that I've figured out what I should do with the jacket meant for Shane."

A couple of hours later, after a round-trip drive into Cody, the woman delivered the finished jackets to the Childerses, and Joe put them aside inside the house.

John Van Valin dropped by that night to help Joe feed his cattle, hopping the fence and grabbing a bale as he walked out to the spot where Joe was spreading hay for his steers. Joe was glad to see him and launched into one of his tales, so that John experienced the familiar feeling of having joined him in mid-sentence. When they finished outside, they went in the barn and carried hay and oats for the horses. When they were done and had stepped outside to the lit barnyard, Joe asked John to wait for a moment. He had something for him in the house.

Joe came back out through the side door carrying a Shoshone Back Country Horsemen jean jacket, the one that had been stitched for Shane.

"Say, John, I had one of these made up for Shane and, you know, Shane's not going to be able to enjoy it now. I'm pretty sure it's your size. Try it on. Considering his feelings for you, I bet Shane would get a real kick out of you having it now."

John was almost speechless but thanked Joe as he put on the jacket, and then turned around into the beam of the barn light so that Joe could admire the bright red and blue of the logo and lettering. They stood there and talked for a while, with lavender and pink tendrils of light out over the Beartooths in the western sky, before John had to leave.

A couple of afternoons that week, while he was waiting for

Shane's body to return and he was distracted by the details of making funeral arrangements, Joe suddenly had the urge to be with John and drove over to see him. He wasn't afraid to wrap his big, bearlike arms around Van Valin and cry until he felt better. Deb Van Valin called this "Joe getting his John fix." John tried to have his new Shoshone Back Country Horsemen jacket on whenever Joe appeared, and he always wore it when he drove over to the Childerses himself.

One afternoon after John left in his pickup, Joe was crossing his yard when he was struck by an idea so contradictory yet sensible that it had to be true. If he said so himself, he had to admire his own thinking about it. Parting with that jacket was all wrapped up in his "separation process" from Shane. A side of him, he knew, still expected "old Shane to come diddly-boppin' down the lane any minute now and say something to make us all laugh." He probably wouldn't be able to get over that wishful thinking until Shane's body was returned and they faced the finality of a funeral. In the meantime he just loved seeing John in that jacket and decided that it was useless to try to untangle all the emotions he had about that.

KNOW HOW TO BE

O n Monday morning Captain Hutchison and First Sergeant Morgan rode back down over the dark, moody Pryors in their government Suburban, glumly reviewing the pile of government forms bulging out of Hutchison's black canvas satchel. They were both concerned that they might overwhelm Joe and Judy Childers with the mountain of paperwork that had to be completed in the next several days and agreed to keep this first visit under two hours. Besides, they were planning on visiting the local funeral home and the police chief in Powell to begin making arrangements for what they expected to be a complicated, crowded funeral event. After clearing the last foothills east of Cody, they bumped across the Childerses' dusty drive. Once more Hutchison's heart sank as he took in the panorama of wobbly fence lines, swayback horses, and piles of farm machinery stretching back to the Polecat Bench, but then he caught himself just in time.

Hutchison knew that noticing the disorganized, Steinbeck-clutter of the Childers place was just a social judgment on his part, and that he would be much better off recalling his lifetime motto, a Spanish concept called *saber estar.* The term literally translated into English as "know how to be," and Hutchison had first heard it from an avuncular, grizzled Mexican janitor with whom he had worked as a boy in southern California, when he accompanied his father to his office on Saturday mornings. (His bilingualism had emerged even earlier when his nanny, Maria, who adored young Kevin, insisted on speaking to him only in Spanish.) In prep school, his Spanish teacher had encouraged Hutchison to write an essay on the importance of not only understanding *saber estar,* but also the usefulness of adopting personal credos to guide his life.

At the time, Hutchison thought that all this devotion to personal credos was embarrassing, the corny sort of thing that prep school teachers tried to develop in their students. A side of him still felt that way, but the problem with *saber estar* was that it worked. Whether he was touring Europe with his college friends, or rescuing one of his rifle platoon recruits from a drunken confrontation at a North Carolina strip joint, he had found that he never met someone new he didn't somehow like. "You know, Barry," Hutchison had occasionally said to Morgan, "I've never met a single person from whom I didn't learn something important." In reply, the first sergeant would just grunt.

Now the dust of a bumpy Wyoming drive was swirling up in vortices over the roof of his government vehicle, obscuring the windshield and settling in a thick film on the hood of the Suburban. Hutchison was reminded again that he would much rather be serving elsewhere, in a real war, not devoting himself to CACO work in this lonely, shitwreck remove of the western prairies. But *saber estar.* Wordlessly he parked the Suburban in between a pile of sun-bleached lumber and a mound of old tractor tires. It was his job now to fold himself into the lives of the Childers family, considering only their situation, not his.

Judy met Hutchison and Morgan at the front door and escorted them through the small sun room inside the shed addition. She had already turned the piano inside the dining room into an impromptu but surprisingly attractive shrine to Shane Childers, with his official marine portrait, flowers, press clips, snapshots, and condolence cards arranged along the sheet-music shelf and the top surface. When Hutchison and Morgan instinctively placed their dress caps on the piano stool, the look seemed to complete the tableau, creating a memorial that was almost too perfect, as if the piano and its mementos to Shane were a photographer's still-life for a Hallmark card.

When they sat down at the large antique table in the dining room, clearly the center of the open floor plan of the house, they could see that they wouldn't be overwhelming the Childerses. If anything, they were a welcome relief. All morning delivery trucks bearing flowers, condolences, and cooked meals from neighbors were arriving, and the phone was constantly ringing. Judy briskly made coffee and Joe came in from the barn wearing his USS *Tortuga* ball cap. They all fell in together around the table and Hutchison felt that the Childerses' informality and warmth was infectious. Observing his best marine officer decorum–actually, it was a default to his prep school manners– Hutchison insisted on calling Judy "Mrs. Childers." The third or fourth time she heard him address her that way, Judy cocked her head sideways, turned her mouth into a mock frown and reached over and touched Hutchison's hand.

"Captain Hutchison," Judy said, grandiloquently stretching out the syllables of his rank and name. "I'll call you Kevin, and you'll call me Judy, all right? That's an order from *Mrs. Childers.* Got it?"

"Right, Mrs. Childers," Hutchison said. "It's Judy from now on. I promise."

"Oh God, Joe, don't you just love him?" Judy said, reaching across the table to squeeze Hutchison's hand again. "So polite. Just like Shane."

"Yeah, that was old Shane all right," Joe said, his eyes misting up.

"The neighbors would all tell me that Shane got all the manners that I never picked up."

It truly was a mountain of paperwork and decision making that they had to plow through that morning, but Hutchison was relieved about it, even happy for himself. Crisply moving Joe and Judy through the forms, explaining everything in detail, for the first time he actually felt that he was doing something productive, really helping them. The first thing he did was hand them a check for $6,000 and a receipt form to sign—the death gratuity automatically paid by the Pentagon to the next of kin of any serviceman killed in training or action, so the family would have funds just to tide them over the first painful weeks. Judy quietly put that aside, beginning the pile of paperwork that she would meticulously maintain as they progressed. Hutchison then explained the payment of $250,000 for Shane's military group life insurance policy, his pay arrears and certfication of combat pay, which had begun as soon as he left Camp Pendleton in February, his military 401(k) plan, the payoff of his student loans, and forms for the disposition of his remains to the family and the payment of a standard government allowance of $4,300 for funeral costs.

The list was endless. Hutchison explained that there were government allowances available for family members to travel to the funeral, but only if they were "immediate next of kin." Judy wanted to use that benefit to help pay for the travel costs of more distant relatives who probably couldn't afford to come to the funeral. Hutchison promised to wiggle that through the Casualty Assistance branch in Quantico. Certifying Shane's ribbons and medals so that his burial uniform could be prepared, transferring his car ownership to his parents and recovering the personal possessions that he'd left behind in a suburban San Diego storage facility, all required a separate set of multiple forms.

One aspect of this impressed Hutchison. All servicemen about to be posted overseas, especially for combat assignments, are required to run through a long series of records checklists to make certain that, in the event of injury or death, their insurance forms, medical history, and records of personal property are in order and immediately accessible by computer and in a single paper file. These personal records were supposed to be checked and double-checked by commanding officers, but often that process became the first casualty of a hectic deployment. Frequently, recovering the records or bank accounts of an injured or killed soldier was a nightmare for the battalion support staff or CACO officers back home. But Shane Childers' files seemed to be in perfect order, with every credit card and its expiration date, every bank balance and college loan meticulously recorded in his small, precise handwriting on the proper forms.

"Judy, I'm really amazed by how these records are kept—Shane must have been very . . ." Hutchison said, and then immediately regretted it, because perhaps he was evoking too painful a reminder.

"Organized," Judy said. "He was very organized. I don't think there's a person I know who packed more in, had more fun, than Shane. It was crazy what he tried to do with a single day, how disorganized it all seemed. But then every paper that was due, every form that had to be filled out, was in order. That was Shane. The most organized disorganized person you could meet."

The succession of paperwork and all the decisions they had to make frequently prompted memories from Judy and Joe, and Hutchison felt that he was slowly learning more about Shane, but in no particular order. The memories were returning disjunctively, flashback piling upon flashback. First Joe would talk about Shane hitching up his team to the sleigh when he was home for Christmas, and then he would digress to the horseshoeing junkets they had taken together in Virginia or Iran, when Shane was still a boy. Judy was the same way, but her stories were shorter and generally led to a point. When Hutchison mentioned how orderly Shane's records were, for example, Judy jumped to something she wanted to say.

During the twelve years that they had lived in Wyoming, Shane was always buying them something new when he returned home. Aging color-television tubes or coffeemakers with broken timers aroused in him a deep, altruistic urge to blow some money on his parents—and he was the same way with his other relatives. While Joe and Judy were off at work, Shane would hop into his pickup and drive into the Wal-Mart in Cody or the Radio Shack at the mall in Billings, buy a new appliance, and then race in at twilight in a swirl of pickup dust. He loved surprising them with a new appliance, theatrically removing it from the cardboard box, installing it in the living room or the kitchen, and then squabbling with Joe about how to work the new remote or program the electronic features. Over dinner Shane would entertain them with stories about the people he'd met—to him, that's what a shopping excursion was all about. The young community college student working behind the counter at Radio Shack—maybe, just maybe, Shane was never certain about this, she was flirting with him—who was thinking of dropping out of school, but Shane was pretty sure that he had talked her out of it. At the food court at the Billings malls, he met old Indians from the Northern Cheyenne reservation, or refinery workers from the big Chevron plant, and argued with them about national politics or Custer's Last Stand. As Shane grew older and matured, especially after he entered The Citadel in South Carolina, these conversations with strangers became both more confident and ecumenical. Shane loved to describe them to his parents, to debrief his "great freaking day." Fun-fun, hop into the pickup and race up through the mountains for Billings, meet an architect or a French teacher at the food court and sponge everything he could from their brains, then ride back home along a new route through Red Lodge or Deaver, meeting still more people at the tourist traps or general stores. He was insatiable about it, addicted to the thrill of meeting new people. And he loved these vacation junkets best because he was wearing civilian clothes and no one could typecast him as a marine.

A few days later, when he left for Camp Lejeune or The Citadel,

Shane would leave an envelope behind on the kitchen counter. It contained duplicates of the warranty forms and service contracts that he had neatly filled out and mailed to the appliance manufacturer. Sometimes he would also include hand-written instructions or suggestions for Joe and Judy. For weeks afterward Shane would pester them with e-mails and calls. Were they following the instructions? Had Joe learned to work the remote?

"Shane wasn't exactly what you'd call a control freak," Judy said to Hutchison. "He was too nice for that. But you definitely knew that he had plans for your life."

Over the weekend, Hutchison had worried about what to tell the Childerses about the return of Shane's body. A full colonel at Quantico had already told him that because of Shane Childers' status as the first killed in the war, and what the marines expected to be considerable media attention, his case was being given high priority–right up to division command. Whatever Hutchison needed in order to expedite the return of Shane Childers' remains, whatever problems he encountered, the captain merely had to inform Quantico and they'd pull rank up through the command. But Hutchison knew he couldn't trust this. After being placed in a body bag and a plain aluminum transport coffin filled with ice, Shane's body would be flown by Air Force cargo plane from a field morgue in Kuwait to Germany. From there, with the timing depending on other casualties and returning cargo, the body would be transshipped to the joint services national mortuary at Dover Air Force Base in Delaware. Again, depending on how busy the mortuary was, the mandatory autopsy and forensic reports, embalming, fitting Shane's body with a dress blue uniform and a proper medals rack, and then a coffin of the Childerses' choice, required at least another two to three days. The flag-draped coffin would then be returned to the family in Wyoming, with a marine officer as escort, in the cargo hold of a scheduled airliner. But the "information flow" concerning the progress of the body toward home was actually distrib-

uted through three military locations–Quantico, Dover, and a navy lo-
gistical support center (the marines are technically a division of the
navy) at the Great Lakes Naval Station in Illinois. Red tape and delays
were almost guaranteed. The wait for the return of a soldier's body
could take at least a week or ten days.

Hutchison worried that if he was honest with the Childerses and
told them that he really didn't know when the body was returning,
they would lose confidence in him and become upset. But if he lied
and adopted a posture of false assurance, that might eventually upset
them more. His marine CACO manual was 150 pages long and had
something to say about everything, but not this.

When he started to explain the procedures for returning Shane's
body, Judy Childers interrupted and held up her hand.

"Kevin, it's okay, you can just tell us," Judy said, holding up her
hand. "You don't know, right?"

"No, Judy, I don't know for sure," Hutchison said. "Not yet."

"Well you don't have to apologize for that," Judy said. "We're a
military family and we understand. Just be honest with us. Just tell us
what you know, and what you don't know. That's all we expect."

Hutchison felt awful about it. He was the CACO officer. The family relied on him to know. But he didn't know and instead of really
being able to help the Childerses by focusing on details, he was frequently distracted by all these queer leaps of intuition, brought on by
the intensity of the CACO experience and the plaintive scene. While
he sat there explaining the return of Shane's body, the prairie wind
moaned around the corners of the ranch house, rattling the gutters
and the windowpanes, and then the sun briefly but intensely broke
through the clouds. Outside, it illuminated the gray-brown striations
on the Polecat Bench. Inside, a bright triangle of light beamed across
the shrine to Shane on the piano, glinting off the gold braid on Hutchison's and Morgan's dress caps and the glass flower vases.

Okay, yeah, now I can tell, Hutchison thought. Judy likes me and she's such a strong reader of body language—just like my mother, always anticipating my thoughts. I just wish my voice wouldn't hesitate and crack when I spoke.

Judy and Joe had briefly toyed with the idea of burying Shane at Arlington National Cemetery outside Washington, D.C., which would have made traveling to the funeral so much easier for the populous Childers clan in West Virginia. Besides, it would have been *so* Shane. Shane, wonking out on every battle of the Civil War, Shane who knew the Normandy invasion and the long slog toward Berlin so well. Now he'd be buried in the company of soldiers he practically knew, overlooking the Potomac and the Washington Monument. But in the end they decided that it wasn't practical. They'd miss visiting Shane at his grave and the family seat was in Wyoming now. Crown Hill Cemetery on the eastern edge of Powell was a beautiful place, high up, with commanding views of the Shoshone River plain and the Bighorn massif to the east. In 1996, when he had returned from marine security guard duty at the American embassies in Geneva and Nairobi, Shane had spent several days staying in shape by pedaling like mad on his bike all the way out to Clark's Fork and then making the big Deaver loop. He loved the snow-capped mountains out there, which reminded him of the Alps and Mount Kilimanjaro, which he had climbed several times. Back from Pendleton, or back from Twentynine Palms on his way to Iraq, he had dreamed with Joe about another run with the mules up to Jack Creek. This was his country and he had loved visiting his parents there. That's where he belonged now, they decided, back in the snowy bosom of the Bighorns.

Hutchison sat at the table and patiently listened while the Childerses discussed the burial plans. It was a useful step, he thought, part of the process. Who knows what shape the body will be in and how we're going to deal with that? The Childerses would be confronting a lot while they waited for Shane to return. Talking about burying Shane, instead of just being flooded by memories of him alive, was a way of facing the awful finality of his death.

Judy told Hutchison that she thought it was best for them to establish a firm date for the funeral and memorial service, because that would make it easier for family members who needed to make plans to travel all the way to Wyoming. Veterans' groups, local politicians, and even the governor's office had called to ask about the funeral, and they would need a certain date too. She was thinking of a week from Tuesday. Hutchison agreed on the need to set a firm date but suggested that they wait, just a day or two, until he knew more.

Hutchison and Morgan noticed something again about the Childerses, which they discussed later in the car. Judy was affectionate and warm, very realistic, but also very composed emotionally. She showed no signs of breaking down about Shane, which worried both of them. Joe, meanwhile, seemed to have no filter on his emotions, and he defaulted in a particular way. Whenever there was a new form to sign or a decision to make, he would instantly derail, put down the pen, and launch into another story about Shane, which just boiled him up toward a long crying jag.

"Oh, my Shane, you know?" Joe would begin in his West Virginia drawl. "You should have seen him come home for Thanksgiving or Christmas, hitch my Belgians to the sleigh and then jingle out across the snow to feed the cattle. You should have seen that boy ride a mule up into Jack Creek. Then he'd come back, break down my combine and fix it. There wasn't anything he couldn't do. Shane."

Two things always set Joe off—events he had shared with Shane, or plans he had made with Shane. Hutchison and Morgan admired Joe for being so frank with his emotions, letting it all out. But his yarns, with all the obligatory Childers digressions, were awfully long, and toward the end of them Judy would start to fidget, lose her patience, and then place a pen in Joe's hand and make him sign the form.

Morgan recognized in the Childerses a prototype from his youth—the Iowa farm couples he'd known around Waterloo in the late 1970s. So many of them were interesting but troubled couples, made so by the dire farm economy of the Midwest. The men were all fun-loving and great storytellers, yapping away about their quail hunts or plans for laying new drainage tile in their fields, even if they were hocked right up to the top of their new silo clusters in bank debt. They literally jawed their worries away, they were adventurers in farming whose narcotic was talk. Meanwhile, back at the farmhouse, their expressionless and preoccupied wives monitored the bank debt, made sure the crop insurance was paid on time, and fretted about the children and whether they'd be able to attend college. The men provided all the colorful identity and dreams on those Iowa farms. But it was the women who established the real center of gravity and kept those farms and families together.

When they were done with most of the paperwork, at a little after 1 P.M., Judy stood up and walked toward the kitchen, suggesting that the CACO team remain for lunch. Hutchison was about to thank her—he thought that they should, if asked, stay for lunch—but then Morgan cleared his throat, stepped over for his officer's cap on the piano stool, and spoke.

"Ah, ma'am, the captain and I agreed that we wouldn't burden you by too long a stay," he said. "And we think that we should get over to the funeral home, to start making arrangements."

Joe Childers just loved this and started to laugh.

"Hey, cap'n," Joe said. "The first noncom is kicking your butt here, hunh? He's the boss and he doesn't want you to stay for lunch."

Morgan immediately felt bad about it, if Joe Childers was going to frame it that way. He hadn't meant to undercut his chief of command.

"Ah, sir. Joe," Morgan said, "I love Kevin. He's my captain, and the best. I'm just saying . . ."

"No, no, sergeant," Joe said. "It's okay. I'm just remembering being the noncom myself, and having to kick that captain's butt. Ship's gotta run on time, you know? You go along. It's all right."

"Kevin," Judy called from the kitchen. "Next time?"

"Judy, it's a date," Hutchison said. "Wednesday we're coming back and we're staying for lunch."

Hutchison was still edgy about it when they got out to the car. They had turned down the Childerses' offer of lunch, but his first sergeant was probably right about it being time for them to leave. How was it best to serve this family? Hutchison sighed as he pulled the Suburban around in reverse. *Saber estar.* Knowing how to be just wasn't at all easy in the situation he was now in.

"Thanks, Barry," Hutchison said. "It was probably time to get out of there. But I just feel so awful for the Childerses. I feel so sad for them."

Morgan felt the same way, but it was his nature to stay focused on practical details, to keep the CACO running on time. The two marines, in fact, were nudging toward a sensible division of labor. While Morgan concentrated on mopping-up details and maintaining the order of the Billings command, Hutchison's purview was emotions, and constantly attuning himself to the Childerses' needs. He was becoming the commander in charge of bereavement.

Hutchison turned east on the farm road, toward Powell. The brisk Wyoming wind was up now, and he noticed in the rearview mirror that it was blowing their dust trail due south, ninety degrees to the bumper.

The Miratsky-Easton Funeral Home stands just off the main commercial district of Powell, two blocks west on Third Street. It's a simple, unpretentious cinder-block structure, painted white on the sides with a tasteful tan stucco facade in the front. Graceful columns holding up a verandah roof, and three large cottonwood trees in the front yard, complete the look and seem to complement the quiet elegance of the residential neighborhood that stretches west to the prairie.

On Monday afternoon, when Hutchison and Morgan stepped up to the front door of the funeral home and rang the bell, Laura Richardson, the matronly, cheerful, brown-haired funeral director, looked through the curtains of her office window and saw the two marines standing under the verandah in their dress blue uniforms and white caps.

Oh my God, they're here, she thought. They're here and please God, or someone, start praying for me. This is going to be tough, honey, real tough.

Richardson stepped through the large reception vestibule of the funeral home and opened the front door for the marines, quickly ushering them in and locking the door behind them so they wouldn't be disturbed, and then introduced herself.

"Laura," Hutchison said, "We're here because a young marine from Powell, Lieutenant Therrel Shane Childers, has been killed."

"Captain, I know that already," Richardson said. "It's such a terrible thing to say, but, well, I was hoping you wouldn't be coming here. But now you're here and Lord help us. We've got *so* much work to do."

Richardson knew a lot about military funerals. A native of Wyoming, she had married and then moved to New Mexico, becoming a funeral director after she was divorced and needed a means of supporting her two young children. She had returned to Wyoming several years before to be closer to her family and her mother, who lived in Lander, and to take over the management of the funeral home in Powell for an owner who lived in Arizona. But while she was still in New Mexico, Richardson had handled the funerals of two active-duty servicemen, one of whom had been killed in a helicopter crash in Greece, the other during parachute training in the United States. She was familiar with the peculiar demands of military deaths–the long wait for a body, which made it almost impossible to finalize arrangements, the meticulous color guards, processions, and gun salutes, the outpouring of curiosity and support from local veterans groups and distant military commands. Burying even the most obscure, low-ranking private required an attention to detail and an ability to coordinate that far exceeded the demands of a civilian funeral.

Richardson had first heard about Shane Childers' death on Saturday morning and all weekend she was worried about something else, a concern shared by several other Wyoming funeral directors who had already called to offer their help with the funeral. In the fall of 1998, Wyoming had been both repulsed and riven with divisions after the death of a young homosexual student at the University of Wyoming, Matthew Sheperd, who had been robbed, pistol-whipped, and then roped to a fence all night on the outskirts of Laramie. During the memorial services for Sheperd, thousands of gay activists and fundamentalist Christian antigay activists descended on Wyoming and there were several ugly confrontations between these groups. This offended the natural decency and the live-and-let-live sensibility of many Wyoming residents, but they didn't blame the activists. They blamed the national media and especially the television camera crews that roamed freely through Laramie for several days, filming the confrontations between the gay and antigay activists and interviewing ordinary Wyoming folks in a way that made them look like hicks. Many Wyoming residents were still resentful about that. Big events, the arrival of the national media, they concluded, were bad for Wyoming. It was as simple as that, and now the funeral drama for the first soldier killed in Iraq would draw too many outsiders—antiwar protestors, veterans groups, the marauding media—into a replay of the Sheperd mess.

Richardson considered these fears to be exaggerated, mostly an expression of how uncomfortable Wyoming felt under the glare of publicity, but they added to the mounting pressure she felt all weekend. The Shane Childers funeral *had* to be perfect, flawlessly executed, and she knew how much was involved.

Hutchison and Morgan sat down with Richardson in the carpeted, tastefully furnished conference room where she met with families to discuss funeral arrangements. They were immediately impressed with her reassuring mix of brisk efficiency and personal warmth.

"Okay, captain, sergeant, we all have to start making up lists," Laura told them. "We need lists on yellow legal sheets, okay? You guys will be going back to Billings tonight and making up lists of everything you need, everything you expect from me, all your needs. And I'll be spending tonight making up *my* lists. Then on Wednesday we'll merge and purge our lists and get started."

They were amazed by her, how much went into a big military funeral, which they could see was not going to be at all like the relatively small, private affair they had arranged last summer in Montana. Had Hutchison thought yet about contacting local car dealers, so that vans could be provided to drive the family back and forth from the funeral and burial? What about blocking out motel reservations in Cody and Powell for visiting relatives? There wasn't a church large enough in town to accommodate a funeral of this size, so they would probably have to arrange to use the community college gym. She advised Hutchison and Morgan to start mentally and emotionally preparing themselves to view the body, once Shane Childers arrived, to help ease the family through the difficult decision about whether the casket should be open or shut during the wake. If they decided on a full military procession through Powell, which many people in town were already asking about, arrangements about routing and security had to be made with the police and county sheriff. And they would have to protect themselves against snafus, especially paperwork snafus, always a problem when dealing with the military. To legally bury Childers she would need a death certificate and an assignment of the remains to the family, and they would have to be in touch with uniform suppliers as well, just in case Childers arrived without a proper medals rack. Everything had to be considered.

While she was running through her mental checklists, Laura would occasionally reach over and squeeze their arms. When she stood up to refill their coffee cups, or check a file, she patted them on their shoulders, bolstering them up, as if to take the edge off her litany of instructions.

Hutchison made a strong, early impression on Laura as well. While he seemed very professional and intent on getting the details right, he was also disarmingly humble. He didn't affect the aura of unquestioned command that she found so common in other military officers. When she asked him whether he had a firm delivery date for Childers' body, or if he'd discussed a burial plot with the family, he wasn't embarrassed to tell her that he didn't know or hadn't checked that yet.

"Laura, how do we make this happen?" Hutchison asked her. "We've never done anything this big before. I need your help."

After they were done in the conference room and had moved toward the front door, Morgan scooted out to the verandah while Hutchison and Laura lingered to talk for a few more minutes. Before Hutchison left Laura squeezed his hand once more and tried to be reassuring.

"Captain," she said. "I know it all seems like a lot to do. But let's work together, okay? I won't let you down."

On the ride back to Billings, Hutchison and Morgan reviewed all their paperwork, started making their lists, and discussed a sensible division of labor for the rest of the week. While the captain would work intensively with the Childerses and Laura Richardson on all the funeral details, the sergeant would have to concentrate on assembling and drilling a color guard and gun-salute team for the funeral. They were in "marine mode" now. It would all get done.

After they got north of the Montana line and were passing through Bridger, it got dark outside, and they had to abandon their paperwork. They rode in silence for a while, but then Morgan just couldn't resist.

"Say, sir, mind if I mention one other detail?"

"Barry, please," Hutchison said. "Go ahead."

"I'll keep your secret about Laura Richardson, okay? Sir."

"Barry, shut up."

"Ah, c'mon, sir. I'll keep your secret. I mean, she kept touching your arm. She held your hand. She *likes* you, sir. I found it very moving and . . ."

"Now look, Barry," Hutchison said.

"Sir! I *will* keep your secret. None of the girlfriends in Billings have to know. Promise."

"Sergeant," Hutchison said. "Shut your pie hole. Now. And that's an order."

But it was good they were laughing now. To the right of the car the Pryors were black and featureless and to the west the high rim of the Beartooths glowed incandescent purple and orange as the sun fell. They were exhausted from the emotions of the day, overwhelmed by the funeral chores they still faced. But at least they could rib each other in the old way, pretending they were on some other mission.

"I'm just saying, sir, you know? I've got to hand it to you. You've really got a way with these older women."

When he got back to Billings that night, Hutchison worked for two hours at the armory faxing all his completed paperwork out to Quantico, checking his e-mail, and generally feeling overloaded about all the details of his command that were being neglected because of his CACO responsibilities with the Childerses. At home, he made dinner, worked for another hour on lists for Laura Richardson, and then decided that he was too ramped up, too overtired, to go to sleep. He was jittery about the war in Iraq and felt disorganized because of the piles of tools and reconstruction rubble littered around his house. But it was still early enough for him to call home to California and talk with his mother and older sister.

Hutchison's parents had divorced when he was a year old. After that, his father had remarried, and his parents lived fifteen minutes away from each other in Palos Verdes. Hutchison spent every other weekend with his father. The demands of adjusting to what would eventually become a very extended Hutchison clan had made him very sensitive, but also very flexible. By the time he was fifteen, when his father remarried for a second time, Hutchison had already gone through the "evil stepmother" experience and suffered the envy of watching his father lavish attention and money on his stepbrothers and stepsisters. Hutchison felt disappointed and lonely after his two older sisters left for college but soon learned to stay in touch with them by phone.

Counting both his father's remarriages and his mother's, he eventually had a total of eleven siblings and stepsiblings, and they were all close. His father established an admirable model by putting all his children and stepchildren through college without complaint, and every Thanksgiving he took the whole madass jumble of the blended Hutchison clan–wives, ex-wives, new husbands, boyfriends and all–down to the Balboa Club at Mazatlan in Mexico for a long holiday. They all had a crazy time together down there and, as a result, Hutchison's sense of family was bumptious but very committed. "I probably have just about the healthiest family in America," Hutchison liked to say. "We put the fun back in dysfunction."

Hutchison was particularly close to his mother, Nancy, and his older sister, Heidi, and frequently spoke with them by phone late into the night. It was a habit that he revealed to only a few close friends, but he retained a confident, self-mocking humor about it. Yes, he was undeniably a tough, successful marine, particularly respected among his peer group of officers for the variety of his "expert" rankings–everything from parachute school to winter warfare. But when something bothered him, or the shit hit the fan in the Corps, he called home and debriefed with Mom. It was a system of personal support and evaluation that worked well for him.

Over the weekend, Hutchison had already told his mother and sister about his CACO assignment. They were solicitous and promised to do whatever they could to help but he really didn't know very much at that point. Now the concerns he shared with them were quite specific. He'd forgotten just how many *details* had to be mastered during a CACO case, and he was afraid that he'd obsess on one or two and then become overwhelmed. Also, he worried about losing his professional detachment. He felt so sorry for the Childerses, so committed to them already, that he was afraid that he might burst into tears and not perform his job. As the week progressed and he became increasingly preoccupied and wasn't able to sleep, Hutchison's entire family–his father, his mother, his sisters–were concerned, and they called frequently to buoy him up.

"Kevin, I don't really have a very good picture of this family yet," his mother said to him that night. "Tell me more. Then I can help you."

So Hutchison told her about the Childerses and Joe's storytelling, his West Virginia rearing and two hitches in Vietnam, then blacksmithing school and his long romantic career in the Seabees. When he got to the part about Joe taking Shane off every weekend on his horseshoeing junkets, his mother began to cry.

"Oh, but, Kevin, can't you see?" she said. "You're perfect for this. You care about people, and they sense it right away. I know you don't want to be doing this, but just remember that you were chosen for a reason."

"But, Mom, I'm so upset I might cry."

"It's okay to cry, Kevin! When you feel like that, just call us. Call home."

Later, when his sister Heidi called–she'd been briefed through the family phone tree–she made Hutchison repeat after her: It's okay to cry, Kev, it's okay, you're supposed to be sensitive. When you feel like that, call us. Call home.

After the phone calls, Hutchison tried to get some sleep, but his mind was still swirling from Judy to Heidi to his mother, their repeat-after-me doting. One thing that both Judy and his mother said affected him. He and Shane *were* very similar and he knew that they would have instantly liked each other. They were only a year apart in age, both bookish and obsessed with marine discipline, devoted to rifle platoon leadership. And like himself, Hutchison thought, it sounded as if Shane had rejected the American creed of comfort and prosperity to pursue a life of meaning, which so often became expressed by excitement over people, especially the intense, nascent, unalloyed pleasure of making new friends. And both of them, too, had achieved exceptionally, despite the very real obstacles in their past.

As thoughts like this caromed around in his head, Hutchison had trouble sleeping. There were so many angles to work here, so many associations aroused by this marine named Shane Childers, and then dealing with his family. He couldn't resolve all of them and bring his mind to a place where he could get some sleep.

But it was quite late now and, through the top panes of his bay window, Hutchison could see the points of stars in the black sky. The mountains outside that he couldn't see in the blackness seemed to nuzzle and protect him, and in the morning just the sight of the peaks again would lift his spirits.

Good to Go

J oe Childers' reputation as a colorful blacksmith continued to define him as he traveled around the world for the navy Seabees, and it also marked him as a parent for Shane. In 1974, when Joe's tour at Roosevelt Roads in Puerto Rico was completed, the Childerses were reassigned to the big Oceana Naval Air Station at Virginia Beach, and Joe quickly reverted to his weekend disappearance act, junketing off to shoe horses. He was also away a lot for the navy, for six to eight weeks at a time, serving with a small unit attached to the State Department that maintained American embassies in places like the Central African Republic or Jamaica. But the Childerses were infinitely happy and busy at Oceana, and Judy had everything nearby that she needed for the children—beaches, amusement parks, the playgrounds and gyms of a cheerful, peacetime naval base. In the summer they made the long drive west over the Appalachians to the Childers family seat in Salt Rock. The family lacked only one thing, the dream farm that Joe could never stop talking about, but now at least they were consistently saving money toward that.

But the horse country, God, there was such great horse country within easy reach of Oceana–the standardbred tracks along the Delmarva Peninsula, the jump-show circuit in middle Virginia, all the new quarter-horse stud farms in the Carolinas that were coming on so strong during those years. For a ferociously energetic and curious boy like Shane, Joe's fun-loving, vagabond style was ideal, but it also served the Childers marriage pretty well. By the end of the week Judy was exhausted from managing the maniacally active Shane and his younger brother Sam. Shane in particular was so active, always pestering adults with questions and looking for something new to do, that Judy couldn't find a babysitter willing to take him on more than once. She was more than happy to hand him off to Joe for the weekend and finally enjoy some peace around the house. Joe had his own theory about it. "Shane was a kid that you just had to distract, keep him busy, *work* him, you know, like a racehorse. But, boy, then he would just calm down real nice, real good. I just loved it, working Shane hard and watching him fall into harness like that."

So Friday night, fun-fun, load up the pickup with tools and the shoes. While Judy fussed in the kitchen making sure that Shane had a proper change of boots, his jean jacket and cowboy hat, Joe gave him a final, military-style inspection at the door.

"Therrel Shane Childers, young man, are you good to go?"

"Good to go, Dad. Can we *leave* now?"

They drove and shoed hard all weekend. By the time he was four, Shane was a capable smithy's assistant, knowing just when to hand over the clippers, the rasp, the nails, then the small ball-peen and the nail stop. They ate in diners or in the kitchens of the grand estates where they were shoeing, they camped together beside rivers and in the barns. Like his father before him–Wilton to Joe to Shane–the new lad of the family learned conversation, storytelling, just the entertainment value of that, the Childers gift, talk, talk, talk, shoe another horse, talk some more, the ethic of hard work and talk. Shane knew that there was a rationale behind his father's restlessness, the frenetic weekend pace, and all the men laughed when he volunteered it. "We've got horses to shoe!" Shane would chirp out. "We're saving for a farm." Joe was proud of the way that Shane matured into a natural horseman and worker. He loved holding the lead line while Joe shoed, talking to a skittish colt, running back and forth to the pickup all day for more shoes. By Saturday noon, Shane was settled down into what Joe called "his working personality, Shane's groove," a boy who was calm now, but still very eager. During the long drive back to Oceana on Sunday nights, Shane slept on the pickup bench seat, using his father's leg as a pillow. They were sunburned and tired when they finally pulled in but Judy was always relieved to see them. For the next day or two, Shane's hyperactivity seemed miraculously cured.

One quality stood out, even then, when Shane was still young. He was insatiably curious about people and burned with inquisitiveness to learn more about them. At first this was expressed by the boyish fascination for men and their tools. "Dad, what's a veterinarian? How do you get into that work?" He was equally fascinated by Midas Muffler welders or horse-sale auctioneers. In the steeplechase country of Virginia, some men trained horses, some owned them, some cropped them over the jumps. "Dad, *why*? What's the difference?"

It drove Joe nuts sometimes, completely nuts. Riding along in the pickup, with all that gorgeous Choptank or Rappahannock River country going by, Shane would push his father right to the precipice of madness with his obsessive questions. *Dad, I don't get it. If you don't need college to become a welder, why do you need it to become a doctor? Okay, okay. But what about a truck driver?* Joe enjoyed off-loading his knowledge for Shane, but he began to notice something important. There were questions that his son asked that Joe couldn't answer, and when that happened Shane would sit quietly in his corner of the pickup cab, push back his cowboy hat and stare through the windshield to the farmlands they were passing, looking pensive and dreamy.

"It was very clear, early on, that Shane just wanted to take his mind somewhere, go places, that maybe his family couldn't really provide for," Joe later said. "He was dreaming big and had the confidence for that. But he just didn't know yet how he would do it."

There were other subtle changes as Shane grew, and the weekend curriculum of horseshoeing journeys proved ideal in other respects. Shane was so gregarious and winning with people that as his confidence grew he just asked men about their jobs himself, and Joe could see that they would share things with his son that perhaps they said to no one else. Shane also graduated from just wanting to know about men and their tools to becoming interested in them as people, who their sisters and family were, why they practiced this religion, not another. Joe gently smiled to himself about it sometimes, looking up from his work on a hoof and watching Shane with people. Shane was a better *listener* than he was and didn't just fill the air with grand talk. And he was very social, effortlessly social, oblivious to class. If something or someone interested him, Shane would ask, no matter who they were. He asked about the meaning of words that he didn't know yet, and then turned thoughtful and bright-faced as it was explained and the knowledge sunk in. Joe's social awareness about himself–that he was the son of modest West Virginia farmers–never seemed to affect Shane. There was a mobility about him, between people, places, ideas, that seemed innate.

It was the emergence of a lifelong trait. The restless Childers gene, the attention-deficit default, was expressing itself through a new and improved model, Shane. Whereas Joe cluttered his life with extra possessions and indulged a hoarding disorder, racing from event to event without much of a daily plan, Shane got his work done first, listened, and then raced from person to person, insatiably committed to them, and curious about what made them tick. He hoarded people, friends. Joe valued conversation as entertainment, engaging bluster that maybe covered up a lot. Shane seemed to need conversation as an engine of personal growth.

The big Childers family move to the Middle East, which would prove so formative for Shane, came about because of a curious anomaly of Joe's. He was famously disorganized about a lot of things except for his military paperwork, which was always thorough and up to date. Joe's records at Oceana showed that the children were all inoculated for foreign travel, certified as fit for school, and that an emergency plan for their care was in place. As it happened, Joe was the only member of his unit to have his paperwork in order when an adventuresome new assignment, a classic Childers opportunity for travel, turned up in the fall of 1977.

The American embassy in Iran was looking for a jack-of-all-trades Seabee to fill its "one man post" at its large compound in Tehran. It was a time of rising tensions in the Mideast, with the regime of Shah Reza Pahlavi unraveling in the face of an uprising by the Shi'ite followers of Ayatollah Ruhollah Khomeini, and renewed threats of an OPEC oil embargo. The shah was one of the last unquestioned American allies in the oil-rich Persian Gulf and a huge military lift was underway to keep him in power. At the American embassy compound in Tehran, a feverish security effort was underway, and someone was needed to supervise the installation of new cameras, locks, alarm systems, and communications gear. In a pinch, the Seabee engineer would also have to be able to fix generators or boilers and make other emergency repairs–anything the compound needed during a hectic time. Joe Childers seemed perfectly cast for the job. His Seabee commanders were already impressed with his record during assignments in other unstable Third World locations. He was ingenious and fiercely independent, and never complained about the lack of tools or spare parts at remote African or Asian bases. He was pure West Virginia and could shit-rig anything. The job always got done.

Judy had trepidations about going to Iran, but this was exactly the kind of foreign adventure they wanted to have. The children would get to see an exotic foreign land, there were good American schools in

Tehran, and Joe, who had done considerable reading about horses, knew that wealthy Persians had been importing choice Arabian and Thoroughbred bloodstock for centuries. The mountains outside Tehran sheltered some of the best stud farms in the world, and he couldn't wait to get there, check out the stallions, and start shoeing. After Joe received glowing recommendations for the Seabee post in Tehran and was told he had the job, the Childerses quickly packed their personal belongings and left their furniture and washer and dryer behind in storage. Their car, a 1973 Mercury Comet, and Joe's blacksmithing tools, were shipped ahead of them. They left in early September 1977, to get to Tehran in time to enroll Sandra and Shane in their new school.

Tehran was beautiful and fun at first, even more exotic than the Childerses expected, but there was an undercurrent of instability and impending violence. At the big American base in Isfahan where they landed, there were hundreds of American fighters and assault helicopters on the ramp, and the hangars and warehouses nearby swelled with shipping crates filled with American military equipment. Ayatollah Khomeini was then in exile in the holy city of Najaf, Iraq, and every time he issued a new fatwa or gave an interview denouncing the Americans and the shah, massive street demonstrations broke out. These were in turn brutally suppressed by the shah's police and military units, which reinforced a strange sense of tension, and very real social divisions, that could be felt on the streets. Most of the Shi'ite supporters of the ayatollah were crowded densely into the bazaars and narrow alleys of Tehran's residential districts, the block upon block of low-rise stucco houses fronting on the main squares, and the large open plazas around the mosques. The shah's middle class and wealthy supporters hardly participated in the life of the city, however. They all lived in the gaudy starter-mansions that climbed the foothills north and east of town. At night, Judy and the children were often awakened by the sounds of gas stations or bank buildings being blown up by pro-Khomeini rebels, and then the pro-shah forces would be bused in from the suburbs and throng into the streets, banging cooking pans with large wooden spoons. Occasionally, Joe would be detached for a month's work in nearby countries–Qatar, Saudi Arabia, Kuwait–and Judy would sit up at night comforting the children while they listened to sirens and explosions rumbling throughout the city.

Still, they thrived in Tehran and loved their life there, roaming the streets and bazaars on warm evenings, with the veiled women and donkeys highlighted against the orange twilight as the sun fell over the smoky city. The Childerses went camping on weekends in the mountains and took the children to the small, goofy neighborhood amusement parks with Ferris wheels and rides that looked as if they dated to the nineteenth century.

After living on the embassy grounds for a month, Joe and Judy found an apartment in a three-family house at 18 Alley Sharood, five blocks from the embassy. (The landlady in the building, who befriended Judy and looked after her while Joe was away, was pro-shah, but everyone else was pro-Khomeini.) While Sandy repeated first grade at the American School, Shane entered kindergarten and made an immediate, strong impression. When Joe and Judy attended their first parent-teacher conference that fall, Shane's teacher was so emotional about having him in his class that Joe thought he might cry. He just loved having a student who was so eager and energetic about learning, and there was one other quality that amazed him. If the class got out of hand, or couldn't settle down in the morning, Shane would stare up front to the teacher, establish eye contact, and then spread his arms wide to the other pupils. The room immediately hushed.

"I just can't get over this boy," the teacher told the Childerses. "What have you done to raise him this way? The other children just want to follow him."

Shane entering school was a relief for Judy–she finally had her rambunctious older son out of the house for most of the day. But neither she nor Joe were deceived by the glowing reports they received from his school. Shane was still very restless and hyperactive, requiring constant activity management. In the evenings or on weekends, Joe would take over and work that hot-blooded colt of his. Joe was obsessive about finishing a project once it was begun, and after dinner at home he often returned to the embassy to work, and would bring Shane along. The five-block walk to the embassy was colorful and fun–*Dad, why do they wear veils? Why do they paint their cars like that?*– and the embassy grounds were spacious and safe, with lots of room for Shane to roam while Joe finished his work in one of the buildings. Shane loved the embassy and soon became a popular foreign-service brat.

Shane's favorite activity was car washing. On cool evenings and on Saturday mornings, the Iranian embassy staff rolled the compound's large fleet of cars–the ambassador's limo, the security-force Fords, all the jeeps and pickups–out of the motor-pool garage and gave them a cleanup. When Joe left Shane one day with the American supervisor of the motor pool, Shane jumped right in. He loved the orderliness of it, the tangible results–spray with the hose, wash, wax, and then buff–with all the Iranians chattering in Farsi around him, the American motor-pool mechanics smoking cigarettes while they enjoyed the cool spray from the hose. They adored him and Shane became the motor-pool mascot. Oh God, here comes that Childers kid again. Boys, roll out the vehicles.

They loved watching him do it. Go-go-go, Shane, wash those jeeps. He was a bundle of energy and purpose, a miniature piece of work. When he was done, they lifted him up to the passenger seat, taught him how to shift the jeep gears, and then careened him around the grounds once or twice before they stowed the vehicle away. It was an enduring image from his childhood that Shane later enjoyed joking about.

"I was an Iranian car-washer once," he liked to tell friends in the marines and at The Citadel. "That was my boyhood. Washing and waxing the ambassador's limo in Tehran. It wasn't good enough until I could see the reflection of my face in the freaking paint. We even ironed the freaking little flags that hung from the fenders. I was a total freaking fruitcake about it, washing those embassy cars."

Joe was pretty good about his family life at first. Islamic fundamentalism made him nervous about life in the city, the safety of his family, and he would often rise early to get over to the embassy so he could knock off in the afternoon, walk the children home from school, and then return to the embassy at night with Shane. They all enjoyed the life of the city, the weekend camping and hunting trips up to the Lar Valley northeast of Tehran, or meeting friends at the embassy while the children splashed around in the pool.

Islamic fundamentalism, however, could not cure Joe's itch. He was as passionately in love with horses and horsemen as ever. One day, at the Farrabad racetrack in Tehran, he met a wealthy Armenian-Iranian businessman, Mike Malikian, and they started talking. Like so many others before him, Malikian fell under the Childers spell. Malikian had his horses spread across several farms around the country and owned a large hog operation as well. Before long Joe was visiting the Malikian farms to take care of his horseshoeing, then handling shoeing for all Malikian's friends, and he became a regular at Farrabad too. Joe loved the track, especially early in the morning—the horses and jockeys warming up, the camaraderie of coffee and cigarettes, the smell of saddle leather and hot iron as he shoed—the way all horsemen do. He became well known and was given a nickname, "the farrier at the barrier," because he was particularly skilled at making last-minute fixes on shoes at the last barrier before the horses entered the track. By the winter of 1977, he was rising at 4 A.M. on weekends to get over to Farrabad, shoeing all day, and then running off with Malikian or his friends somewhere, and not getting back home to Alley Sharood until midnight.

"Judy would complain, you know, but then I would just buy her flowers," Joe said. "She appreciated that I was making extra money. We were saving for that farm."

But if Joe was an absentee spouse again, he wasn't always an absentee father. He took Shane on most of his best horseshoeing junkets, all around Iran. They mostly traveled by train and were picked up at distant stations by the farm employees of large estates. It was just like their earlier times together in Maryland or Virginia, except that now the moody views were of brown, sandy mountains and cypress stands, falling off to the Dasht-e-Kavir desert or the aquamarine horizon on the Caspian Sea. There were trips north, almost to Azerbaijan, where Joe shod the horses of friends of the shah. At the Malikian farms, Shane chased hogs, learned to ride ponies or ran for more nails. Everyone enjoyed it when the "farrier at the barrier" showed up with his son. Yes, it was a strange country with different views, and not many people to query in English, but Shane was happy. He was off shoeing horses with his father, listening all weekend to his incomparable talk.

One particular image, a photograph in his mind almost, became fixed for Shane–he would often describe it later to relatives and friends. It must have symbolized to him the joyful beginning of those distant, dreamy weekends in Iran. Joe and Shane would arrive quite early on Saturday morning at the main train depot in Tehran, find some food in the small bazaar outside the station, and then board the train. First, Joe hoisted his son up through the passenger door of the car, and then Shane would chase along the aisle until he found an empty seat and throw open the window. Then Joe lifted his box of blacksmithing tools up to Shane.

"Good to go, Dad. Get on the train."

The continued American support for the hapless shah was based on a faulty premise, mostly because Islamic fundamentalism had not overthrown a government yet. The Shi'ite branch of Islam had generally disdained politics in the past, its mullahs and fervent followers devoting themselves to doctrinal matters relating to the interpretation of the Koran. But this began to change in the 1970s as the shah instituted a series of reforms that directly attacked Islam—emancipating women, changing property and domestic relations laws to favor secular principles and not the Koran, even seizing the vast lands of the Shi'ite clergy. The pace intensified in October 1978, a year after the Childerses arrived in Tehran, when Ayatollah Khomeini was deported from Iraq after issuing a series of virulent condemnations of the Pahlavi regime and its American supporters. From his new base at a chateau outside Paris, Khomeini was now free to reach his followers through the international media and issued new tirades almost every week. The street demonstrations and clashes between the anti-shah and pro-shah forces were now almost a daily occurrence.

In the fall of 1978, when Joe returned to Tehran from a brief Seabee detachment in Bahrain, he could immediately feel the difference in the city. Marshal law had been declared and life became a blur as the shah's regime began to collapse and the street demonstrations intensified. One afternoon, several buildings and a car dealership near the embassy were torched. As a precaution, Joe was delivered home in a security van. But the violence on the streets was so bad that the driver couldn't risk stopping when they got to Alley Sharood. Instead, Joe was pushed out the door while the van was still moving.

In December that year, the embassy finally made the decision to evacuate all dependants of the compound's personnel, and Judy hurriedly packed and took Sandra and Shane out of school. Judy and the children flew home to West Virginia, where they would wait until Joe got out of Iran. He remained behind in the apartment at Alley Sharood for two months and then moved to the military barracks on the embassy. In February 1979, as tensions continued to mount, the shah was deposed and Ayatollah Khomeini made his triumphant return.

Joe was briefly involved in a perilous but forgotten prelude to the more famous takeover of the American embassy in November 1979. This was the so-called Valentine's Day storming of the embassy by Islamic militants in February, a one-day siege during which the American compound was swarmed by angry Shi'ite crowds and most of the embassy personnel were held hostage. Joe was among them, but was eventually released under an agreement with the Khomeini forces that allowed the Iranians to maintain a temporary presence on the compound. Joe remained on the embassy grounds for six more days, repairing generators and electrical equipment damaged during the takeover, and then was ordered out of the country. He was relieved to escape Iran unscathed, but for years afterward he still harbored regrets about his hurried departure.

"Those damn Iranians got an old rifle of mine that had been in the Childers family for years, and they also snitched some of my blacksmithing tools, dangit. It still pisses me off. Some Iranian over there is building a hut in back of his house with *my* tools, you know?"

But Iran also meant something more to them later, even after they settled back in America for the best ten years of their lives and the children grew. Joe would call it "the turning point for Shane."

One Saturday evening in the summer of 1978 after he'd been shoeing at the Farrabad track, Joe arrived back at Alley Sharood to find Judy in a dither. Shane was bouncing off the walls again and she just found it so hard after a day like that to be herself, to enjoy life. Joe told Shane to put his swimming trunks on underneath his clothes and they headed off to the embassy together, enjoying the walk up past the food stalls and rug shops. When they got there, Joe tossed Shane into the pool to enjoy himself with the other embassy brats and sat down on a chaise longue to read an English-language paper.

It was a quiet night across Tehran. An orange disk of sun was falling in the smoky sky, embassy cars were whooshing in and out as the diplomats left for their dinner parties, and a group of marines from the embassy security guards were drilling on the lawn just down from the pool. The marines were practicing flanking steps off a point, presenting arms, and twirling their rifles around like airplane propellers in front of their faces. Shane swam to the side of the pool, propped himself over the edge on his arms, and stared down the hill at the marines.

When Joe finally pulled Shane out of the water, he wrapped him in a towel and they sat together on the chaise longue, with Shane between his father's legs.

"Dad. What are marines? What do they do?"

Joe loved a question like that, not simply because he could go on for hours on this one, but because the knowledge shared with his son was so personal. He was a navy man and had always worked with marines. So he told Shane all about amphibious forces, first wave assaults, getting in there early and tough, and then leaving the cleanup work to a bunch of pansies from the army. Marines dropped from the air, landed by sea, they took beaches and mountains and deserts for which no one else was trained. Of course, there was nothing sophisticated or mechanical about the work, not like being a navy Seabee. Still, marines were the best. That was Joe's opinion.

"Dad, I think I'm going to become a marine," Shane said. "That's what I want to do."

Shane was five years old that summer, but there was never any doubt about it after that. It just became an accepted part of his personal progression, the family reality. Shane was growing up to become a marine.

"It's a strange thing to say that you could hear a boy of five say something like that and then know that he was growing up to do it," Joe later said. "But that was Shane. He was very confident and set when he made a decision. I was never concerned about the safety of it, or that he would qualify—he was too bright and ambitious to worry about that. I did worry though that the military could provide everything he was looking for, that it would be enough for someone who had so much going on in his head. But that was it, pretty much. At five years old he told me that he was going to be a marine."

Iran remained an important memory for the Childerses, not simply because Islamic fundamentalism had deposed the shah and they had witnessed history there. It was a risky adventure, a family crucible that they had survived together. And Shane returned to America with wonderful images—the orange sun over the minarets at night, the embassy grounds, the views as the train climbed the mountains toward Tajrish. He didn't know yet that he would reckon again with those Arabian sands, many times, in fact, or that his rendezvous there would become a personal obsession. Now it was time for him to resume a thoroughly American childhood among the cattail thickets of another memorable place, the banks of the Little Biloxi River.

After Iran, settling down in America felt effortless, safe, familiar—what life should be. For the next ten years Joe would serve at the big Seabee base in Gulfport, Mississippi, near the naval yards on the Gulf of Mexico, and the Childerses would enjoy their first long stretch of stability. Joe continued to travel overseas for the navy, shoe horses on weekends, and devote himself to the welding or tractor-repair needs of his neighbors while his own projects languished at home. But the Childerses still felt strongly that Judy should remain home with the family, and Joe needed the extra income to supplement his modest navy pay. The three Childers children would grow up ambivalent and even a little hurt by passing through adolescence without their father around, but later they came to love Joe for it. By then they were out of the house and working second jobs themselves.

But Joe did find that dream farm, which compensated for a lot at the time. It was six acres of rich bottomland near a horseshoe bend of the Little Biloxi River, just outside the remote hamlet of Saucier, Mississippi. The place wasn't much at first, just a four-bedroom brick ranch with a garage that Joe converted into a den, some open fields, and then thick, impenetrable stands of cattails and tall canary grass that fell to the massive willow trees along the river. But Joe soon made the place over in his image. "Within two years, there was farm machinery everywhere," Sam Childers said. "Whenever Dad got back from an overseas trip, he bought more." Over time, Joe and Shane laid in fence lines to pasture horses and mules, and they all cleared some land together to build a barn. Horse vans, hay wagons, and antique tractors in various states of repair completed the mix, and Sam later said that he and Shane grew up with that curious insecurity of the most popular neighborhood kids. "Our place was a train wreck, with *way* too much going on most of the time," he said. "So how come all the other kids just loved being at our house?"

Shane's first pony was a palomino named Honey, and Joe enjoyed exploring with him just how the equestrian relationship worked. If he told his son not to ride Honey up past the stop sign on the corner, Shane automatically did it. When he told Shane not to try and break the pony to harness without his help, Shane did it anyway and wrecked the cart. Later, Joe bought Shane his first horse, from the divorced wife of a Seabee pal. It was a three-year-old bay mare, a Thoroughbred–quarter horse cross named Anay. This time, Shane listened and watched pensively as Joe taught him how to train the mare. Anay meant freedom for Shane, his own Childers wander. On Friday nights after school, he saddled up the mare, loaded her down with camping gear, food, a lantern, even his homework and the cat. Then he rode off for the distant woods or a sandy clearing along the river that he particularly liked and camped until Saturday afternoon. They never really knew what the hell Shane was doing back there, but he always returned bright-faced and happy, talking to his horse. Clearly, he enjoyed being alone and naturally took to the woods.

Shane and Sam, along with four or five other neighborhood boys, spent most of the summer down along the Little Biloxi, running barefoot and swimming all day. "That's where Shane and I grew up, right there," Sam said. "He was our leader-king and we loved following him down there." Pillaging from Joe's piles of lumber up in the yard, they built Huck Finn rafts and a tree fort, hung a swinging rope from a bough over the river, fished, and snagged bullfrogs. All the other boys would run and wait at a safe distance when they came across a copperhead snake, watching as Shane caught and killed it.

Everyone who knew the future marine as he emerged into adolescence unfailingly mentioned three points—ferocious energy, fearlessness, and the endless curiosity about people. Leadership came naturally to him because he had that knack, even in a group, of making everyone feel that he was there just for him.

Becky Moore, the wife of a navy chaplain from the base down at Gulfport, got to know the Childerses well in Saucier after Joe began shoeing their horses. Her son Scott was Shane's age and ran around with the Little Biloxi gang.

"I remember my son coming up from the river one day and telling me that he was never afraid of anything as long as he was with Shane. That was the effect Shane had on people. He was never afraid of anything. And the boys would follow him anywhere because he made it clear that he liked them so much."

In school, Shane emerged as a capable if barely interested B and C student. The Mississippi schools weren't very good, with few inspiring teachers, and after Shane began attending high school in Gulfport, the bus during the long ride south from Saucier was filled with bullies who called all the other kids "fags" or "Jews." Shane spent an inordinate amount of time intervening to protect the weaker kids and then having to explain himself to teachers. By his sophomore year Shane had purchased a marine physical fitness training manual and rose every morning at dawn, wolfed down raw eggs for breakfast, and then pushed himself through a grueling regimen of calisthenics and then a five-mile run. He also played sports—baseball and football—and most years held down one or two part-time jobs after school and on weekends, becoming the same blur around the house that his father was. The bristling intellectuality and love of books that he would later display as a mid-twenties marine—for history, literature, psychology, the arts—just couldn't come out yet. There were too many other issues to work on. Shane wasn't so much a case of arrested development as development that just had to wait until all the energy could come out that way.

Besides, by now the wall of silence that so often falls between fathers and their adolescent sons had closed in on Joe and Shane. Joe was either away with the navy or off shoeing horses most of the time; Shane was coming in late after working at Quincy's Steakhouse. They passed each other like guests at a motel and found it hard to discover things to talk about. Joe was annoyed that Shane and Sam were fighting a lot now, always yelling in the house. And Shane was annoyed by Joe's nonstop chatter and storytelling, his complete lack of summary function, which embarrassed Shane in front of his friends. Meanwhile, Joe was increasingly preoccupied with discovering new things about himself. Frequently, but particularly in he fall, he was plagued with long spells of the blues, melancholy, and guilt over his mounting list of unfinished projects, which just made him more lethargic about getting anything done. Eventually, he was diagnosed with a thyroid problem that the doctors said might contribute to depression. For the first time he heard about a syndrome—attention-deficit disorder—that he cheerfully agreed probably explained his eternal restlessness and ennui.

"I had a lot of things that I wanted to do, you know?" Joe said later. "It was only when I got into my fifties that I realized the impact it all had on Shane. I would get lethargic and couldn't get things done, which just made me more ADD, and then Shane would come along and get *all* his projects done. I guess we were frustrated with each other, that's all. I take the blame for it now, as long as I get the credit for improving our relationship later, after he became a marine. But, you know, it's there. I didn't spend the time with him as a teenager that I should have, just showing him that I cared."

In the summer of 1988, when Shane was sixteen, he escaped the tensions of his immediate family by spending three months up in Salt Rock, West Virginia. He was already adored as a kind of hero grandson in the Childers clan and that summer annealed his connection to the family for the rest of his life. He lived with his uncle and aunt, Dave and Mary Bias, who considered him almost a son, and worked at their used-car lot and garage, rebuilding sedans and pickups for auto auctions. Shane was a blur of activity, and everyone called him "All-Shane, All the Time." Every morning he rose before dawn and ran three miles over the hollows to his grandparents, laughed with them all through breakfast, then ran to another uncle's house, visited some more, and was home and showered by the time Dave Bias was ready to leave for his car lot. Shane organized hay rides for the younger cousins, dredged ponds with the neighbors, blushed and laughed uneasily when his aunts teased him about the way he turned the girls' heads at county fairs. But his work always got done and none of the Childerses had much difficulty figuring him out.

"Shane was absolutely fanatical about finishing what he started," his aunt Mary said. "It came from watching his father never get anything done."

Shane's big project that summer was his first car, a 1977 Mustang II, which he and Uncle Dave fastidiously rebuilt from bumper to bumper—a new block and cylinders, shocks, drive train, exhaust, the works. Back in Mississippi, however, he became hell on wheels, and indeed for the rest of his life, everyone who knew him would draw straws *not* to ride with Shane. The impatience, the overconfidence, the urgency to race to the next event, all came out when he was behind the wheel. In February 1989, while racing home after his job at

Quincy's Steakhouse on a rainy night, Shane hit the bad curve just south of the house and rolled the 'Stang.

Joe called a wrecker and went over with Shane to inspect the crash site.

"Oh God, did we laugh our asses off at Shane that night," Joe said. "He was all hell to tarnation about it, kicking the bumper and using language that I had to pretend to be shocked about. He loved that vehicle, his first car. But now it was a total loss, bottoms up in the reeds."

In 1990, while still a senior at Harrison Central High School in Gulfport, Shane preenlisted in the marine's "early entry program." He'd been eating raw eggs every morning and practicing self-defense moves from a marine manual for three years, so there wasn't the least doubt about how well he would do. But there was one quality, one consistent display of self-restraint, that astounded everyone who knew him. They were immensely curious about how it would play out once this engaging and unforgettable boy reached the marines.

Over the years, during literally dozens of fights in the tough Mississippi schools, Shane had evolved a unique martial style. In high school, Shane was wiry and muscular, but never particularly big–five foot seven and 160 pounds. After boot camp he finally filled out to five nine and 175. He was fearless about taking on much larger boys, even a couple of very mean, dirty fighters at once, and he remained calm, almost relaxed. But he never applied more force than was needed, and preferred less. Not once had he ever slugged another kid, even in self-defense. Not a single punch, ever. That fighting was psychology, not physical combat, seemed to have arrived naturally and at a young age.

When Shane was seven or eight, an older boy slugged him while he was coming off the school bus. When he got home, he asked Judy, "Mom, why did that boy do that? I wasn't threatening him at all." It was almost as if he was saying, "Could someone be that stupid? Hitting *me*?"

In the fall of 1988, just after he got back from West Virginia, Shane and Sam were at the horse arena outside Saucier one night when a much bigger bully from town, a six-footer named Chuck, sauntered over to tell Shane that he was taking him out. Shane had insulted a friend of Chuck's by telling him to stop calling a girl a "slut."

Shane stood there calmly and waited for Chuck to make his first move, which came quickly enough, a punch to Shane's chin.

After a couple of quick karate moves, Shane moved deftly behind Chuck, locked up his arms, and then kicked out his legs. Now he had Chuck pinned to the dirt by his stomach and cheek.

"Let me up, you bastard."

"If I let you up," Shane said, "you going to hit me?"

"No!"

Shane let him up, and Chuck slugged him again.

"Oh God," Shane said, before pinning him to the dirt again. "This is *sooooo* boring."

They cycled through it two or three more times, and then finally Shane was truly bored and tossed Chuck into the crowd that had gathered. They all laughed at Chuck and told him to go away. When Shane dusted off and stood up, they all cheered.

After that, no one wanted to take on Shane Childers. It wasn't that they were worried about trouncing him, because they probably could. They just didn't want to face the humiliation, that he would prove by shrewdness and restraint that he was tougher.

Shane's first leave-taking for the marines was not particularly eventful. Joe and Sam drove him down to the navy recruiting office in Gulfport, and he left on a bus for Parris Island boot camp in South Carolina. It would take a couple of years of everyone growing up a bit, and Shane coming back from his first war, for the departures and arrivals to be marked by evident expressions of love.

"Shane was ready, and I do mean ready, to get his ass out of Mississippi," Sam said. "It was apparent to everyone that he needed to get away from all of us, especially Dad."

When they got back from Gulfport, Sandra Childers was in the kitchen. Joe looked confused and sad about Shane leaving, but also relieved and optimistic. Most of all he was proud, really proud of Shane, but that was still a hard thing to get out.

"Dad," Sandra asked him. "What can they possibly do with Shane at boot camp? He's already a marine."

The Russians Are Coming

It was now Wednesday, five days after Shane had been killed, and Judy Childers woke that morning with a fleeting but intense sensation. A light snow had fallen in northern Wyoming overnight, and when she looked out her bedroom window, the landscape was expansively white across the prairie and all the way up the Polecat Bench. A pink ribbon of cirrus glowed where the rim met the sky.

Snow made her feel joyful, expectant. Snow covered all the piles in the Childers yard and Joe would always wake up looking revived, boyish again. He loved harnessing his team and watching them prance in the powder, hitching them to the sleigh, and then jingling off across that big white security blanket of prairie. When he was back inside the house, he would overflow with the Childers gift, red-cheeked from the wind and happy, yap-yap-yap remember the time it snowed in West Virginia and Shane spun down the hill on the Flying Saucer. Yap-yap that snow we saw in the mountains up above Tehran. Memory and snow and the house filling up, the light overcast sky, so moody but soothing. It felt like Christmas. Fleetingly but intensely, that's what she felt, it was Christmas.

It felt like Christmas because in the morning when she walked out to the end of the lane the mailbox was full of letters and condolence cards, more than fifty a day now. She and Joe would sit over coffee at the dining-room table reviewing them, like Christmas cards, remembering all the old friends they were hearing from now. Sandy and Richard had arrived from Texas and Judy was looking forward to spending a quiet morning with her daughter, cutting out newspaper articles and photos of Shane and then pasting them into a set of leather-bound albums they had bought. Sam and his wife, Cori, had called from Mitchell, South Dakota. Their minivan had broken down but the car dealer there had rented them a car to make it the rest of the way to Wyoming. Joe's old Seabee pal, Robert Reagan, their favorite—just such a fun, fun guy, gravelly voiced and sarcastic all the time—had called from London, and he was on his way. The Moores were coming from Texas, the Whittens from California, and all the Childerses were converging from West Virginia. By tonight the rooms upstairs would be filled with grandchildren, two or three bundled up together in the same bed. They would pay for it big in the morning when the small house exploded with activity.

Oh, and Shane at Christmas, more fun-per-hour than anyone else. Hey, Mom, I'm into telemark skiing this year, let me tell you about that. Drinking Joe under the table at the Christmas party for the Northstate Corp., and coming back in just the right amount of drunk. Buying them TV sets, VCRs, new tires for their cars, yap-yapping away about this girl he met at the mall. So much fun, Shane at Christmas. It was fleeting but intense, just the amount of time it took for her to rise and head for the kitchen and coffee. Then she remembered and sighed deeply. No, this is March. It's a spring snow. This is not Christmas. Perhaps this morning when Captain Hutchison arrives we'll finally learn more about the return of Shane's body.

Joe and Judy had a good long chat that morning, perhaps their best since they'd heard the awful news. Joe was worried that Judy might be feeling that he'd been crying too much, but he tried to reassure her that he was all cried out for now and even feeling better, exhausted but resigned. In the night, a couple of times, he had heard her wake and gently cry, and she woke up looking tired. But he knew it was best not to push her for now.

"I would just really like to be *alone* a little bit, you know?" Joe said. "People come, I get to talking about Shane, and then I cry when I'm all cranked up."

"Joe, it's the stories," Judy said. "Maybe just cut back a little on the stories?"

"Yeah. I need to do that," Joe said. "Spend some time alone and not tell so many stories."

The new snow reminded him that he'd promised to get the team and pull the sleigh off the lawn, so that they wouldn't have that particular memory of Shane out front all during the funeral. John Van Valin was supposed to come over and help him by holding the gates, but John didn't show. Then a visitor who knew horses arrived, and Joe recruited him for the chore. They went out to the barn, and Joe introduced the stranger to his horses and mules, they harnessed the cream Belgians, and then pranced them through the yard and hitched up.

At the first gate, Joe jumped off the sleigh and nodded his head toward the lead horse, Amigo.

"Say, that Amigo horse there is going to shy at this gate, okay? Don't fight him too much. Just swing wide to the right, let him shy, and then just harness that energy by pulling him back through the left. Good to go?"

"Good to go."

Amigo shied gently but wide as soon as Joe opened the gate, but the visitor was competent enough to sail the sleigh through, with a few inches to spare on the left post. Then Joe hopped back on the sleigh and took the reins, which was a pleasure for someone else to see. He is a more than competent horseman and talks to his animals, doesn't yell, with very little rapping on the rump with the lines. His grip on the reins is firm but gentle and the horses feel guided but not contained.

The harness jingled smartly in the crisp air as they bobbed the sleigh across the prairie.

The Childers branch of the Smithsonian Institution's Antique Farm Machinery and Tool Dump takes up most of an acre. There are about forty rusting artifacts in all, plus a great deal of used irrigation pipe and attachments. There's actually a spot where the sleigh is usually parked—it's just in between an old McCormick thresher and a potato-washing sluice—and Joe expertly side-slipped Amigo and April right in.

"Well, good, that job's done, then," Joe said, unhitching. "Jeez, this is hard, though. I just keep expecting old Shane to come diddly-boppin' down the lane any minute now. Gotta stop doing that."

Joe drove the team back to the barn on foot. The Belgians still wanted to go and were acting up, prancing and farting and pulling all these goof-off shies to the left and the right, but Joe was enjoying it. He made an extra loop with the reins around each hand, leaned back hard, and just let the team sled him across the slippery prairie by his rubber boots. The wind was on his back now and he looked handsome and fun, a tough, muscular smithy, dragged by his horses across the snow as his red navy ball cap was etched against the white of the Pole-cat Bench.

Shane Childers' timing about entering the marines was fortuitous. He entered boot camp at Parris Island on July 17, 1990, two weeks before Saddam Hussein stunned the world by invading Kuwait. As President George H. W. Bush rallied an international coalition and began a rapid buildup of forces in the Persian Gulf, everyone in the marines was now on a fast track. After boot camp and basic Marine Combat Training at Camp Lejeune in South Carolina, Shane was assigned to a light armored vehicle driver's course at Camp Pendleton near San Diego. The marines, like the other branches of the military, had been caught flat-footed by Saddam's invasion of Kuwait, and the pressure was intense to quickly transition from peacetime to a wartime footing. At Pendleton, the size of Shane's light armored class was doubled, and the eight-week curriculum was crammed into four weeks. Shane quickly mastered the handling and systems of the eight-wheel drive, semiamphibious vehicles, and was considered good enough to be recommended for extra training. He learned map reading, reconnaissance, and communications, so that he could either be assigned to a regular combat unit or one of the smaller recon groups that worked ahead and probed enemy lines.

Shane didn't particularly stand out at first, but there was a good reason for that. All the recruits just out of boot camp and basic were pretty much the same—gung-ho, especially now that a war was on, incredibly physically fit, and as hard-working as their officers asked. But there was one attribute that a few marines close to him noticed, a quality more personal than professional for the time being. Fellow recruit Bill Hendry first met Shane at Camp Lejeune in 1990 and would later serve with him in Saudi Arabia during the Operation Desert Storm deployment against Saddam Hussein.

"Shane was very reserved at first, and he wouldn't clown around and talk about people behind their back like everyone else," Hendry said. "He was very selective about who he would confide in. Sure, if we all went out some night after our courses were over, Shane could be a party animal with the rest of us, but not a lot. If there was a book to read that would put him ahead in the course, something he could do with his equipment, he preferred that. There was a sense, even then, at eighteen, that this was a guy who would take the opportunities offered by the marines and stretch it very far. Self-improvement and personal growth just interested him a hell of a lot more than running around and being a normal grunt."

Along with Hendry, Shane was assigned to a five-hundred-man rear replacement unit that would supply new men as marines up front were injured or got sick. The unit arrived in Saudi Arabia for Desert Storm in February 1991, just ten days before the ground war commenced. Everyone bitched because they were in a replacement unit, not an active fighting force, and they all could miss the action if the war was short. The disappointment was even more severe after they were all ordered to unload ships at the Saudi docks. They were stevedores now, not marines, and it was insufferably hot under the sun. But then Shane received the first of many lucky breaks.

A few days after the war started, he was ordered forward as a light armored driver and ended up seeing limited action as the remnants of Saddam's Republican Guard were chased north out of Kuwait. Shane would later say very little about his experiences in Kuwait, professing a veteran's modesty about his war exploits, but there was a good reason for that. He was assigned forward at a time when Operation Desert Storm had only about a week more to go, and there were massive transportation snarls in northern Kuwait as U.S. Air Force and Navy planes pounded retreating Republican Guard armored units that were trapped along the main highway to Basra in southern Iraq. Shane saw a lot of scorched tanks and decaying bodies on the shoulder of the highway north, and his unit was briefly assigned to provide perimeter security for Kuwaiti oil fields that had been torched by the Iraqis and were then repaired by American oil-service companies. The truth was that most of the heavy fighting was over by the time Shane got to Kuwait.

Still, the rest of the replacement unit grunts back in Saudi Arabia were jealous as hell.

"I don't think anyone in the marines said, 'Hey, get me Childers,' " Hendry said. "They went down the list, got to C, and there was Shane, good to go. But getting up into Kuwait just contributed to his legend. Shane was lucky and then made the most of it. That's who he was."

Desert Storm was a big personal milestone for Shane, even if he was reticent about it. "Shane felt real proud and lucky about Desert Storm," Joe said. "He didn't want to be in the marines unless they used him for something real." It was part of Shane's mystique now. Eight months after he enlisted, he had served in a war and now had a theater combat medal to prove it. He was a veteran at the age of eighteen.

While Shane was readying himself and then fighting in Kuwait, major changes that would have a profound effect on his relationship with his family were underway back in Mississippi. After twenty-one years in the service, Joe was finally ready to sign up for his pension and leave the Seabees. He was sick of working triple jobs, sick of Mississippi, tired of all the overseas junkets for the navy that interrupted his plans. And now he was really thinking big, not just a marginalized "dream farm" along the Little Biloxi, but a real horseman's place, this time a dream *ranch*. After a scouting trip west, Joe and Judy settled on northern Wyoming, and they closed on their house in Mississippi in early December 1990. They would find a place in the Bighorns once they got out there, and departed for Wyoming ten days before Christmas that year.

It was an epic transcontinental crossing, the real Childers experience. "Oh, please, do not get me started on that trip," Sam Childers later said. "Compared to us, the Beverly Hillbillies are just for show." The lead vehicle of the Childers family caravan was Joe's 250-Diesel Ford pickup, towing a sixteen-foot flatbed trailer overloaded with farm machinery. Sam drove the middle pickup, a 1981 Toyota, also pulling a flatbed, this one bearing a hay wagon that had been temporarily converted into a shipping container for the tools, blacksmithing equipment, harness, and tack. Judy and Sandra brought up the rear in their 1983 Buick Regal, burdened down in the rear with luggage.

They had their first breakdown a few miles out of Horn Lake, Mississippi, when the fuel injectors on the diesel crapped out, which for some reason took three days to repair. In Arkansas, during a bad rainstorm, Sam rear-ended a car in the Toyota pickup, so the front end of that had to be completely rebuilt. Joe's trailer lights failed in Saint Joseph, Missouri, and the tires blew in Lincoln, Nebraska. When Joe and Sam temporarily abandoned one vehicle, in order to save another, they got stranded in snowstorms and the family ended up being separated a lot. It was a train wreck, a Donner Party farce, all the way from the Little Biloxi to the North Platte.

"Yeah, I guess you could kind of maybe say that we set a record, I would admit that," Joe said. "Thirteen days and five major breakdowns between Mississippi and Wyoming. We pulled into Casper two days after Christmas."

But nothing stopped the Childerses. After staying in motels and renting in a trailer park for three weeks, Joe and Judy found their 124-acre dream spread in Powell, moved in, and began making basic repairs. A week later, Joe and Sandy returned to Mississippi to trailer his horses and donkeys to Wyoming. Then he bought some more mules, met the Van Valins and the Shoshone Back Country Horsemen, built a big barn behind the house, and started working at sugar-beet processing plants and local ranches to supplement his navy pension. He loved owning a place with irrigation rights, big open fields to hay, and waking up in the morning to see his own small herd of beef cattle browsing on the high plains.

Shane made his first visit to the new spread in Powell in July 1991, just after he came back on leave following Operation Desert Storm in Kuwait. For Joe and Judy, it was wonderful having him home, safe from the war, and seeing how enthusiastically he responded to their life now. The move west had significance way beyond geography, acreage, or the beautiful vistas the family now enjoyed. The residual tensions of Shane's adolescent conflict with his father, the confusion introduced by Joe's navy schedule, and the tough Gulfport schools, were fading. That was all a memory now, framed by the phrase "the

Mississippi years," and they'd gained separation from all that. They were living in the Bighorn country of Wyoming now, a place they were really meant for, and Shane had fought in the Persian Gulf War. Mississippi was behind them.

Shane loved Wyoming, everything about it. As the years passed and he grew in sophistication and experience—he was returning now from Pacific cruises, or Paris, Nairobi, Tel Aviv—each visit to the new home place would be remembered by what Shane did that year, all the manic projects and crazyass fun. During that first visit, Shane repaired Joe's combine. Later, they laid in new fence lines and irrigation pipe, broke horses together and fixed the barns, even did a little bit of shoeing for the Shoshone Back Country Horsemen. When they patched the shed roof, Shane snuck beers up in their nail buckets so that Judy wouldn't know they were drinking in the middle of the day. The meticulous and varied obsession with physical fitness also thrived out west. Shane chased on his mountain bike five miles or more in the morning, ran ten miles along the rim of the Polecat Bench, then drove into Cody to buy camping or sporting gear, whatever he was into that year. Shane was always returning to Wyoming after some great mountaineering junket—the Alps, Kilimanjaro, Mount Shasta in California, which he climbed four times—and the snowy Bighorns reminded him of those peaks.

But Wyoming wasn't just about the gorgeous views and Shane's epic rides. It was the new feelings between them now. The Joe-Shane relationship had survived, prospered, and they were back together—literally—in the saddle. "Freakin' A, Dad," Shane would say. "We're shoeing horses again." It was thrilling for Joe to watch Shane's progress and to enjoy such a wonderful son.

At Camp Lejeune in North Carolina, Shane signed up for every kind of specialized training he could wrangle out of the marines—survival camp, night navigation training, jump school—during two more years of seasoning as a rifle infantryman. With Bill Hendry and his other marine pals, he did his share of carousing, hitting the strip joints in Jacksonville or careening off for wild weekends in Savannah or Wilmington Beach. But he was also becoming known as an enlisted man with exceptional potential.

"Shane made sergeant faster than anyone I ever saw in the marines, after about eighteen months," Hendry said. "It wasn't simply that he was always one hundred percent effort or spent his free time working on his uniform. If he had a problem with one of his peers–and there's a lot of that in the marines–he would take the initiative and resolve it. If he had a problem that had to be reported up, he was very direct about going to an officer and working it out. He just became marked as a solutions person, someone who didn't create or accept problems, but fixed them."

In 1993 Shane was selected for poster-boy duty in the marines, the highly coveted Marine Security Guard course at Quantico in Virginia, which would make him eligible for work at embassies abroad. The training represented a lot more than just an opportunity to enjoy exotic travel and the comfortable routines of embassy life. Marine security guards don't just man the gatehouse at the embassy entrance. They escort embassy wives and visiting VIPs to parties and conferences, help coordinate intelligence, and must be able to work with a wide variety of embassy officials–economic and political attachés, protocol and passport employees–in ways that go way beyond the skills of a rifle platoon grunt. The experience would nurture a number of latent qualities in Shane and lead to considerable change.

When he was done with the course at Quantico, Shane was assigned to the American consulate in Geneva and given an eight-hundred-dollar allowance for civilian clothes, which he would need for his evening security work at social functions. But he had never bought civilian dress clothes before and translated his need for help in an interesting way. The Childerses' old navy friends from Gulfport, Paul and Becky Moore, were stationed at Quantico then. Paul Moore was a naval officer who had spent his career in the chaplain corps, and the Moores were a sophisticated, college-educated couple, worldly and always well-dressed. Shane called Becky, explained his problem, and she took him out one Saturday afternoon to the Potomac Mills Shopping Mall.

Boy, was that an enjoyable afternoon for Becky. The hunkiest marine at Quantico, twenty-one years old, had eight hundred dollars to blow on new clothes, and she was the one who got to dress the Ken doll. Becky knew the naval officer's life and even a lot about embassy functions, and she gave Shane advice that she considered useful for the future. Okay, buy one really nice suit for formal occasions, but for the rest of the time just have one high-quality blue blazer, gray wool slacks, and shoes that are right. Keep it elegant, simple, be the effortlessly tasteful man. The most noticeable feature finishing off the look–shirts and ties–can always be changed and refurbished as you go along. Don't be afraid to ask the sales staff to help you pick out the shirts and ties.

Shane was delightfully obsessive-compulsive about it, the way he always learned something new. Get the basics down, move on to the shirts, shoes, and belts–whoa, new concept, thanks, Becky–match a tie to your skin tone. He was completely self-assured about admitting what he didn't know and was grateful for all Becky's fashion tips.

"Shane was so cute that day," Becky said. "I kept coming up and telling him what looked good, and it was wonderful being with a boy who responded so enthusiastically. He would be well dressed from then on. I just knew that."

For the next three years, Shane lived a life straight out of a glossy Marine Corps brochure. He pulled down plum assignments in Geneva, Paris, and Nairobi, at first putting in a lot of uniformed duty at the guard post but then coming to the attention of his superiors as the ideal nonuniformed security presence at glittering parties and high-end economic conferences. The work was steady but not particularly demanding, and Shane had plenty of free weekend time. In Switzerland, simply because the lakes were there and it looked like such an interesting thing to do, he took sailing lessons. He kayaked, joined a bike-touring club, and began to climb the Alps. Within a month of reaching Nairobi in 1994, he climbed Mount Kilimanjaro, Africa's highest peak, and after that he went on safari almost every weekend. He was well-liked by the State Department regulars he was now circulating with and becoming something of a legend for blowing in on Sunday nights with great stories about his latest mountain-climbing or camping junket.

In Nairobi Shane stood out for two other reasons which became important elements of his personal lore. In the U.S. Marine barracks, which wasn't a barracks at all but instead a spacious house with wide lawns in the middle of an upper-class Nairobi suburb, Shane was assigned a comfortable room. But he pushed the bed aside and used it as a storage rack for his bike equipment and mountain-climbing gear, preferring to sleep on the floor. "I don't want to get soft just because this is a cushy assignment," Shane told friends. "Marines sleep on the floor." He continued this practice for the rest of his marine career, often sleeping on the hard cement of apartment balconies or bedroom floors with thin industrial carpets.

There were also signs of an emerging passion for social justice, more typical of a college student than a marine his age, which markedly defined him later. Shane was embarrassed and even mildly angry when he learned that the marines in his barracks paid impoverished Kenyan women fifty cents a load to do their laundry. He refused to participate in a system that he considered nothing more than foreign wage-slavery and did his own laundry for more than a year. Later, when he was promoted to a supervisory job in Kenya and had less time, he sent his laundry out but insisted on paying *his* Kenyan laundress five dollars every time she did his clothes. It was still a pittance, Shane thought, but actually a very high price according to Kenyan wage standards. Typically, Shane was willing to suffer the consequences of his altruism. The other marines in the barracks were annoyed at him when their laundresses heard about what Shane was paying and insisted on a higher price. But Shane didn't care and confidently rebuffed the criticism. Exploiting foreign labor to get your laundry done, he felt, did not befit a United States Marine.

Shane's elan, his athletic appeal—particularly the brooding sense that he had hidden ambitions, that there was something still unrealized about him—was noticed by everyone, but they also laughed about another trait. He was charmingly clueless about women. He'd been that way ever since high school in Mississippi, awkward around girls, too busy with his many interests, and then his marine career, to really understand the effort of dating.

"I just don't know what happened to Shane in that department anyway," Joe Childers said. "I mean you'd take one look at that fellow and figure that most women would be pleased as punch just to buy that deal right off the hoof. But, you know, then Shane would buy some girl a corsage, or wax up the car before he took her to the dance. Then she'd dump him."

Part of the problem was that young Shane was still very much a man's man. It would take him five or six more years to fully transition to the throb who was "macho sensitive," which was how virtually every woman who knew him later described Shane. The recessive West Virginia gene, which made him so entertaining around men, made him shy and noninitiating with women. And he was very picky about the opposite sex. They *had* to be what he called "perfect foxes," that is trim, with very pretty faces, smart, and nonsmokers. But his values and personal tastes—country music, marine discipline, politics that leaned right—made him come off as a redneck who couldn't attract those kind of girls. If someone disagreed with his ideas, or maybe just smoked a little pot, control-freakism took over and he chased them away.

Robbin Whitten was married to Shane's commanding officer in Nairobi, and they became close friends during his security guard years. She had first met him in Paris in 1993, when Shane was briefly assigned to the American embassy there to provide security during a diplomatic conference.

"Oh, Shane Childers, wow, you know?" Whitten said. "He was like the *Esquire* model, the picture in *Vanity Fair,* the poster boy that every commander wanted in his unit. Very courteous, very military in bearing, but also very, very charmingly informal, even vulnerable. We called him 'The Traffic Stopper.' Believe me, when that marine walked down the Champs Élysées, every girl in Paris noticed. But Shane was completely out to lunch about it. He couldn't believe that he was adored by women."

But then it finally happened for him, in Nairobi in 1994, a beautiful and romantic relationship that lasted for more than a year.

Adi Arad was the daughter of an Israeli consulate official who had lived in the expatriate community in Kenya since 1988. She was ranked third in the country in the one-hundred-meter breaststroke and spoke flawless New York English from attending the American School in Nairobi. She was outgoing, sexy, and super-bright, with soft, olive skin and a wild mane of brown curly hair with blond highlights from the African sun. On Friday nights, with her other expat girlfriends, she regularly attended Movie Night at the suburban U.S. Marine barracks, which were staged after an elaborate picnic on the broad lawns outside the house. The American marines loved to flirt with her, crowding around and telling her who they were, pulling all the usual moves, but Adi was profoundly disinterested in them all. She just wanted to see good American flicks.

The night she met Shane the movie was *8 Seconds,* a cowboy film about a bullrider played by Luke Perry.

"Oooooh. Who's that marine over there? I think I might go for that."

"Forget it," one of Adi's girlfriends told her. "That's Sergeant Childers. He just got here. He's completely square and all he does is climb mountains and ride bikes."

But she was intrigued because of his great looks and mysterious contrasts. When he was at rest and not saying much Childers looked somber and withdrawn. But the minute he spoke and smiled, his eyes sparkled and his demeanor seemed cheerful and fun. What a hunk, and so polite looking. Adi was not bashful and after *8 Seconds* was over she walked across the room and asked his name.

"Shane," he said.

"Oh, come off it. That's too good a line. Shane. Are you a cowboy, too?"

"Well, no. But I mean yes, in a way. The full name is Therrel Shane, actually. I didn't just make it up for tonight."

Oh boy. The southern accent, which she loved right away, and the Robert Duvall voice. Hunky, courteous, probably a little bit vulnerable, self-effacing around women. Adi, girl, this is going to be one fun pile of work.

"He was textbook marine," Adi said years later. "So textbook, so marine, and so unbelievably square that it was completely attractive. I couldn't wait to roll up my sleeves and start loosening this guy up."

But it was work at first. Technically, Shane was not allowed to date Adi because she was only eighteen and marine regulations forbid dating "natives" that young, even if Adi was obviously sophisticated way beyond her years. Shane was a real stickler for the rules and resisted her for a while, even though they talked for hours now after movie night. She found him fascinating, this unique blend of working-class hero and brainy intellectual trying to break out. He was in Kenya now, so he was reading every book he could find on British colonial Africa, which he loved to share with her and discuss. It was a classic brainfuck that was going well.

Everyone in the barracks was laughing about it–Shane was following the rules and wouldn't date Adi. Finally a commanding officer got wind of this and pulled Shane aside.

"Childers, you miserable bonehead. Frig the rules, man. That girl can easily pass for twenty, so get a life. You're good to go on this one."

They immediately "clicked," as Adi put it, as soon as they started dating, and they did all of Nairobi and Kenya together. She gave him tapes of the latest European rock bands and he introduced her to Willie Nelson and Garth Brooks. She loved going to the Carnivore nightclub with him because it was fun showing him how easy it was to break the law in Kenya and buy her drinks. Lighten up, Shane. They spent long, dreamy weekends at her parents' house and went on photo-safaris at the bush resorts. At the pool, when he stripped down to his trunks to swim, the body was unbelievable. All those years of calisthenics and weight-lifting had produced a physique that belonged in the magazine spreads about Muscle Beach.

They were together almost every day. On weeknights Shane would occasionally take her to meetings of his mountaineering club. The group mostly consisted of middle-aged European and British ex-pats, very serious about climbing, and they sat around all night in dens decorated with paintings of giraffes and Mount Kilimanjaro, watching slide shows and talking about snakebite kits.

"Hey, Shane, mind if I ask you about the meeting back there?" Adi said one night while he was driving her home.

"No, no," he said. "Anything wrong?"

"Shane," Adi said. "You climb the mountain, right? Then you walk back down. Is there really anything more to it than that? I mean, all those guys back there. They were talking about *compasses*."

Shane threw his head back and howled, and oh did she love him that night. He could really laugh his ass off about himself. He had self-knowledge, so much of it, and such good self-mocking humor.

"Adi, sorry, sorry." Shane laughed. "Christ, I'm such an idiot. But look, they're not really that bad, right?"

"Shane, they're total losers. I'm never climbing a mountain with those guys."

"Okay! Okay! I'm an idiot. Want to go for a drink?"

Still, she couldn't completely liberate Shane from the marine mentality, or his West Virginia roots. Adi's family was very Israeli, which is to say Euro-hip, globally cool, not at all square or clueless. The Arads adored Shane, expressed out loud that they were adopting him as a son, and trusted him completely with their daughter. When the Arads went to bed for the night, Adi and Shane in turn headed for her room, pushing the two small beds in there together so it was more comfortable to sleep together. In the morning, when he woke to change for his run, Shane would start fussing around the room, hurriedly cleaning up and insisting that they separate the beds back to the original floor plan.

"Adi! C'mon, get up. Let's get these beds squared away," Shane would say. "Your mother might come in here and be shocked if she finds the beds are together."

"Shane, go for your run," Adi would say, refusing to wake up. "If my mother comes in here, she'll be shocked if the beds are apart."

"Oh my God, don't say that, please. I mean, she doesn't know, right? You're joking me."

"Shane . . . Shane?"

"What?"

"Take your run. Please?"

And the Shane Childers obsessive-compulsive technique for making new friends, falling in love. He was becoming a Jew now. Shane went to a book store in downtown Nairobi and bought every volume he could find about Judaism and studied them all. He sat up with Adi's parents until past midnight, discussing Jewish history, Zionism, and the founding of Israel. Of course, he became particularly adept at Jewish military history, all the way from the Maccabees to Yoni at Entebbe.

"Shane was fascinated by my Jewishness and just couldn't get enough of it," Adi said. "He had to know everything about everything, of course, but now it was everything about Jews. That's not an exaggeration. It was totally adorable and pathetic. By the time we broke up, he knew more about Judaism than I did."

They were first lovers and thought it would last forever. But in 1995 Adi, after much anguish, decided that she should return to Israel and perform her national military service. Shane was great about that, putting his self-interest aside to discuss it with her. Adi, what's good about this for you, what might be bad for us. He was lovingly supportive and wanted her to do what she believed in. After she left in October that year, Shane wrote her long, morose letters from Nairobi–life at the embassy, the expat scene in Africa, was boring without her.

In February 1996 Shane made a ten-day trip to Israel to be with her and tour the Jerusalem historic sites, but the trip was a disaster. Because of her language skills, Adi was based with an Israeli Army intelligence unit up on the Lebanese border, acting as a liaison with the multinational forces enforcing United Nations border agreements. The day Shane visited her base up north, it was shelled by guerilla forces from Lebanon and Shane had to leave as soon as he reached the gate. Then when she got back to Tel Aviv to be with him, the shelling started again and she was ordered back to base. Shane spent his time visiting the Mediterranean beaches and touring the ruins with Adi's mother. They were at an impasse, and they bravely faced it. Adi was serving in the Israeli Army and would certainly want to date a few more men before she decided on a commitment. Shane was a U.S. Marine and would be perpetually on the move. It just wasn't working.

Over the years, they corresponded sporadically and talked on the phone late at night. They even reunited once in New York. But their hearts were broken now and they could never reclaim what they'd had once in distant, dreamy Kenya. Kissing that first time outside the nightclub in Nairobi. Hiking back into the bush and photographing wildlife, then reclining by the resort pool as the sun fell over Kilimanjaro. The memories remained the most potent of their lives and, five years later, when he described Adi to close friends, Shane's eyes would still well up with tears. But they could never quite get it back and Shane and Adi never "clicked" again.

But the Arad family connection proved provocative for Shane, and he used it in the usual way. Back in Nairobi, he sat up long into the night discussing his life and his dreams about the future with Adi's mother, Micheal. Shane and Micheal became quite close—he called her his second mother—and Adi thought that she could sense what was going on, when she heard about their talks by letter or phone. It was the old available-mom syndrome. He was in Nairobi now, love-sick and pondering his future, and Micheal was a patient, solid enabler.

And Micheal could see what was going on. Shane was super-bright, completely adorable as a personality, burning with ambition. He was perfectionist and tended to default toward control-freakism when he wasn't sure of his way. At twenty-four, he still had some personal and family baggage to resolve. Intellectual growth would round out a lot of these edges and give him something new to achieve. It was with Micheal that Shane started pondering the idea of finally getting with the program and realizing his potential. It was time to consider college.

Everyone else could see it as well. It had been a quick climb in the marines for a boy from Harrison Central High School in Gulfport, Mississippi. But now Shane was edgy, impatient, almost manic about his future. Classically driven, he needed a new challenge just to enjoy life. And now he was opening up a little and saying something new to his friends in the marines and diplomatic corps, a clear result of having tasted embassy life. It nagged at him, socially, that no one in his immediate family had a college degree. He knew that he wouldn't rise further in the marines—not to mention in life—until he acquired a college degree.

Back in Wyoming, the Childerses knew that Shane was considering college, but he deliberately kept them in the dark about his plans until he knew for sure. When he visited home on leave from his embassy assignments, they could tell he was distracted now. Once, when talking with his sister in the kitchen, Shane had blurted out something that she could never forget.

"God, Sandy, what am I going to do? I haven't accomplished a single thing with my life yet."

Sandra laughed hysterically.

"Oh God, Shane, that is just so *you*. Do you mind if I tell you about just one tiny little fact?"

"No! No! I don't mind. What's the fact?"

"Shane. Get a grip. You're twenty-three years old."

Steve Whitten, the master sergeant who ran the marine detachment in Nairobi, mentored Shane quite a bit, but also relied on him as a supremely competent manager who could take over at the embassy when Whitten was on leave or detached assignments. Shane was personally close to the whole Whitten family. Robbin Whitten became one of many marine wives to join what they called the "Shane Childers Fan Club," and the three Whitten daughters clapped with joy and defaulted to goof-off mode as soon as he arrived at their house, joking around with him and playing sports. They called him "Uncle Shane."

"Shane was always thinking ten steps ahead of where he was," Whitten said. "We would talk endlessly into the night about that because he knew he had to get that college degree. I was the one who told him about the marine enlisted commission program, which would allow him to get his degree and jump to the officer class. He was instantly crazy about doing that."

The Marine Enlisted Commissioning Education Program, MECEP, was in fact quite a prestigious thing. Every year, about one hundred prior enlist marines of exceptional promise are selected to attend four-year colleges on a full military scholarship while collecting regular pay, after which they would be commissioned as officers. "Getting MECEP" was a huge deal in the marines not simply because the program was very competitive and the benefits lavish. It marked the future officer for life because it proved that he was socially and professionally capable of vaulting through the military's rigid class structure of rank.

Shane was under a lot of pressure now. The age limit for applying was twenty-five, and there weren't a lot of people around who could give him sound advice about completing college applications, writing all those essays and finding a location overseas to take his SATs. But he went at it with maniacal energy and typical attention to detail. By the spring of 1998 he was hearing from schools. He'd been accepted at The Citadel in Charleston, South Carolina, his first choice, but also all the state universities he'd applied to—in Colorado, Virginia, and Florida.

"Freakin' A," Shane exulted to his friends. "I can't believe this. I got into all of my colleges."

Everyone was overjoyed for Shane. And, as he left Nairobi for a brief reassignment to Camp Pendleton in California and then a Western Pacific cruise before he enrolled at The Citadel, it was clear what the college milestone would mean. He was getting past the limits of family now, past his personal background. He had become that most interesting kind of person, the compelling and achieving late bloomer, finally addressing the development delayed back in Mississippi. Shane was keenly aware of all this and often spoke about it to friends. He was scared about the amount of academic work required by college, and he had chosen The Citadel because he felt more comfortable in the environment of a military college after rejecting the "hippie girl" culture of the other campuses he visited. And he knew that he couldn't fuck up now, he *had* to perform. Everyone would be watching the first Childers to attend college.

That summer, the Childerses had been in Wyoming for seven years and Joe had been privately dreaming about a college education himself. He had his navy pension now, picking up an extra job somewhere was always a snap, and he could attend college at night, or whenever. There was a good community college right there in Powell, a place called Northwest. Then Shane came home for his summer visit, he and Joe broke some horses together and laid irrigation pipe, and it was just great to see how excited Shane was about leaving for his MECEP prep course in California before he traveled east for The Citadel in the fall.

"Well, you know, when Shane told me that he was going to college I just said to hell with my own plans for school," Joe said. "Shane would be going to college for both of us. That was the feeling between us now, I just kind of sensed. Shane was accomplishing whole bunches of things that were dreams for us all."

On Wednesday morning, when the CACO team arrived at the Childerses, it took a few minutes for the initial awkwardness and tension to wear off. That was because they all knew that they were operating now with a deficit of information. Hutchison still couldn't get a firm ship date for Shane's body out of Quantico or the Dover mortuary, mostly because there had been a lot more casualties in Iraq and the field morgue shipments were coming back in unpredictable waves. The pressure on Hutchison was infuriating. Don't screw up this CACO assignment, captain, is the funeral all planned yet? It's getting there, sir, but I need the body. Sorry, we can't help you on that yet. As soon as we hear from Germany or Dover, we'll let you know.

That was marine life, right there, all of it incredibly compressed by the agony of burying the first killed in Iraq. We don't have the information you need, captain. Oh, and by the way, Hutch. Don't fuck up.

The Childerses were being pressured from a lot of different directions. Governor Dave Freudenthal had already announced that he would attend the funeral. Wyoming's congressmen and state senators had all called, and there were all the local veterans' groups, the media, and now family and friends converging from London and California. But when was the funeral? They all had to know. It was maddening to have given up your son in a war but then nobody in the military really knew when he'd be back.

"Kevin, I think we should just say Tuesday and establish that as a firm date for the funeral," Judy told Hutchison as they sat at the dining-room table. "We can always hold a big memorial service for everyone who's here and then bury Shane privately when he's back."

"Judy," Hutchison said. "I promised to agree on a firm date, and Tuesday is fine. That just motivates me to work harder to get Shane back."

"Ah, listen here, Kevin," Joe said. "We're not blaming you, see? You do know that, right? We know that the thing is out of your control."

"Thanks, Joe," Hutchison said. "I do know that. But let's work toward Tuesday, and I'll push hard for that."

There were a few more forms left to sign and they talked about the funeral and Laura Richardson's suggestion that it be held in the gym at Northwest College in Powell. Hutchison explained that he and Sergeant Morgan would be making visits in town today to discuss all the arrangements with the funeral home and the police—they would even be speaking with the editor of the Powell *Tribune* to get the proper word out. He explained that Morgan would probably be spending the rest of the week in Billings, drilling his honor guard team at the armory, while Hutchison worked all the details from Powell. When they again declined lunch because they had an appointment in town at the police department, Judy insisted that they take some coffee and Girl Scout cookies.

Before he left, Hutchison managed to maneuver Judy into the living room and talked to her alone. He'd been worried about her, and so was everyone else. She still wasn't showing much emotion about Shane's death, and he was concerned about her well-being, the emotional consequences of her holding so much in. But he wasn't sure how to handle it so he had checked his thinking with his mother out in California the night before. And she had made a useful suggestion.

"Kevin, make it a request for information, okay? Don't tell her what to do, how she should feel. Just ask, all right?"

That's how Hutchison handled it. He told Judy that he was concerned about her, that she wasn't expressing much emotion at all, and that he would just like to know how she was feeling. Was there anything more he should be doing?

"Oh, Kevin, please," Judy said. "I'm fine, really. I'm so used to being the rock of this family after keeping everything together when Joe was traveling for the navy. Just give me time. I'll be okay."

"All right, Judy," Hutchison said. "You're sure?"

"Kevin? Kevin Hutchison? What did I just say?"

"All right, Judy. All right. But I'm here. You just have to tell me."

Hutchison and Morgan left the house a few minutes later, heading for town. Hutchison still felt vaguely uncomfortable about how Judy was doing and made a mental note to ask his mother for more advice. But it was certainly possible, he thought, that he was being *too* sensitive about Judy, and that he should just relax about it.

When they reached downtown Powell, Hutchison and Morgan began to sense that Shane Childers' death, and the prospect of hosting the funeral of the first soldier killed in Iraq, was having quite an impact in the community. If they stopped somewhere for coffee or lunch, or just bought a paper, no one would take their money. They stood out in their dress blues, obviously the CACO team handling the Childers burial. Strangers would stop them on the street and ask if there was anything they could do to help.

Over at the Skyline Café on East Coulter Avenue, Hutchison and Morgan overheard some farmers talking. They were all huddled together in a booth, finishing lunch, discussing the war in Iraq and the upcoming funeral. The farmers were expecting a lot of peace protestors and demonstrators from out of town. If the demonstrators acted up, the farmers were all planning on bashing heads and kicking some ass. They all laughed when one of them pointed out that this is why Wyoming farmers own too many tractors. You can always use one to make bail.

When Hutchison and Morgan met with the deputy chief at the police station, he was also concerned about handling such a big event. The governor's office, CNN, and veterans' groups had all called about attending the funeral, and they all wanted to know if there was going to be a procession of the hearse through town. Many other residents of Powell had asked about it as well. Hutchison said that they were planning on a procession, which the deputy felt was going to create crowd control and security issues.

But, really, the deputy was mainly concerned about something else: peace protestors. That was the big worry. For sure, a lot of them would be showing up in Powell to demonstrate at the funeral, and the police department was readying plans to recruit extra state troopers and set up partitions so that all the peace protestors could be conveniently herded out of harm's way. They would be trying to turn this event into another Matthew Sheperd media spectacle, but the police didn't want any trouble like that in Powell.

Hutchison thought these concerns were exaggerated, but he didn't want to say so directly and offend the local law. He made eye contact with Morgan, who was suppressing a smile, and then felt Morgan's size eleven shoe applying pressure on top of his own. The meeting was beginning to remind Hutchison of his favorite cold war farce, a movie starring Carl Reiner and Alan Arkin called *The Russians Are Coming, the Russians Are Coming*, during which a small New England town reacts to the grounding of a harmless Soviet submarine. He was burying a marine in a Wyoming town so remote that there was road-kill elk a few blocks from city hall. But the Russians were coming now, the Russians were coming, and for sure there would be marauding peace protestors on the streets.

Hutchison thought fast and replied, "Well deputy, we appreciate your thoroughness here. But I think that the military might have a position on this."

"Sure," the deputy said. "What would that be?"

"I can check with command," Hutchison said. "But I think they'll suggest that we keep any partitions or extra police officers out of sight, unless we really need them. We want the public to feel welcome. We want to show proper respect. I'm burying a fellow marine."

The deputy agreed but suggested that they just keep the problem of the protestors in mind. You never know.

Hutchison and Morgan started roaring with laughter as soon as they got out to the Surburban and headed out of town, taking the Belfry cutoff north.

"Oh Christ, sir," Morgan said. "What bullshit. There isn't a frickin' peace protestor within three hundred miles of this town. The last hippie sighting was in 1968."

"The Russians are coming, Barry," Hutchison said. "The Russians are coming."

Morgan was really roaring now, and Hutchison appreciated it, that they could get traction on some levity and get away from the pressures of the CACO work.

"Fuck me," Morgan said. "The Russians are coming. Hey. Do you think we should tell Joe? It's so funny."

"Yeah, let's tell Joe. He's got a great sense of humor, don't you think?"

"Oh God, yes. Let's tell him. Old Jedd Clampett back there will love it. The fucking Russians are coming to Powell."

It started getting dark once they were past the open range of the Two Dot ranch and then, in the gap between the Beartooths and the Pryors, the peaks blocked what remained of the sun. It was all just one vast blackness outside now, with two good marines in their car trying to stay loosened up as they drove north through the void. The Russians were coming, but in the Montana sky ahead the familiar lights of Laurel and Billings beckoned them safely home.

THE CITADEL YEARS

B y the end of the week, Captain Hutchison was getting close to melting down and everyone around him saw it. The whole Billings command was affected by it. He wasn't exercising in the morning, a violation of marine and personal doctrine, he wasn't eating or sleeping well, and paperwork for the Childers CACO was strewn all around his desk. He worked late every night, CACO-obsessed. Hutchison had always liked to lead by example and loosely at that, and had never been sharp-tongued with his men. But he was now. Even the Mexicans working on his house noticed the change. Normally when he came in from his morning run, he'd make coffee and chatter away with them in Spanish for a while. But now they were just in the way, a nuisance waiting around for further instructions about shutters and paint. Hutchison was anxious to leave early for the armory to deal with the Childers CACO.

One of his most trusted noncommissioned officers, Staff Sergeant Travis Ridgeway, stepped into Hutchison's office on Friday afternoon and expressed the concerns of the other marines.

"Sir," the staff sergeant said. "You're taking the Childers CACO way too seriously, way beyond the call of duty. Take some time off."

But Hutchison felt that he had no choice except to ignore that advice. One of the problems was that Joe and Judy Childers were more than willing to accept Hutchison's many generous offers to assume responsibility for the paperwork that families often did themselves. He was mired down in completing insurance forms, closing bank accounts, and chasing down the location of Shane's storage locker outside Camp Pendleton in suburban San Diego. Meanwhile he had to coordinate all the details of a funeral parade in Powell with the local police, monitor carefully that they weren't overreacting to the threat of peace protestors, field calls from the national media, and deal with the flood of reply faxes from Virginia and Washington on Shane's CACO case. Headquarters branch at Quantico had now concluded that the crush of media, dignitaries, and veterans groups could overwhelm tiny Powell, and they didn't want to botch the PR during a very public funeral for the first soldier killed in Iraq. Quantico was sending out two additional Marine Public Affairs Officers to assist with the funeral, help that was welcome. But each new layer of contact required additional complexity—motel reservations, transportation, more reporting up to a distant command.

And he still had no firm news for Joe and Judy about when Shane's body would return. He did know at this point that Shane was at the national mortuary in Dover, Delaware, being prepared. Faxes had been exchanged about a proper medals rack for his burial uniform and the Childerses had selected a coffin. But it was nearly the weekend now, the Tuesday funeral and burial date loomed, and he still couldn't provide specific information for funeral director Laura Richardson, the Powell police, or the family on when Shane would arrive. With casualties mounting in Iraq, Dover was backed up now and the mortuary couldn't release a firm ship date. Thanks for your concern, captain, FYI, we'll keep you up to date. It was the old military hurry up and wait routine. But this was positively maddening when the job at hand was burying a hero marine.

Hutchison's meticulous approach to the Childers CACO created tensions in his important relationship with First Sergeant Morgan as well. Morgan adored the Childerses—all Joe's crazyass projects around the ranch, the way Judy was the quiet force that held the family together, the impressive son they had raised. The CACO manual required only that a local command make the next-of-kin notification, keep an appointment or two to familiarize the survivors with all the paperwork, and then provide an honor guard and assistance with the funeral if the family asked.

Hutchison was going way beyond that and then not listening to his second in command, who was advising that the Billings marines might just consider reducing the CACO effort a bit. Morgan reached his limit when he heard about the photo albums. Hutchison had gone out to Staples and purchased fifty of them, so that every friend and family member who came to Wyoming for the service could have a fitting memento, replete with newspaper stories and pictures of Shane. It was a noble gesture, the sort of generosity that came effortlessly to Hutchison. It was just his way of living out the marine motto, Semper Fidelis—Always Faithful—for the Childers family. But the photocopying and the runs back and forth to Staples for color copies of Shane's official marine portrait ate up a lot of time.

Christ, photo albums. First Sergeant Morgan saw the problem clearly.

"Okay, it probably wasn't Kevin's fault—he's just a super-conscientious marine," Morgan said later. "It's the military, the officer system. They take a guy with a normal upbringing, two good parents, and a nice town somewhere, and what do they do to make him an officer? Send him to *college*. He gets sensitive, you know? It's a total waste of energy. Christ, we went so overboard with sensitive on the Childers CACO it isn't even funny."

On Friday another small wrinkle came up. Joe Childers was planning on wearing his old Seabee dress uniform to the funeral, but he didn't have a pair of regulation navy enlisted chief petty officer's trousers that fit him anymore. Joe also needed the regulation belt. Because this was a CACO case, the uniform supplier, the Navy Exchange, was willing to ship by FedEx overnight. But the CACO manuals didn't say that government funds were authorized for this expense. The pants and belt would cost forty-eight dollars, plus shipping, but no one in the Billings command felt like calling Joe Childers and asking for the money.

"Sir, what should we do about the chief petty officer's pants for Joe?" Morgan asked Hutchison.

"Oh, I don't know, Barry," Hutchison said distractedly, looking up from his desk in the middle of a dozen other CACO details. "Can you handle that one? Do you mind?"

Hell, no. Morgan didn't mind. At that moment he realized the problem that he had with this super-sensitive, Pomona-educated California surfer boy captain of his. Fucking Hutch. Morgan liked the guy too much.

"Done, sir," Morgan said. "I'm on it."

Meanwhile, down on the Childers ranch, Joe and Judy were receiving visitors and graciously accepting the anonymous gifts and outpouring of support from the town of Powell. In the morning, cars drove in—they were women from the American Legion auxillary, or Judy's friends from Avon—bearing containers of casseroles, country-fried chicken, and baked goods, even cartons of soda and coffee. Joe received a delegation from his employer, Northstate Corp., and stood out on the front patio with the men, talking for half an hour beside the flag that was hanging at half-mast. Joe was subdued, but cheerful, almost his old self—telling stories, joking—because he was all cried out for now. He could see the anguish on the faces of his visitors, the awkwardness about what to say, and felt an obligation to entertain. The men, many of them, wrapped their big arms around his shoulders and hugged him sideways, pushed their ball caps up and then were insistent about one point.

"But, Joe, there must be something we can do for you. How can we help?"

"Oh, I'm all right, really," Joe said. "It's hard to concentrate on much at the moment. We're fine for now. The marines are taking really good care of us."

It was interesting, though, how people translated that. The Northstate men asked the Childerses what they could do. Joe suggested that they order some gravel for the driveway. A couple of hours after the Northstate group left, two ten-wheeler gravel trucks showed up at the Childerses place, started dumping and smoothing, and by midafternoon the driveway looked brand new. There was only one bathroom in the house, and the Childerses were expecting a lot of company. Northstate also sent over a truck bearing two Porta-Johns and had them installed behind the toolshed.

Shane Childers arrived at The Citadel in Charleston, South Carolina, in the fall of 1998. For the first time since he was a teenager, he was liberated from the tedium of intensive military training, deployments, and the perpetual scrutiny of professional and personal review. Charleston and The Citadel were an ideal mix for him, pure Shane in a lot of ways, and it's hard to imagine him flowering as he did in any of the other schools where he'd been accepted. Now he was a mid-twenties cadet at one of the nation's most prestigious military colleges, revered in legend, Civil War histories, and novels, most notably Pat Conroy's *The Lords of Discipline*. The Citadel appeased Shane's military side, his need to channel his ferocious energy in a disciplined, martial environment. As he settled into an off-campus apartment on Smith Street near Charleston's gracious historic district, Shane also was exultant about discovering civilian life, rounding out as a person. In letters to friends he excitedly described the city's night life and his evening and weekend excursions now–pub-crawling at the touristy bars, listening to contemporary folk musicians at the coffeehouses, discovering antiquarian bookstores. He shopped for furniture and rugs at antique stores, taught himself to cook nouvelle cuisine, and filled his apartment walls and every flat surface with books, hundreds of books.

While The Citadel years would eventually change him, at first Shane was as manic and driven as ever. The word universally used to describe him was *intense*. On weekends he competed in triathlon events in Florida and the Carolinas, junketed off to Georgia or Virginia to hike the Appalachian Trail, or made the long drive back to Salt Rock to goof off and kayak with his favorite West Virginia cousins, Jessi and Jonna Walker. Friends continued to be amazed by the pace he could maintain. Every morning he rose at five to run and then put in twelve miles on his bike, and then he attended classes, dealt with his Marine ROTC unit, and studied all night. At midnight he was still going strong, The Citadel Energizer Bunny, yap-yapping away on the phone with friends about his girlfriend problems, his history term paper, or goading someone he loved to pay attention to their goals and explore personal growth.

The Shane Childers legend would grow immensely while he was at The Citadel, but more than anything else it derived from his passionate sense of justice. Within weeks of arriving at the campus that fall, one incident in particular established Shane as an unforgettable force who would leave his mark in ways that challenged The Citadel's rich but inflexible traditions.

Hazing was still a big part of Citadel life then. It was ritualized abuse that enforced a traditional rite of passage during which incoming freshman cadets were introduced to "discipline" and "humility" by mostly out-of-control upperclassmen. Less than half The Citadel's graduates actually go on to military service—the college is also a reliable feeder system for the South's banks, insurance companies, and law schools—but hazing kept alive a caste structure that guaranteed that Citadel graduates would some day become tough, unbreakable company men. All fall the green lawns of The Citadel's stately quadrangle echoed with the shouts of senior cadets running the newbies through push-up drills, uniform inspections, and verbal taunting. The late-night antics in the barracks-style dormitories were a lot worse.

Shane Childers, a MECEP marine and a Gulf War veteran—not to mention simply how he carried himself in general—was supremely immune from this treatment, of course. No one dared asked him to do push-ups on the grass.

But one day he was crossing the campus and saw a large group of upperclassmen standing around and watching an eager bully at his work, humiliating a freshman with verbal abuse and comments about his uniform, not letting up and clearly enjoying the laughter of his senior peers. The young cadet was showing signs of stress, but still the seniors wouldn't let up. Shane's sense of justice surfaced—there must have been residual frustration left over from boot camp eight years ago, or marine life in general, where abuse of the weak is so common. Or maybe it was just Shane's innate impatience with morons.

Shane didn't snap or overplay his hand. He simply walked over to the bullying cadet, stepped up on his toes a bit to stare him down face-to-face, and said one thing, calmly, "That's not a soldier."

That's all he said. "That's not a soldier."

Then Shane just stood there facing the senior down eyeball to eyeball, seeing if he would react.

The senior cadet was too astounded to say anything, and was clearly intimidated by Shane. After a long, pregnant silence, he turned on his heels and left, and the crowd around him quickly dispersed. Shane remained on the quadrangle grass for a few minutes, quietly introducing himself to his fellow member of the freshman class, chatting and making sure that he was all right.

News of the Childers stare-down spread quickly around the campus, and was particularly admired by faculty members, most of whom detested the hazing system for its impact on campus morale and student attention spans. What Shane had done was a dramatic violation of protocol, a direct affront to tradition. This simply wasn't done at The Citadel–freshmen didn't confront seniors like that and interrupt hazing. Now this new man on campus, an uber-marine named Shane Childers, had done exactly that and made an important statement about a practice that he didn't like. Hazing didn't change, of course. But everyone was talking about it and Shane was now known as someone completely different at The Citadel, and certainly not to be trifled with. "It's fun being the black sheep," he later wrote about his Citadel experiences in a letter to Adi Arad, but it was much more than that. Shane's unique mix of sensitivity and strength made him a standout on The Citadel campus, and the event was still spoken about years later.

"Shane was always doing things like this and he stood out at The Citadel right away," said Guy Toubiana, a native of France who is a member of the school's language faculty and became one of Shane's closest friends. "If the cadets were acting up in class, he would stare them down and say 'Show more respect,' and they did. It wasn't simply his sense of justice and the code of military discipline. And he certainly wasn't big or scary. But you could see the strength in his eyes."

Academically, Shane performed poorly at first and clearly showed signs of a student unprepared for college and intimidated by the workload. In both French and English, his sentence structure was poor and in one spring-semester French course, his test grades kited between the low forties and high sixties, until with a final push he managed to pull off an eighty-four on the final exam and just barely pass the course. He obsessed about subjects rather than truly understanding them, often taking out more than a dozen library books just to complete a five-page paper. Scholastic humility—just a willingness to settle down, listen, and learn—did not come easily to him, especially in military history courses where he believed that he already knew the material. He considered those professors arrogant "know-it-alls" and conducted semester-long battles with Ph.D. historians over such topics as the U.S. Air Force's strategic bombing campaign against Japan in World War II or Napoleon's defeat in Russia. The one complaint about him to reach administrators at The Citadel was revelatory. Shane Childers owed so much in fines for overdue books at libraries all over town that three of them were threatening to shred his borrower's card.

But Shane was engagingly persistent. With professors that he trusted, he was constantly asking for help and extra work, appearing in their offices without appointments and chatting with them until he demanded that they correct his papers *before* he turned them in. Wisely deciding against majoring in history—he detested the department, a feeling that apparently was mutual—he settled instead on French, concluding that language skills would be of inestimable use for him as a marine officer. Later, he thought, a degree in languages might help him develop a second career as a State Department official, or he could always take advantage of generous military support for officers pursuing graduate degrees and get his masters and doctorate in French. Serving some day as a diplomat at one of the embassies where he was once just a marine guard, or teaching at a college, were active fantasies he discussed a lot with friends.

Besides, the routines of the language department—French-language banquets once or twice a semester, monthly roundtables at a French restaurant downtown, summer study programs abroad—were very appealing to Shane, and he thrived in the environment. By the fall of his second year he was pulling down straight As and after that never left the dean's list. He became legendary in the department for cramming in every extra-credit opportunity he could find around the world, and spent his summers on academic and mountain-climbing junkets to France, French Equatorial Africa, and Middlebury College in Vermont.

"Shane did extremely well at The Citadel, but not because the material came easily to him," Toubiana said. "He worked very, very hard. He was one of the very few students I've ever had who would come back every time after a test and insist on figuring out why he got a single question wrong. And he was obsessed, truly obsessed, with getting a B.A. in French because he could speak the language fluently. He *had* to be perfect all the time—that was his personal standard."

Shane was unavoidable for another reason. By Citadel tradition, cadets deferred either to the ranking cadet or the academic leader in a class, and Shane usually qualified as both. The student leader received the professor's first question, helped lead discussions, and even occasionally assisted in the presentation of lectures. There were groans all around when cadets realized that they'd enrolled in a course with Shane.

"It was basically an attitude of 'Oh, crap, we're in this course with Childers,'" said French professor Christopher McRae, who also became a close friend and fan of Shane. "Shane would shine and dominate, no matter what."

McRae's girlfriend, Barbara Blatchley, was the chairman of the psychology department at Agnes Scott College in Decatur, Georgia, and frequently made the weekend commute to Charleston. One Friday in the spring of 2000, McRae asked her to deliver a guest lecture on language and the brain to his French class, an experience that proved memorable because it was Blatchley's first experience with Shane. Before her lecture began, Shane approached the visiting professor outside the classroom and asked that she include in her presentation as much as she could say about Tourette's syndrome—he simply wanted to know more about it. After the class was over he approached her again. Shane felt that the students had been lethargic and nonresponsive, asking too few questions when she was done, and he just wanted to apologize to her for the disappointing performance of the class.

"In seventeen years of teaching, I had never seen a student doing either one of these things, and now here was someone doing both at once," Blatchley said. "First, this very earnest and obviously intense student wants to set the agenda for the lecture and tell me what I should talk about. Then he apologizes for his class. And all through the class, I noticed, he was clearly the alpha dog in the pack. Before all the other students asked a question, they would glance at him as if they were asking his permission 'Wow, who is this guy?' I just had to ask myself. You just couldn't forget Shane Childers once you had encountered him."

And that alpha dog just wouldn't let go of his sense of justice either. Like many Citadel professors, McRae was often annoyed that the hectic schedules maintained by cadets—early-morning marching drills, military events all day, the distractions of hazing—were exhausting and left too little room for social development and the kind of wishful thinking that should occur during the college years. His biggest problem was cadets falling asleep in class. The student body was drawn mostly from the South and from military families and their social outlook tended to be narrow, typecast. To expose his cadets to broader possibilities, McRae occasionally liked to steer his classes toward open discussions, especially when he was teaching sociolinguistics.

Shane could always be relied upon to be provocative during such discussions, one reason McRae appreciated having him in his class, and his views were not always as predictable as they seemed. His political mind-set was generally right of center—pro-military, of course, pro-Republican, a Reagan-style thinker on economics, taxes, and the size of government. But he had no patience at all for the social agenda of the conservatives and detested both intolerance and self-righteous religion. One day, the subject in McRae's class turned to homosexuality and gays, a high-profile issue just then in a military environment like The Citadel. After initially botching an attempt at reform, the Clinton administration's stance on gays in the military had evolved to the controversial policy "Don't Ask, Don't Tell."

"Homophobia is a big part of the culture at The Citadel," McRae said. "But Shane defended gays. He was more adamant about it than persuasive, I would say, but it was a very moving experience for me. *I couldn't be very effective preaching tolerance, because the cadets would just dismiss me as a typical civilian instructor, probably a closet liberal. But Shane was a marine, studying to become a commissioned officer, with all the political assumptions involved. And here he was at The Citadel, in this pressure-cooker environment where homophobia is rampant. He wasn't afraid to speak up, defend gays, and denounce prejudice. His basic position was that this is America. Personal freedom counts. Gays have a right to be who they are. He wasn't going to listen to anyone bash gays, not in his class, not in his country."

McRae left the campus that day convinced that Shane Childers was one of the most remarkable and open-minded people he had ever met. It was Shane's courage to think on his own, the personal growth track, that impressed McRae the most, because he knew a lot about Shane now. He had grown up in Mississippi, in a military family, and spent the last nine years as a marine. But personal freedom and independent thinking mattered more to him than the standard military line on gays. For McRae, Shane had just "saved the reputation of the marines."

And it didn't bother Shane in the least that word quickly circulated around The Citadel about what he said in the class, and that some cadets were labeling him "pro-fag." Shane was Shane, that was it, and this was the American way. Tolerance, period. Sure, Childers could be a pain in the butt to have in your course. He just wouldn't stop achieving or shut up in class. But McRae was deeply touched by his performance that day and knew that he would never forget this uber-marine named Shane.

And no matter what, Shane just couldn't stop building on that legend. It was his style now, the irrepressible Childers default. Go somewhere exotic, study hard and climb a mountain, confront injustice, save a damsel in distress, then return to campus with the Shane mystique enhanced.

In the summer of 1999, following his freshman year, Shane traveled to France with a group of cadets for the five-week Citadel Summer Program in Montpelier, near the southern coast along the Mediterranean. Students lived with French families, studied until noon at the French Institute, and then took afternoon excursions into Marseilles or the bullfights down near the border with Spain. Professor Guy Toubiana, who was along on the trip, noticed an old trait of Shane's on those afternoon jaunts. The touring cadets seemed less intimidated by the foreign culture and the difficulties of using public transportation as long as Shane was along. "The other students felt very, very safe in his presence," Toubiana said. "His confidence was infectious."

Late one evening in June, The Citadel cadets were returning from a particularly enjoyable junket, a visit to the topless beach at Palavas. In a crowded bus, a group of Arab-French toughs began harassing two teenage English tourists, both female. The thugs jabbed cigarettes in the girls' faces, made sexual taunts, and then began aggressively pushing them around the back of the bus.

Shane was furious that no one on the bus was intervening to help the girls, and he quickly pushed forward through the crowd for the classic Childers rescue act. When he told the thugs to stop hassling the girls, they mocked his poorly accented French and pushed the girls around some more. Shane moved on all of them at once and then one of them pulled a knife.

It wasn't much for Shane. He easily disarmed the member of the group with the knife and then kept the others at bay while telling the English girls to move to the other end of the bus, where The Citadel cadets would protect them. When the tough lunged at him to recover his knife, Shane held him back and addressed him in French.

"Dans ton estomachi, ami"–"This knife is for your stomach, not mine, friend."

The bus howled with laughter over Shane's atrocious pronunciation, and the thugs kept trying to lunge at him again or get behind his back, but he held them off with his back to the window.

Then another Arab man on the bus, believing that Arab pride had been offended, leaped forward and confronted Shane, but quickly got off the bus at the next stop when Shane muscled him around, too. At the stop after that Shane threw all the rest of the Arab-French gang off the bus, and then went back to comfort the English girls.

At the institute that night, all the other cadets were talking about it, rhapsodizing about Childers and his ability to take on so much opposition at once. Freakin' Shane. He could disarm one guy with a knife, while holding three more off with his free arm. Professor Toubiana asked the other cadets why they hadn't moved forward on the bus to help Shane.

"We didn't even think about it," one of them said. "Shane obviously didn't need us."

"I don't think Shane really had that much of a problem handling those Arab kids," Toubiana said. "He was a marine and exceptionally capable at things like that, taking care of trouble. Shane's biggest problem was that he felt that his French wasn't good enough to make it clear to these kids that he was in charge. But the other cadets were very impressed, and I think the story just got away from him after that."

Indeed, by the time The Citadel Summer Program cadets had returned to campus in the fall, the details had become exaggerated, and Shane had taken on half the Arabs in southern France. Shane being

Shane, the hyperbole seemed warranted, however, and it was just another tale about him that contributed to the mystery and his outsize legend.

But Toubiana considered one thing that Shane said about the incident to be strange, and so would others when the bus fracas in France came up in conversation.

"You know, Guy, I've been up against Arabs before," Shane told his professor. "Now I am back here in France and they are confronting me again. It will be me or them someday. The Arabs will end up killing me. I will be killed by an Arab."

Toubiana had no reason to receive this as a premonition–September 11, 2001, and the war on terror, was still two years away. Besides, Shane would occasionally say things like this. "I'm going to freeze to death up on Mount Shasta," he would say, because bad ice storms had pushed him back from that California summit two times. An avalanche would take him out in the Alps, or he would smash his pickup. Shane was single, intense, and a fascinating bundle of contradictions–sometimes effortlessly social and fun, other times a moody Tennessee Williams loner–and this was the kind of thing that driven, lonely guys would say. An Arab would kill him someday. There was no reason to take this seriously at all, but it did speak to the underside of Shane's character. People often had the uncomfortable feeling around him that one day Shane just might blow.

"Yes, Shane did stand out, but not simply for his qualities," Toubiana said. "His defects were right on the surface too. He was impatient, very tightly wound, short-tempered, too intense. You could be with him and have the sense that he was about to crack. He spoke very openly about his athleticism, all that biking, hiking, and running. He needed that outlet, maybe even in excess, just to stay balanced."

Shane's workaholic ways and frantic pace had by now produced another amusing behavioral trait, a reprise, actually, of his habits as a boy. By the early evening, often at dinnertime, he was so exhausted that he could collapse anywhere—on a friend's couch, on the floor of The Citadel ROTC unit, in a library cubicle—and sleep soundly for an hour. One friend dubbed Shane "the caveman" for his ability to simply drop wherever he ran out of energy. Then he recovered ferociously, running himself back down all night. The resulting insomnia, a classic symptom of overwork and its distractions, led to the legendary late-night calls to family members and friends. These calls frequently stretched for hours, until well after midnight, with Shane droning on so monotonously that the person on the other end of the line fell asleep.

But everyone could see other, refreshing changes in Shane. His tastes and habits were maturing. Now he was spending forty-five minutes in a video store picking out a movie, and it was usually a foreign art-house flick—*Run Lola Run* by the German writer-director Tom Tykwer was a favorite. Willie Nelson and Johnny Cash were getting ditched for Sheryl Crow, U2, or the Dave Matthews Band. The summer language arts program at Middlebury College in Vermont was clearly a seminal experience for Shane, and he came back marveling to his friends about what had happened. "Liberal rich bitches" from schools like Mount Holyoke or Stanford, the sort of women he couldn't attract before, not only seemed to accept him now, but they actively chased him. He took them hiking up Vermont's tallest peak, Mount Mansfield, or over to the Adirondacks to do Mount Marcy. They invited him to join their study groups, asked him to go dancing, and then back to the room to smoke pot. And Shane wasn't inhibited now about spending the night with a woman he knew he'd never see again once the summer program was over. That's what happened to college men who could offer a girl something she'd never had before, a hip uber-marine who traveled the world and was very earnest about learning French.

"The Citadel years were huge for Shane, huge, college changed him so much," said Jessi Walker, one of two West Virginia cousins with whom he became exceptionally close while he was living in Charleston. "He was becoming more human. He was listening better, chilling a little when he was away from his studying and work. He would always be this incredibly driven guy, but now he was open to different people, different ideas. There was a real sense we all had that Shane was turning. It was his turning moment and he was emerging so much."

Jessi entertained another compelling theory about Shane. His upbringing and formative years had occurred in a succession of relatively isolated and unusual places—foreign countries, naval bases, then a rural Mississippi hamlet. He'd missed out on the major leavening force of his generation.

"Shane was never exposed to the moderating force of living in the suburbs or a relatively sophisticated community like that," Jessi said. "He didn't get while he was young the benefit of what he needed—a lot of bright kids his age, good schools, things like that. So all the discipline and the atmosphere of extremism about him came from working out that issue. He'd had to push so hard for normal things that everything he discovered seemed new, new to him. The Citadel at least exposed him to more of a peer group, but of course he was already formed by then and so driven."

Jonna Walker, Jessi's sister, had a slightly different take on it. The cyclone of Shane could be understood only in the context of the Childers family, the genetic leaning toward hyperactivity that had to be contained. Joe Childers was a compelling example of rebellion and accomplishment, too, rejecting the family's born-again Christianity, getting out of West Virginia as a young man, always kicking out of the domestic traces to run off and shoe horses somewhere. Shane had simply taken these frenetic gifts and channeled them toward different achievement, and a bit more upward mobility.

"He was this fascinating contradiction between attention deficit disorder and intense focus, always racing from interest to interest,"

Jonna said. "That's where the marines and The Citadel came in. He needed that discipline to somehow focus his energies and love of people."

The changes in Shane were also being expressed by a sort of adorable bachelor style that evolved as he prospered in Charleston. Weekend apartment guests were welcome because their pending arrival forced Shane to decorate and make his place comfortable. Jessi and Jonna were particularly prized as Charleston visitors because the Walker cousins had refined tastes and loved to teach Shane how to shop, how to pick out accessories, match colors, and the like.

"Oh, wow, Jess," Shane said one day after a shopping session. "That's what you do with this thing? Just stick it on the end of the couch like that?"

"Yes, Shane," Jessi said. "It's called a throw. It can actually go anywhere along the couch, just casual, you know?"

"Great, a throw. Jeez. And the colors, all right, you have to figure that out too I guess. Is there a book about this I can read?"

"Shane. Shane, please."

"What?"

"You don't need a book about it, okay? You've got your throw now, and you don't need any more. All right? Chill, Shane. Chill."

"Okay! Okay! I'm just saying. If there was a book on the subject, I could read up on throws."

These weekend visits always followed a plan, because Shane was meticulous about having a written agenda before they got there. It was a mission, an objective to be seized, weekend fun was an activity to be organized just like the marines. Wake up the guests at 0700 (Shane's calisthenics and run began at 0500), grab a quick breakfast at the apartment or a downtown café, careen out to the suburban Wal-Mart in Shane's pickup and buy new glasses and towels. After that, they were scheduled to take the 1100 tourist ferry out to Fort Sumter. There Shane wonked for two hours about the opening battle of the Civil

War, explaining in detail about how it had evolved primarily as an artillery event. By 1530, they were back in Charleston for a buggy ride through the historic district and then Guinness stout at Tommy Condon's Irish Pub on Church Street. Back at the apartment, Shane would collapse on the couch for an hour before dinner, rebound, and then they would eat and listen to some new folk artist downtown or go dancing. For a good deal of this time–1030 to 1430, pretty much–Shane was yakking away with one of his ongoing "book reports" about the title he was reading at the moment, which could be anything from a new biography of Napoleon to the Alan Moorehead classic, *The Blue Nile*. It was maddening, and Jonna would tell Shane several times that she'd heard enough about the book. "Okay! Okay! I'm done, then. I promise. But look, let me just tell you this one more thing." Like his father, Shane completely lacked summary function.

"You were always aware when you were with Shane that he was born to be a great marine, born to be this star achiever that made the family back in West Virginia so proud," Jonna said. "But dealing with him on a daily basis? Forget it. You couldn't keep up with him. Sometimes I thought that his only purpose in life was wearing other people out."

In the spring of 2001, as his graduation approached, Shane pulled another classic Childers stunt, a fitting send-off to his unique Citadel career. His B.A. in French from The Citadel would now qualify him for the marine officer corps, and he would have to be formally commissioned. The event meant a lot to Shane, but was essentially pro forma. Before an audience of family, friends, and his fellow MECEP marines, Shane would receive his lieutenant's bars and swear loyalty to his country and the Corps in an officer's uniform. Those were the regs.

But Shane Childers had no intention of being commissioned a marine lieutenant in an officer's uniform. He was an enlisted man who had climbed through the ranks, and a part of him would always be that person. He loved the Corps and he loved those men. To show proper respect, to symbolize his origins, Shane told the executive officer of The Citadel marine MECEP unit that he would be commissioned in his utility fatigues.

This was "undoable," the XO told him. Marine regs were marine regs. He wasn't even going to bother requesting up through command about what to do with Childers, because they would just say no. We love you, Shane, you've been a standout here, but the regs are the regs and you've done enough already trying to rewrite the rules. You're getting commissioned in an officer's uniform.

The contest went back and forth for several weeks, but Shane wouldn't budge, even when he was given a direct order to comply. He was Bartleby the Scrivener about it, I prefer not to, sir. To Shane, high personal privilege and belief were involved.

"Sir, I am not disobeying an order," he told his XO at one point. "I am merely interpreting it in my own way. I came up through the ranks. I want every man who ever serves under me to know how much I care for them, that I showed proper respect for who they are."

The XO had wisely not advised higher command about his obdurate working-class hero, and so a convenient fiction was arranged. Shane would be inducted as an officer before family and fellow marines in a "private commissioning" ceremony. It was bull, pure Shane getting his way. There wasn't any difference between a private commissioning and the very public one Shane received in The Citadel's Thompson Hall on June 15, 2001. But the Mississippi-Wyoming boy, the marine who was a Gulf War veteran at eighteen, was commissioned according to his own standard of symbolism, in his utility fatigues.

It had been a strong run for Shane. The full baccalaureate course in three years, lots of summer study, and dean's list most of the way, all that legend-building that was now known among his peers in the Corps. And during those three years, too, he had climbed Mount Shasta twice, the Pryors, the Alps, the Pyrenees, the Presidentials, the

Appalachians, the Adirondacks, and the Greens. It was a hell of a climb and now he was good to go for the Basic School and the Infantry Officer Course at Quantico.

And they all could never forget the sight of Shane being commissioned in Thompson Hall.

"He stood there at attention throughout the ceremony with his arms locked against his sides, shaking, literally shaking, with excitement," Jonna Walker said. "His eyes were staring forward and glazed over, so intense. He just couldn't wait for the commissioning to be over so he could start work as a marine lieutenant."

After lunch on Friday, Hutchison and Morgan sat down together in Hutchison's office at the Billings command to review their updated plans for the Childers funeral. This might be their last opportunity to meet face to face because Morgan would be drilling his honor guard team all weekend in the armory while Hutchison ran back and forth to Powell coordinating details. There was still a lot of paperwork to complete, and they were busy with all the police liaison and preparation for the funeral parade through town. Now Hutchison was running through the points of a long checklist that he had compiled on a yellow legal pad.

"Okay. Navy enlisted chief petty officer's trousers for Joe Childers," Hutchison said. "Where are we on that?"

"Like I said this morning, it's done, sir," Morgan said. "When I told FedEx what this was about, they promised to make us the first drop in the morning. The pants will be here in time for you to take them down to Powell."

"Great, Barry. Thanks," Hutchison said. "Now how are we paying for them? I don't think the government covers this expense."

"It's taken care of, sir. We passed the hat for Joe's pants."

Hutchison let out a long sigh, looked up to his first noncom, and reached across the desk for his wallet.

"All right, well let me contribute too," he said. "How much more do you still need?"

"Sir, it's covered," Morgan said. "You've already done enough."

Hutchison sighed again and looked up.

"First sergeant, thanks. And look, I was short with you this morning about this and I apologize. I think we're all overloaded by this CACO, but you've done a great job holding things together for us. How are the men?"

Oh, here we go, Morgan thought. The Hutch. My California-dreaming, super-sensitive Beach Boy head of command.

"Sir, they're fine, really. But listen, why don't you take the rest of the afternoon off? You should relax so everything we've got to do over the weekend isn't too much."

Hutchison thanked Morgan again, but said that he didn't want to leave the Billings command. He was pretty sure that they would receive word before the weekend about a ship date and flight number for Shane Childers' body, and he wanted to be close to all the phones and computers to be able to act quickly once they heard.

Morgan stepped up to return to his own office.

"All right then, sir. It's another thing to scratch off your list. We've got the chief petty pants for Joe."

Down in Powell, there were large, drum-shaped winter cumulus, blue-gray in the sky, hanging over the snowy Bighorns. The wind had picked up and blew from the southeast, pointing the half-mast flag for Shane off to the Pryors. But it was sunny, too. The fields around the Childers house were a crystalline mosaic of melting snow and freshened earth.

Inside, at the dining-room table, Joe and Judy were marveling at the bounty of mail, gifts, and expressions of grief reaching them from all over the country, even the world. Friends they had lost touch with years ago and people who had simply read about Shane in their local papers were sending cards, gift certificates for flowers, long letters, and even CD tapes with patriotic or religious music. The alumni from Shane's high school class back in Mississippi sent a gift certificate good for a seventy-five-dollar purchase at the local nursery, and there were already inquiries from prominent graduates of The Citadel about establishing a scholarship fund in Shane's honor.

Judy was particularly impressed because she felt that a lot of the people who were reaching out to the Childers family now were more emotional about Shane's death than they were. This was interesting and, in a flash of insight, she felt that she understood what was happening. She and Joe were *here*, in a house full of memories of Shane, confronting grief everywhere they stepped, fielding phone calls all day, which forced them to emotionally resolve, if only for the moment. But the other marine mothers out there who were writing, or just strangers who cared, had no markers of Shane around, nothing real to confront. They were grieving into a void, abstracting Shane as the first killed in Iraq and imagining what his family must be going through, with nothing tangible or immediate to relieve those feelings. So they all sent letters and gifts. She and Joe appreciated that, but their overloaded mailbox meant something else. There was just an abstracted need out there for people to grieve the losses of a new war, and Shane's death provided focus for that urge.

By the end of the weekend, tired after so much attention and media interviews, Judy would often say that she was "tired of sharing Shane." But for now the surplus of mail made her appreciate how far off Wyoming and its funeral drama for Shane must seem to people who were reading about the Childerses in Wisconsin or Georgia.

"Oh! Joe, look at this," Judy said. "Here's one from Beetle Bailey of Gulfport. Didn't you used to talk about a Beetle Bailey from Gulfport?"

"Oh, yeah. Yeah. I think I remember him."

Then they were interrupted by the delivery woman from the florist in Powell, who by now had made so many runs to the house that Judy was starting to think of her as an old friend. After the flower delivery, Judy stepped over to the phone. A producer in New York from ABC's *20/20* needed help with some information about Shane. They were cobbling together a segment for that night's broadcast about soldiers killed in Iraq and would be using footage shot by a local television station of the Childerses.

As soon as the line was free another call came in, this one for Joe. After he had mumbled into the phone in the kitchen for a while, Joe returned to the living room, wiping tears from his eyes.

"It's just all these memories people think they are helping us with," Joe said, "but it just gets me all worked up again. That was some old boy from West Virginia. He says that we were blacksmithing friends and he was over at our place the day Shane was born."

To get away from the phone, and all the letters, Joe pulled on his USS *Tortuga* cap and stepped outside to the front of the house. He wanted to run a new line and straighten out the electrical connection for the lights illuminating the flag at half-mast. If a lot of visitors congregated on the front patio, which they were likely to do, he didn't want anyone tripping on an electrical cord.

He felt better as soon as he got out there. Monkeying around in his shop, finding just the right tools and U-shaped nails to get the job done, was vaguely satisfying. He was rushed again with the feeling he'd had as a teenager back in West Virginia, running down the hollow with his father and some wooden boxes of tools to help the neighbors or members of their church prepare their little farm for a big funeral.

When he stepped back to survey his finished work, Joe pushed up his ball cap and took in the panorama of prairie and mountains stretching off toward Cody. The sun had dropped a bit and now the winter cumulus were pink underneath from the shallow angle of light.

In the breeze, the trailing edge of the flag for Shane snapped like a whip.

Oh, Wyoming. It was a small comfort, but Joe was grateful that he was enduring the loss of Shane in the Bighorn country, on his own dream ranch, with so much beautiful scenery and his browsing steers and horses all around. The openness and familiarity of the land seemed to touch and protect him. And the new gravel on the driveway looked good, crisply lined at the edges and gunmetal gray, like a frigate with fresh paint. The house seemed ready for guests.

THE WEST VIRGINIA COUSINS

T he steady arrival of old friends and family members had a calming influence on the Childerses, particularly Joe, who soon fell into comfortable routine. As more and more people appeared, he would harness Amigo and April, hitch them up to his hay wagon, and then take each visitor in turn for a run out to feed the cattle and enjoy a private chat. By now his son Sam and son-in-law Richard Brown were at the ranch, then his old Seabee pal Robert Reagan and Shane's former marine buddy Bill Hendry. They were all military men and Joe considered it a luxury just to be with them, chatting in a familiar argot, catching up on their news, jawing away about his cattle or how he had rerouted this particular irrigation trench so that the field got better coverage. It was good to get away from the house and its sadness, the bustle and the ringing phone.

Joe was particularly glad to see Reagan, his old Vietnam War buddy. Reagan and Joe had been close friends since 1967, worked on a number of Seabee projects together, and stayed in touch over the years, even after Reagan retired from the navy and settled in London for a life of working at the American embassy and trout-fishing on weekends. He is tall and rangy with a mottled complexion, a smoker, and has an irrepressible sarcasm gene. Reagan believed that the bond he and Joe had formed in Vietnam was as strong as "blood kin," and indeed joined the boisterous dynamics of the Childerses as someone who was nearly a member of the family. "Joe is my little brother and I'm his big brother, and that's that," Reagan liked to say. "Of course, that sometimes means that Judy and I fight like cats and dogs." Reagan had also stayed in close touch with Shane. When Shane was traveling through London on his way to various marine assignments or studying overseas, he stayed with Reagan and his wife, arriving at their apartment with a huge, ninety-pound pack of mountain-climbing gear. Over the years, Reagan felt that he had watched Shane progress from a "typical country kid from the South" into a "very squared-away marine" who had made impressive intellectual growth during his Citadel years.

But Reagan had never seen the Childers spread in Wyoming and now it was a joy for Joe to show him around and discourse on his various possessions—the collection of MacClellan saddles, the one-man plows, the foxtrotter filly. Joe and Robert took long walks up on the Polecat Bench and rode into town together. Robert had a strong reaction to seeing the Powell ranch, because everywhere he turned there were markers of Shane.

"When Shane came through London, he would talk about all these grand plans he had some day of getting a long break from the marines and helping Joe fix up all the farm implements, or make improvements to the house," Reagan said. "Seeing all these piles of farm equipment around just reminds me a lot of Shane and his dreams."

Reagan is both direct and psychologically intuitive, a man's man with a sensitive touch, and Joe seemed more relaxed as soon as he arrived. They went back so far together that Joe could say nearly anything to Robert and be confident that he'd receive an honest reply. Joe, for example, shared with Robert his recurrent thought about "Shane coming diddly-boppin' down that lane again," and reproached himself for saying that phrase too often.

"I told Joe that he shouldn't worry about saying that, or dreaming that Shane would just come diddly-boppin' down that lane again some day," Reagan said. "It was a perfectly healthy response, part of his coping with just how much he'd lost here. I could tell that Joe appreciated my attitude. It wasn't wrong what he was saying to himself at all, and people in that kind of stress need a friend just to say that. 'Hey, it's okay, bud. In your shoes I'd be saying the same thing.' "

Shane's friend from his Persian Gulf days, Bill Hendry, was another welcome sight. When they sat up late at night in Saudi Arabia, or later at Camp Lejeune, Shane would tell Hendry all his favorite stories about his madcap family back in Wyoming. Joe knew that and was anxious to show Hendry the place Shane had described. It was an education for Hendry, a useful filling in. Like so many others he'd always been amazed by Shane Childers, his rare blend of toughness and flexibility, the knack for handling any battlefield or training contingency, the ability to just ride right through personality disorders in others. And the caring for people, the passion for life and a friend's personal growth. It all had to come from somewhere, and now Hendry was seeing it firsthand–the story-a-minute dad, the buckaroo ranch, the ambient mania of the Childers experience. But it filled Hendry with sadness to be meeting Joe and seeing the ranch without Shane. That was his first reaction. "God, I can't wait to tell Shane about this." But he couldn't, of course.

With Reagan and Hendry, Joe was able to talk about another thing–what had happened to Shane in Iraq. He wasn't morbid about this, and the subject didn't make him cry. As a military man and a father, he was fascinated by Shane's fate, and with Reagan and Hendry they worked out all the angles. How had Shane, so capable and smart–brave, but never a yahoo about personal safety–gone down like this? They knew that a complete battlefield report would not be available for months, but certain details were already obvious. Shane was shot early in the morning *after* the platoon he was leading had taken a critical, first objective of the war, Pumping Station Number 2 at Rumaila. The marines were determined to secure these fields, just north of the border with Kuwait, to prevent Saddam's forces from torching them before they retreated. Shane's unit had received very high marks during training at the Twentynine Palms desert warfare grounds in California in the fall of 2002, which was why they were chosen to be among the first assault groups to charge over the berm into Iraq.

Shane's unit had taken the objective, with no other men killed, which meant that he had been successful, efficient. That made Joe proud, but it also meant that Shane's death must have occurred during the early-morning mop-up phase. A sniper maybe? A breakout by Iraqis not yet captured? Friendly fire? They just didn't know yet but it seemed such a waste. Shane had gotten there and made it, he'd obviously led his men well. But how do you go from being first victor in a war to first killed? It was still such a mystery.

Marine platoon leaders operate under two prevailing but essentially contradictory doctrines. Officers lead from the front to set an example for their men, but this can make them an especially visible target during combat. Platoon leaders often travel with radiomen as well, which also makes them stand out. However, marine doctrine also encourages platoon leaders, nearing an objective, to establish a protected place that allows them to see all the action and fields of fire while leading their men from a safe command point. Platoon leaders receive intensive training and run through every conceivable scenario during live-fire exercises. They are taught to improvise constantly on both points, but in actual combat it's a confusing, deadly juggle between the two principles.

Talking with Joe about what might have happened to Shane, Reagan favored the first doctrine.

"In London, the minute I read Shane Childers' name on the casualty list in the *Stars and Stripes,* I wasn't at all surprised that he'd been killed," Reagan said. "If you spent five minutes with this kid you instantly knew he would be right out front and not accepting risks for his men that he wouldn't assume himself. He would have been so obviously the guy in charge that the Iraqis just took one look and decided to take him out."

But Hendry wasn't so sure about this and tended to favor the more cautious doctrine. Shane was unquestionably fearless–he just didn't know fear the way other people experienced it–but he was also very analytical and results oriented. He disdained false notions of bravery, or crazy risk takers. If you were recklessly brave and got shot, now you weren't leading your men.

"There was a shrewdness about him, a caginess, all that southern boy who had been in the woods a lot," Hendry said. "When we were in training together, you could almost hear the wheels turning in Shane's head. When we got back at night, he would say, 'Okay, here's what they said to do. Here's how you can improvise. But here's what is *smart.*' Shane would have been like that in Iraq. He wouldn't have been rattled because Shane wasn't rattled, period, but he'd also been in combat before. Whatever killed him was something freakish, unexpected."

But they couldn't really say for sure now. Perhaps the autopsy record, and later the battlefield report, which Hutchison promised he would eventually obtain for Joe, would solve the mystery. But it was profitable for Joe to speak about this with Robert and Bill. It took his mind off things that he'd done with Shane, the recollections that made him cry, the constant reprise of memory that had become exhausting.

So jingling out across the prairie behind the Belgians, with their legs dangling over the front of the wagon, they all did the big Wyo-Iraq mind-wander together, trying to figure out what happened with Shane. But they enjoyed themselves too, throwing bales of hay to the cattle, joking, laughing, pointing out antelope or mule deer chasing up toward the Bench. The early spring weather was variable at the end of the week, with overcast skies a good deal of the time, then sunny and bright with broken clouds for a few hours, with the wind shifting southeast to north. But it was always brisk, so they were chilled to the bone when they got back to the house. Robert wanted to smoke outside, so Joe made coffee and then carried two steaming cups out to join his friend.

The two Seabee pals sat out in the toolshed on white Rubbermaid patio chairs, with the wide double doors open to the prairie and the views southwest. Robert smoked while they both drank coffee and talked. They caught up on each other's lives and told amusing stories about Shane. Out toward Cody and Yellowstone National Park, the sky was moody, inclement. One of Joe's donkeys brayed from the corral. It was good, really good, for Robert to be there. Robert was a strong friend who made Joe feel like he could get through this.

Shane's Charleston years and the valuable hiatus from military life that they provided had another important chapter, the deepening of his connection with Jessi and Jonna Walker, his cousins from Salt Rock. The Walker sisters had grown up on West Virginia and southern Ohio farms so isolated they had to walk almost a mile to the school bus and rarely saw other children. Their father worked long hours as a railroad foreman and left behind detailed lists of chores for the Walker children to perform during the planting and harvesting seasons–the backbreaking work of bean picking and stripping tobacco, mostly. Their mother, Natalie, is Joe's sister, and like all the cousins in the extended Childers clan, Shane spent a lot of time at their place in "Walker Holler" when he was visiting Salt Rock in the summer.

Even when he was just twelve or fourteen, Shane stood out as different. When there was farming to be done at the Walker place, all the other cousins had the sense to scatter or not show up in the first place, but Shane loved the field work. He made it fun, laughing and teasing Jessi and Jonna as he devised contests or imaginary adventures to take the drudgery out of staking bean poles or hanging tobacco to cure. "We considered Shane a brother, not a cousin," Jonna said. "While we picked beans, we shared secrets or discussed our frustrations about other members of the family." The summer he was sixteen and spent three months in Salt Rock, and then later when he returned as a marine, the Walker sisters had a favorite exercise they performed with Shane. While they sat on his shoulders, he did push-ups.

During the big family picnics at the Wilton Childers homestead at the end of Smith Creek Hollow, Shane, Jessi, and Jonna often wandered off together and climbed the steep hill behind their grandfather's farmhouse. It's a lovely incline with a natural cobble of rocks, velveteen expanses of green moss, and a grove of beeches that climbs halfway to the summit. To the side, the cobble opens into upland meadows where, as a teenager and as a marine, Shane wandered with his cousins and chatted, goofed off, and discussed his dreams. Their favorite hangout was at the edge of the beech grove below, a small clearing and a single hundred-year-old beech on an escarpment overlooking the farm and the hollow. Jessi and Jonna have always called that beech the "Shane Tree." On the uphill side of the tree there is still a prominent marker, carved with a penknife when the future marine was fourteen:

SHANE CHILDERS
8/8/86

The Walkers and Joe and Judy Childers were different from the rest of the extended family in one other critical respect. They were not Missionary Baptists, and in Joe and Judy's case, not churched at all. This was rarely spoken about openly, but was of great concern to the rest of the family. Membership in the small, conservative denomination and adopting its values–Sunday church, strict moral values, teetotaling, and a belief in the importance of being "saved"–was a Childers family requirement, and indeed many family members were either full or part-time pastors. The Missionary Baptist and United Baptist congregations along the Childers hollow in Salt Rock were so small and schismatic that there were "upper" and "lower" Smith Creek Baptist churches. Shane's disinterest in what religion had to offer showed early. At the big Childers family dinners at his grandparents' or uncles and aunts', when Jessi and Jonna glanced around during the long grace, they would always make eye contact with Shane. He was smiling, suppressing a laugh, joining them in not taking the religious devotion seriously.

But as a teenager, and right up through his Citadel years, Shane displayed an admirable flexibility about the family religion. On his visits to West Virginia, he attended the small white churches on Sunday to show respect for his family and to please his grandparents, and he greatly enjoyed church for socializing. It was a chance to catch up with family members and old Salt Rock friends he might have missed during his morning runs over the mountains. He was unchurched himself and found evangelical Christianity narrow and intellectually lifeless, and he was annoyed by the persistent efforts of aunts and ordained uncles to convert him. Platitudes of any kind, personal smugness, had never appealed to him, and he didn't like the prejudice against gays, Catholics, and Jews that were a submerged but very real agenda of the church. Jessi and Jonna were the same way. They all called the old-time Baptist churchgoers of the West Virginia hollows "hypocrite Holy Rollers."

There were other reasons for the strong bond with Jessi and Jonna, which grew as they entered their teenage and college years and Shane continued to visit, now as a very engaging and fun marine. Jessi, spunky-bright and effortlessly witty, the artist of the family, and Jonna, pensive and soulful, were lovely sisters together, pretty, well-read, and ambitious. While the others Childers cousins were moving in one direction—remaining in West Virginia—they were moving in another, dreaming of escaping the state and its limited social and economic horizons. And Jessi and Jonna were fun, loads of fun. They didn't consider it scandalous, after a day of study or work, or just goofing off across the mountains with Shane, to head for a bar in Huntington or across the river in Ohio for a drink.

"That was the connection, the reason for us all being together," Jessi said. "We were the three cousins who had problems with the family religion, went out drinking, and wanted to get out of West Virginia. It's what we shared at first, and then a lot more. And Shane, you know, he was this interesting marine who was always coming back to West Virginia from somewhere new, Europe or Africa. It wasn't simply that he was exotic and so much fun. He could support what Jonna and I wanted to do with our lives."

And that support was both enormous and touching, going both ways. When she was nineteen, Jessi became pregnant, got married, and then divorced, and then did a remarkable job raising her son as a single mother, working to provide, getting her B.F.A. at Marshall University, and finally moving on to a new, successful marriage and settling in Columbus, Ohio. With long letters and late-night phone calls, Shane nursed her through the vicissitudes of her tough, early motherhood and then the decision of choosing a major in college. She nursed him back, understanding that Shane was someone for whom talk was therapy, and that he required a constant debriefing of life's challenges and events. One of Jessi's earliest fears was that young motherhood would trap her in the female stereotype that she saw all around her in West Virginia—women who never followed their dreams or achieved independence because they married too early and started a family before they were ready. While she was pregnant with her son, Jessi went canoeing one day with Shane along Symmes Creek in southern Ohio, just across the river from West Virginia, where her father had bought a new farm.

"Shane was great that day because I was nineteen, pregnant, terrified that my situation was going to prevent me from doing what I wanted with my life," Jessi said. "But Shane said, 'No, don't think that way.' This does not have to mean giving up your dreams. Lots of people, he said, had recovered from worse situations, and he wasn't going to let me forget my goal of becoming an artist."

As a personal enabler, Shane seemed to have intuitively understood something important about providing support. Talk is cheap, and thoroughly forgettable if it occurs in a context where being sympathetic is pro forma, something a relative or close friend is expected to say. Of course, on the canoe ride, Shane said the right thing–Jessi could have her baby *and* become an artist. But that was the expected thing to say. What was remarkable about Shane was how he would assiduously follow up and reinforce what he said through letters, gifts, thoughtful postcards, other kinds of attention.

"Wherever he was with the marines or his Citadel groups after that, it might have been London or Europe, wherever, Shane would scoop up all the brochures from galleries he visited, buy me art books, whatever, and send them with a note," Jessi said. "I don't think he even realized half the time how supportive and inspiring it was. But he was always saying, Jess, I'm not letting you forget your dreams about becoming an artist. He made it clear that this was his expectation for me."

Jonna, the younger sister, faced her own set of issues. It was a long struggle for her to leave the family farm, get started with the right job and move beyond West Virginia and southern Ohio. After studying environmental prelaw at Ohio University and then changing her college major to communications, she worked at an insurance agency across the Ohio River in Kentucky and then as a clerical employee at Marshall University Medical School in Huntington. But both were dead-end jobs, and she wasn't meeting very many interesting new friends or finding reliable men to date. The high point of her week was mowing the lawn, which she actually did enjoy. Shane saw all this and just wouldn't accept it for Jonna.

"There was no sugar-coating with Shane, no bullshit, which was one of the things I liked about him so much," Jonna said. "He would just directly confront and say, 'Why is this such a problem, Jonna? Why can't you get away? There's a big world waiting out there and other people have done this.' He was very, very big on Jessi and me escaping West Virginia, seeing a larger world and pursuing careers."

For Jonna, Shane cruised the self-help and résumé-writing shelves of bookstores. For Christmas in 2001 he sent her a title called *Résumé Magic.* While he was at The Citadel, Shane kept up the pressure, and every few weeks a new packet of personal growth books or articles, with a note attached, would arrive for Jonna.

"Jonna. Here are some books that might help. Semper Fi, Shane."

Shane's West Virginia visits could be even more manic than his Charleston life, and for good reason. As the uncontested star of the family now, he felt under pressure to visit as many relatives as possible during a long weekend, so that no one was insulted. But he complained to Jessi and Jonna about his heavy family obligations and had trouble fitting everyone in. Generally he stayed at either Jessi or Jonna's apartment, rising at dawn and clunking around in his cowboy boots so loudly that the tenant downstairs would complain, and in any case Jessi was now awake. It was so early that, when they got to Shoney's for breakfast, the restaurant wasn't even open yet. Then Shane would take his long run over the mountains visiting relatives, frequently dead-reckoning straight across the hollows and peaks when a route through the woods was more direct than the roads. In the afternoon they'd go kayaking or hiking, or just caterwauling over the mountains in Shane's pickup, Jessi and Jonna telling Shane to shut up about his latest book report, and then screaming at the top of their lungs at the AC/DC tape on, or because of Shane's crazy driving, sometimes they didn't know which.

By the end of the day Shane's overcommitted schedule was all backed up and he was late, again, sometimes for very odd reasons. He was notorious for this. Over Christmas 1999, all the Childerses were waiting for him at the Church Fellowship Hall in Salt Rock for dinner, and began to worry when Shane was two hours late. On slick roads, he'd been driving too fast, took out a mailbox, and felt so guilty about it that he drove all the way out to the interstate in Huntington, found a Home Depot open, and then returned to Salt Rock to install a new mailbox. When he finally arrived at the dinner, everyone was relieved to see him, and impressed that he'd replaced a stranger's mailbox when he could have easily just driven away. He was completely forgiven for keeping the family waiting–typical dispensation for Shane.

Shane's own attempts at cosmetic self-improvement could be comical. In the spring of 2001, as his commissioning as an officer approached, Shane felt he needed better casual wear for the kind of events he would now be invited to on weekends–barbecues at fellow officer's houses, informal cocktail parties, and the like. "I need khakis and polo shirts, something like that," he told Jessi and Jonna while he was in West Virginia for the weekend. "Maybe you two should help me shop."

"It was an important request," Jonna said. "Shane's unfailing weekend attire was cowboy boots, blue jeans, a T-shirt in summer and a plaid workshirt in winter. Now he was asking for fashion tips because he was moving up in the world."

So the Childers-Walker trio hopped into the red pickup, screamed to the music as they raced down the interstate, and then turned off at the exit for the Huntington Mall.

Shane prided himself on being a speed shopper. Get into the Men's Department, push the buttons, get out of there within fifteen minutes and then race to the next event. But Jessi and Jonna had other ideas. He was *their* Ken doll today and they were going to stretch it out, savor the shop, really provide Shane an excellent fashion education.

When they got to the first department store, Jessi found an elegant pair of Perry Ellis wool trousers with just the right look—a kind of suburban Connecticut off-green, herringbone twill, with a pleated front. She'd seen the same trousers in *Esquire* and *GQ* and considered them fantastic for Shane.

"No way, Jess, I'm not wearing those things," Shane said. "It's got a pattern on it. Men don't have patterns on their pants."

"Shane. It's called herringbone, okay?" Jessi said. "It's the look now. A little dressy, but it takes a real guy to wear them because you're not afraid to be stylish. They're perfect for you."

"Jess, we're deviating from the mission here. The objective was khakis and polos. Now you're changing the objective."

Disappointed, Jessi gave up on the trousers, but then Jonna came over from the shirt department with her picks for Shane, also the new look. Solid cotton dress shirts with a matching solid silk tie, no pattern, black-on-black, blue-on-blue, and so forth. Shane would be Brad Pitt or George Clooney heading off for dinner in L.A. or New York.

"What is this, a conspiracy or something?" Shane said. "I mean you've got this kind of like green shirt here with a freaking tie that's the same freaking color. Who wears this stuff?"

Jessi and Jonna gave up on the shirts, too, and badgered Shane to take them to Olive Garden for a nice lunch instead. On the way out of the Lazarus department store Shane quickly pushed the buttons on khakis and polo shirts, and then agreed to buy a blue blazer and gray wool pants—the old Becky Moore default.

"We were demoralized, but laughing about it," Jonna said. "It was classic Shane. He would ask for your help, and then tell you *how* to help him. The controlling instinct was always there in some way."

The family Baptists had their designs on Shane too. It was completely unacceptable to them that the star of the Childers clan, about to be a Citadel graduate no less, remained unbaptized. Just think about it. Shane, born again. That dynamo of obsessive-compulsive genes, all that energy and capacity for hard work, reading, explicating the text, now in the service of the Bible. It had to be accomplished. This would be a huge gain for Jesus.

At weekend church socials down at Smith Creek Baptist, or family parties around Salt Rock, the Childerses assiduously worked on their marine agnostic. Several Childers aunts and uncles were in on it, and there was a fierce competition to "get" Shane for the Missionary United Baptists. Jessi and Jonna would smile to themselves and make up excuses to get Shane out of there when they saw him cornered by a member of the older generation. Shane was very good at rebuffing the conversion talk, one of the few examples anyone could remember of him suppressing his personality or views to get along with people. He smiled at them, told his uncle or aunt that he was living cleanly, and promised to consider their thoughts about his future.

When they got out to the pickup, Jessi, Jonna, and Shane would wait until they were out of sight down the hollow before they roared with laughter.

"God, I wish they would stop pulling this shit," Shane said. "We talked about eternity today. Freaking eternity, you know? I can never be saved and never know Jesus without eternity."

The relatives had also mentioned another painful subject. Drinking. They'd heard through the gossip mill that Shane consumed alcohol from time to time. Shane reassured the relatives that he would think hard about this problem, too.

Then, just to be fair to the family Baptists, they all went out for a drink. Shane turned the pickup left out of the hollow and they headed west on Route 10 and into Huntington, where there are some decent sleazeball bars down along the waterfront on both sides of the river. They played pool, drank stout, and enjoyed a respectable goof-off for a couple of hours before heading off to dinner. It was a major annoyance every time he visited Salt Rock, being evangelized by the relatives, but it was a reliable bonding agent for Shane, Jessi, and Jonna. They always had to go somewhere afterward and laugh it off.

Shane was generous with his money and sent Jessi or Jonna airline tickets if they couldn't pay for their next junket to Charleston, and the trips held a lot of meaning for them. Jonna's first trip to see Shane at The Citadel, just before Christmas in 1999, was the first time she had been away from home alone, the first time she'd flown in an airplane. For Jessi, the Charleston runs were a welcome respite from her routine of child care, work, and college. She always had a wonderful time with Shane, they debriefed their issues together, and Charleston might not be the art capital of the world, but it certainly had better galleries and museums than Huntington, West Virginia.

Jessi had majored in photography in college and was planning on going to graduate school for a fine arts M.A., so she could teach while practicing her art. She had the personality that comes with being the artist of the family and was known for showing up at picnics and dinners with spiked hair, funky clothes, and all kinds of outrageous dreams about her future. Shane goaded her mercilessly about her lifestyle and looks, and she teased him right back about being so square.

In the spring of 2000, during his second year at The Citadel, Shane called Jessi one night and explained that he didn't have a date for the big social event coming up–The Citadel's spring Marine Corps ball. Would she come as his escort?

"Oh, it was so comic," Jessi said. "He wanted me there, he knew that we would absolutely have a great time together, but he was terrified that I would embarrass him in front of the marines with how I looked. I immediately told him I would go, just to box him in, you know?"

Shane sounded happy, but an hour later he called back.

"Ah, say, look, Jess, what color is your hair now?"

"Red, Shane."

"Okay, red. Now is that artsy-fartsy red? Or just red?"

"Red, Shane. My hair is red now. Is that okay with you?"

"Okay! Okay. Red. Now look, about the dress. Can you just pick out something plain, like black? I mean, you know. We don't need to be shocking people or anything."

Jessi got him back good for that one. She picked a shimmering, hot purple gown.

When she got to Charleston for the weekend, all the marines beamed to see her and Shane together at the ball. Shane was dashing in his dress blues and effortlessly courteous and fun, and Jessi enjoyed the marine atmosphere—all the hunky guys in their crew cuts, their manners, their lingo, their striped trousers, and brightly polished shoes. It was obvious that they all considered Shane a star and would do anything for her. If she needed her drink refreshed, a marine ran to the bar. If Shane wouldn't dance a fast number, there was always a younger, even hunkier marine good to go for the floor. She had a wonderful time. That night became one of their strongest shared memories and she just loved doing The Citadel up right with Cousin Shane.

Shane's love life—except for one final and climactic relationship—was mostly a mystery to his family, and by the time he was in his late twenties they had all concluded that his manic schedule and devotion as a marine ended most relationships. One Charleston romance, with a woman named Robbin whom he met at his French roundtable dinners downtown, ended after she found his controlling instincts and frantic schedule just too much. She told friends that it was just too difficult maintaining a relationship with "Sergeant Carter."

"We never saw Shane with girls, but that was partly because he was in such a league that was way different from all of us," said his aunt Mary Bias of Salt Rock. "The girlfriend would be an Israeli that he met in Kenya, and he was flying off to Europe to see her. We heard about them but never met them. But it was all very contradictory information because it was obvious to us that he just didn't have time for relationships. He was so busy."

Over the winter of 2000–2001, as he was approaching his last semester at The Citadel and his departure as a commissioned officer, Shane dove headlong into his last great love affair. This, too, was classic Shane, for the love affair was impulsive, 100 percent of effort and even somewhat naïve.

Leo Kelly, a beautiful single mother, lived in the apartment above Jonna in Ironton, Ohio. She was tall, willowy, and blond, with a Hollywood-quality face and a model's fit body—an exercise buff, she did two hundred sit-ups and ran five miles every day. A teacher originally from across the river in Kentucky, she supported herself and her daughter, Olive, by substitute-teaching jobs in southern Ohio and had also worked as a case worker in a foster care agency. There was an air of mystery and wild girl about her. She had once driven to Alaska and back in her Jeep, washing her daughter along the way in the streams beside the Alcan highway.

Just before Christmas, Jonna had been planning a West Virginia skiing vacation with Leo and Olive and then Shane said that he would come along too because he would be traveling back to West Virginia anyway for his long Christmas break. Typically, Shane handled it like a marine mission. He obtained a nice suite of rooms on his military discount at the Glade Springs Resort near the WinterPlace ski area and organized maps, an itinerary, and even radio walkie-talkies borrowed from The Citadel's ROTC unit, so that the party could communicate and organize "reconnoiters" while on the slopes. After driving through a heavy snowstorm to get there, Jonna, Leo, and Olive arrived at their suite to find everything meticulously arranged by Shane, right down to the mugs of hot chocolate he had waiting when they carried their skis and bags through the door.

Shane and Leo immediately hit it off for a number of obvious reasons. They were both great skiers and fitness nuts, well-traveled and read, and there was much to talk about. She was beautiful and he was the hunky uber-marine. Shane had another quality irresistible to a single mother. He was great with children, they always adored him right away, and Leo could instantly see how well he handled Olive, how willing he was to rise early and run her off for lessons at the bunny slope or help her pick out sandwiches at the luncheon cafeteria. By the second day of the vacation, a pattern had emerged. Jonna, a less experienced skier, was exhausted by the evening and preferred remaining back in the resort babysitting Olive. Shane and Leo headed out for long runs down the WinterPlace slopes under the lights.

Shane worked fast at everything, but this one set a record. By the time they had returned to Salt Rock for the annual round of Childers family Christmas parties, Shane and Leo were an item. The behavior amazed everyone. All through dinner at the relatives, Shane and Leo exchanged loving glances, Shane jumped up during dessert to fetch Leo pie à la mode, and when he called home to Wyoming to speak with his parents, Shane nuzzled in a big La-Z-Boy rocker with Leo, holding the phone in one hand while applying Leo's nail polish with another. Whoa, Jessi, Jonna, and Aunt Mary thought. Was this a Romeo who had emerged out of sight in Europe and Africa or a new Shane? Public displays of affection had never been his style.

But Shane was Shane and did everything in a hurry.

"In anyone else a love affair this sudden would have seemed impulsive," Aunt Mary Bias said, "but with Shane, who threw himself at everything so intensely, it seemed natural."

The relationship developed quickly after that. Every other weekend Shane began making the nine-hour run back to southern Ohio to see Leo, or sent her plane tickets to meet him in Charleston. They frequently met halfway, in Charlotte, North Carolina. In February, Shane brought Leo to Salt Rock for his grandmother's eightieth birthday party, and everyone considered Leo a great catch for Shane—warm and bubbly, gorgeous to look at, and always stylishly dressed. She made Shane laugh, was loosening him up, and allowing him to flower as a full person, not just a Marine. And Shane was so good with Olive that everyone was touched. He bought her glitter kits and books to read, pulled her along on a plastic sled when he and Leo went running in the morning, took her to Saturday afternoon Disney movies when Leo needed a child-care break.

Although they were concerned about how quickly the romance had developed, many of the Childerses thought that Shane and Leo represented a solid attraction of opposites, an exchange of baggage that might be good. They seemed to solve each other's problems. Leo had a pronounced wanderlust, and she had no clear life plan that anyone could detect. Shane was directed and focused but could use a little bit more spontaneity in his life, which Leo would help introduce. It just might work.

Besides, the new couple were so obviously in love, deeply. "I love him, I just love him so much," Leo would write in e-mails to Jonna. "And Olive loves him too."

By late February 2001, when it came time to propose, all Shane's perfectionism came out. This had to be done just right, the details were important—the kind of room he would rent at a Charlotte motel where they would meet, the engagement ring, Dom Perignon champagne. Typically, Shane was ahead of himself and had already picked out wedding bands, too. By early March, when Leo had accepted Shane's proposal and the family was told, she and Jonna were out looking for wedding dresses, and Leo had even driven as far as Lexington, Kentucky, and Cincinnati to find the right gown and bridesmaid dresses. The plan was that Shane and Leo would exchange vows in The Citadel chapel on the day before he was commissioned as an officer in June, and then they would travel to Quantico for his basic officer's courses and then settle somewhere near San Diego as he began work as a platoon leader at Camp Pendleton. Shane was exultant and Leo was telling friends that she was excited too–she'd found a great man to marry and southern California would be a welcome change after slushy, cold Ohio. Shane changed the beneficiary on his service-group life insurance policy from his parents to Leo.

But now, on the verge of marriage, Shane also seemed to be going overboard on the relationship with Leo, making erratic decisions that seemed shocking. He'd always dreamed of becoming a platoon leader in the marines–leading men in a combat rifle platoon is considered the most exciting, demanding job in the Corps–and now he had feverishly worked for three years to get a college degree and become commissioned. But he was ready to give it all up for Leo.

"Shane was even willing to change his MOS (Military Occupational Specialty) in the marines away from the infantry to another area so he and Leo could live together more, without a lot of deployments," Jonna said. "He was willing to completely change his life and career track for her. We all couldn't believe it."

Then, by St. Patrick's Day that year, it had all fallen apart and Shane and Leo had called it off. There had been a confrontation, mostly about Leo's fear that she was being rushed and that all the arrangements for a wedding just three months away were too hectic. She had also begun to harbor worries about marrying a marine, one who might be quickly deployed anywhere around the world regardless of his military specialty, and Shane had insistently tried to talk her out of her fears. Shane told family members that Leo had backed out because she found him "too controlling."

But it was clear too that the whirlwind romance and sudden engagement hadn't given them enough time to really explore each other or discover obvious incompatibilities. Shane's marine career and the quick moves to Virginia and California with a daughter in tow were certainly a concern. And Shane's intensity and need for total commitment must have been intimidating. In Charlotte, where Shane had proposed, Leo must have felt cornered, without enough time to really consider. And what would marriage be like to an uber-marine planner who was now maniacally organizing floral arrangements for the chapel, renting a banquet hall, and even selecting wine and entrées for the reception?

The breakup was ugly, with all the usual recriminations of a canceled engagement—Shane was too demanding, too committed to the marines. Shane was clearly devastated and embarrassed to have been jilted just a few weeks after he had made the big announcement to the family and his friends. It was a crazy period in his life anyway because he was writing a senior thesis, wrapping up his final semester at The Citadel, and battling his MECEP unit over being commissioned in his utility fatigues. He spent a lot of time on the phone with Jessi and Jonna feeling sorry for himself about the botched engagement, and this became one of the few times in his life that Shane was openly unhinged and willing to expose his vulnerability to others. He seemed to understand that impulsivity, which in the past had served him so well, had hurt him here, and he was humbled.

His Citadel professor Christopher McRae was one of those to whom Shane turned for help. Right after spring break he collapsed on a chair in McRae's office, close to tears, obviously in need of a mentor over the cancellation of his engagement.

"It was the first time Shane had spent a long time in my office," McRae said. "Usually he was in and out in such a hurry. Leo had told Shane 'You scare me,' and he was very confused by that. His personality was so straight-ahead, persist, confront head-on, and that had always worked for him. But it didn't work for this gal from Kentucky, and he just couldn't understand that."

Shane buried his hurt and embarrassment over the breakup with Leo by telling family members and friends that he would probably just remain single. "Well, I guess I'm never going to get married," he said. "I'm married to the marines." After his commissioning Shane was busy throughout the summer of 2001 attending his officer training classes at Quantico, and then taking over his new platoon at Camp Pendleton in southern California. Then September 11 happened, training intensified, and all marines realized that they might soon be deployed overseas. It really was better for now that Shane was married only to the marines.

Shane's commissioning week in the middle of June that year was a Childers family beaut. Joe and Judy flew in from Wyoming, Jessi and Jonna came down from southern Ohio, and they all bunked down together in a rented house at the local air force base. Shane's itinerary for them was typically dense—the buggy rides through the historic district, Fort Sumter, tours of The Citadel, dinner reservations, and then Tommy Condon's Irish Pub. Joe and Shane went for haircuts and to look at pickup trailers and came back late, annoying Judy on her birthday. When the Missionary Baptist Childerses arrived from West Virginia, Shane and Jessi scrambled madly around the house to remove all evidence of beer.

The night that he was commissioned, Shane, Jessi, and Jonna hit the town. They started at Tommy Condon's, and when that closed they moved to several other bars, finally ending up quite late down at Folley Beach. To sober up, they stripped to their underwear, dove into the water, and then Jessi got carried away by the current and cut her foot on some rocks. Shane swam over and rescued her, pulled her back to shore, and then they headed back for the house in the pickup, laughing, shrieking to the music, remembering all their ridiculous times together. They were expectant for Shane now, but there was also a heavy sense that their period together was passing. Their Charleston–West Virginia years were over.

At the air force gate, Shane flashed his new military pass. The security guard snapped to attention and saluted.

He was a lieutenant in the United States Marine Corps now, and that was his first salute.

On Friday afternoon, Captain Hutchison finally learned that Shane was coming home. The casualty branch at Quantico informed him that Shane would be arriving in Billings in the cargo hold of a United Air Lines flight at 9:20 P.M. Saturday, with a marine escort riding as a passenger on the same flight. Hutchison immediately called Laura Richardson at the funeral home in Powell to make arrangements for transporting the body and coffin to Powell. Airport pickups of deceased residents or former residents of town are common for funeral directors, and generally they are made with a windowless van. But Richardson informed Hutchison that in this case, out of respect for Shane's status as a military hero and the first casualty of Iraq, she would be returning him to Powell in her best funeral hearse.

Hutchison and Richardson discussed how it would be best to tell Judy and Joe. They agreed that Hutchison would inform the Childerses right away and escort the hearse carrying Shane to Powell on Saturday night—another step way beyond the CACO manual that Hutchison wanted to make as a reassuring courtesy to the Childerses. Richardson advised Hutchison that lifting Shane's coffin out of the airliner might have to wait until the other cargo was removed, and that it would probably be almost midnight before they left the Billings airport.

But Richardson was also enormously relieved. Shane's arrival on Saturday would allow them to view the body and make a decision on Sunday about an open or closed casket at the wake. The wake and reception could then take place on Monday, and the funeral and burial on Tuesday. The complicated details of an honor guard at two locations and a funeral parade through town were mostly in place and could be fully activated now. She and Hutchison had been under considerable pressure, but now they could move ahead with their plans for what was expected to be one of the biggest funerals in northern Wyoming in ten years.

"Kevin, you've just done such a wonderful job holding together the details on this," Richardson told him over the phone. "I'm so impressed."

"Well, Laura," Hutchison said. "I've just been doing my job. You're the one who's really be so helpful on all of this, knowing what to do. I've enjoyed working together."

Richardson hung up deeply touched, but also mildly frustrated by her dealings with Hutchison and his Billings marines. This group was so wonderful, so warm and detail-oriented, and never pushing work off onto others that they could do themselves. It reminded her of how different Hutchison and his team were from other officers she had dealt with on military funerals. Captain Hutchison, however, was so self-effacing and hard-working that she worried that he was too devoted to take time out for himself.

But she would be busy now putting all the rest of her plans for the Childers funeral and burial in place. She would have to arrange with the airline to have the proper conveyor truck available for off-loading, clearance to get her hearse through security, and so much else. She didn't have much time after that to dwell on the personality of Captain Hutchison.

Down in Powell, when he reached her by phone, Judy Childers received the news calmly, renewing Hutchison's concerns about the emotions she was holding in. But he also knew that focusing on the specifics seemed to be comforting to Judy, so he explained about the late-night arrival, the escorted hearse ride to Wyoming, and how things seemed to have fallen in place for the Monday wake and the Tuesday funeral.

"Judy, we're going to ride from Billings with the hearse," Hutchison said. "We will be with Shane all the way."

Judy told Joe when he came in from feeding his cattle, and he took it hard. He was all cried out now and didn't break down, but instead sat at the dining-room table with his USS *Tortuga* cap on and a glum expression on his face, eyes welling with tears as he stared at his folded hands. He and Judy briefly discussed the arrangements for delivering Shane to the Powell funeral home and then Joe sat quietly at the table before returning outside, staring at his hands and the walls.

Later, Joe would say that it was the words, just the words that Judy said, that made him feel so profoundly sad.

"Joe, Shane's coming home," Judy said. "Kevin Hutchison called and said that Shane is flying in on Saturday night."

Shane was coming home. Those words had once made his heart sing. Shane was flying in from Geneva or Nairobi, Shane was driving cross-country in his pickup after completing his officer's courses at Quantico, and then heading off to Camp Pendleton to lead a platoon of marines. For three or four days before Shane visited, Joe would be passing through the routines of his day–driving off to Northstate Corp. for work, cruising the hardware stores, working with his horses in the barn–and then his heart would momentarily race about his son's arrival. It would be so wonderful to see him, and Shane was a sudden burst of energy on the ranch, alleviating the loneliness of Joe and Judy's empty nest. But now Shane was really, really coming home, for good, in a coffin selected from the choices in a government CACO manual.

It was very hard on Joe and, after sitting for a while longer in the dining room, he headed out for the barn to find some work to do.

A SOLDIER COMES HOME

On Saturday morning the Bighorn country was sunny and bright, a pristine landscape out of a photography book on the American West. Before dawn a broad cold front had moved east over the Rockies and now the ceiling and visibility were unlimited in the dry air. The big sky was an intense azure blue, with purple fringes radiating along the peaks of the Beartooths and the Pryors. It was a perfect day to be out with the team, and Joe and his son Sam were up early to feed the cattle. The jingle of harness and the pounding of hooves echoed across the prairie, thrown back by the fortresslike walls of the Polecat Bench.

Like the weather, which would finally turn balmy later in the day, the towns of Powell and Cody had extended a warm generosity to the Childers family and those arriving for the funeral. The motels in both towns were now offering steep discounts and even free rooms to family members and friends who had traveled to Wyoming, and three Powell florists had pooled their resources to prepare flowers for the funeral and grave service. Funeral directors from all over Wyoming had provided the free services of their regular hearse and limousine drivers for the procession through town, and the Powell Chamber of Commerce covered the cost of decorating the lampposts and storefronts for the funeral parade with ribbons in red, white, and blue. Later, to get away from the funeral bustle around the Childers house, Jessi Walker drove into Cody to hit the downtown tourist strip. At a crafts store, she found a kachina doll she really wanted, but the two-hundred-dollar price tag was too much. When the owner learned that she was Shane Childers's cousin, she insisted that Jessi take the kachina doll for half price.

Sam Childers and his wife, Cori, were the recipients of similar generosity in far-off South Dakota. As they were traveling west on I-90 for the funeral, their minivan broke down near Salem, South Dakota, and they were towed to the Salem Auto Center there. The mechanics at the dealership informed Sam that repairs to his van would take several days, but finding a rental car in that remote part of South Dakota proved impossible. When the dealer realized that Sam and his family were traveling back to Wyoming to attend the funeral of his brother killed in Iraq–they had read about Shane in their local papers–they pulled a new minivan off of their sale line, put on dealer's plates, and rented it to Sam for the bargain price of thirty-five dollars a day.

This would be the first of many transforming moments that Sam experienced during the funeral week for Shane, a brother for whom he held troubled, unresolved feelings. Their sibling relationship, scrappy and typically competitive as boys, had been a series of missed approaches once they were adults. The difficulties between them had bothered both brothers for years, and Sam had always felt that once they were in their forties and Shane would have enough time after retiring from the marines, they would patch things up. But with Shane's death in Iraq, that wouldn't happen now, and for the first time Sam was shouldering family responsibilities and confronting old feelings without the shadow of a strong and domineering older brother. For his first few days in Wyoming, Sam was mostly trapped in a conundrum of confusion and doubt. If Shane had been there, Sam would have known exactly what to do—stay in the shadows and follow Shane's lead. Sam had always been the quiet, younger brother, the one who could afford to dodge family functions by going fishing alone, or entertaining himself in the corner with a few like-minded friends, because Shane was effortlessly social and dominated the room. But now that family dynamic was irrevocably over. Sam was the only son left.

In the evenings, after Joe had finished with his hay wagon and team, he would monkey around in the barn for another hour, enjoying some quality time with his horses and mules. Sam and the other men who were visiting that night—a couple of Shoshone Back Country Horsemen, Bill Hendry and Robert Reagan, a West Virginia Childers or two—would linger in the barnyard, just to be near Joe while leaving him alone to enjoy himself in the barn. The men outside talked and smoked and watched the gorgeous pink and lavender sunsets out over Heart Mountain and Dead Indian Pass.

Sam was painfully aware, talking with the men outside, how much they all worshipped Shane. There were other reminders of his brother's long shadow. When Bill Hendry had arrived, Judy had exclaimed, "Oh! You remind me so much of Shane." Sam didn't blame his mother for saying that—in fact, he liked her for it. She was very good at making people feel welcomed by the family. Still, it did hurt. His mother didn't exclaim the same thing to him.

Several times, out in the barnyard with the men, Sam had openly expressed his confusion about his role in the family now. Shane was gone and Sam couldn't get past the feeling that he somehow had an obligation to immediately fill the void.

"How is a younger brother in my situation supposed to react?" Sam repeatedly asked. "I just don't know what to do."

Robert Reagan felt that Sam was asking this question too early. Shane had been an important presence in all their lives and the pain of losing him was immense. But Sam was really the only one who measured himself against Shane, because he had to. They were brothers. It would just take a long time for Sam to adjust to a life suddenly missing the competition.

Outside in the barnyard, Reagan and Sam enjoyed a smoke together and talked about it.

"Stop trying to figure your ass out on this deal right away," Reagan told him. "Give it time, Sam."

"Yeah, but, Robert, what am I supposed to do? I should be helping Dad more."

"You *are* helping your father, kid," Reagan said. "You fed the cattle with him today. That's all he needs. Just time, you know, just spend some time together. You can figure your ass out on this deal later."

"Fine, Robert. We fed the cattle together. But there must be more I should be doing. How is a younger brother in my situation supposed to react?"

Sam was stalled there and Robert was frustrated by it, but he wasn't giving up.

"All right, kid," Robert said. "Whenever I've got a friend with a problem like this there's always a simple solution, and let me tell you. It works every time."

"Okay. What's that?"

"Listen to your Uncle Robert, all right? He's a washed up old navy Seabee, but the guy just happens to be totally fucking brilliant. All right?"

Sam was laughing now, relaxing. He and Shane had always thought that it was thoroughly typical of their father to have a headcase like Robert for his best friend. Robert always nailed you with his sense of humor. His sarcasm was therapeutic.

"Okay, Robert," Sam said. "I'm listening."

"That's the program, listen to your Uncle Robert," Reagan said. "All you've got to do for the moment is chill your ass and feed the cattle with Joe. Spend time with him, bullshit him a little. Go down to the hardware store. Things will just develop from there."

"All right, Robert. I'm chilling."

"Chill your ass, kid. Uncle Robert says you're doing just fine so long as you chill your ass. Don't try and wrap your head around a problem before you can figure it out. Right?"

"I'm chilling."

"Chill, kid. Chill the ass."

As the sky grew dark, the pastel sunset was reflected in their cigarette smoke. The purple fringe along the Beartooths returned as the sun fell. From the barn they heard horses whinnying and kicking their stalls as Joe distributed oats, and then they heard the murmuring of Joe in there, talking to his animals. The men in the barnyard smiled and exchanged knowing glances. Joe's conversation with his horses and mules in the barn was a soothing night sound, belonging to the prairie as much as the distant lowing of cattle.

Shane was a year and a half older than Sam, two grades ahead of him in school, and they were very different in their outlook and personality as they grew up together in Mississippi. Shane was popular and social, strong in sports, clean cut and square. Sam's idea of a good day was fishing along the Little Biloxi alone. He wore baggy blue jeans and left his shirts untucked, and drank beer with his friends out in the barn. As boys, their sibling rivalry played itself out in the usual ways. If they were home alone while Judy and Joe were out visiting the neighbors, and Shane told Sam to put the napkins or dinner plates away, Sam just ignored him and then they fought—once, Shane even gave him a black eye. Joe's attempts at disciplining his two sons for fighting were mostly unsuccessful, and it was often difficult for Judy to impose order when Joe was away on his long Seabee trips. But really the problem for Sam was the one that any younger brother would have had. Shane was successful at almost everything, enormously self-confident, and both verbally and physically arduous. Sam felt that he could never win an argument with Shane because it was just so hard to get in a single word of reply.

"Here's the thing about me and Shane, though," Sam later said. "Even though I resented him for dominating everything, including conversation, at the same time I usually thought that he was right. It just would have been a lot easier if maybe he allowed *me* to say something once in a while? Shane was the only socialite in the family, other than Dad. He had no problem talking with anybody. He loved taking from people what he could learn. I just wasn't like that at all."

Shane's departure for the marines in 1990 had solved many of his problems, particularly the need to get away from rural Mississippi and his family. But Sam's entry into the service in 1992 was at least partly defined by his need to differentiate himself from his unavoidable older brother. Sam deliberately chose the navy, he said, so that he wouldn't have "to fill Shane's shoes." He spent the next eight and a half years as a damage control specialist on navy ships and bases, mostly stationed in San Diego when he wasn't on a cruise. On and off in the mid-1990s, Shane was based at either Camp Pendleton or the Miramar Air Station nearby, but his relationship with Sam became a tragicomedy of missed connections. Shane missed Sam's wedding to Cori in 1996 because he was home on leave in Wyoming, but managed to rush over to the hospital in 1997 to hold Sam's first child, Aksel, in his arms. Incredibly, even though they sailed on the same Western Pacific cruise in 1996–a contingent of Expeditionary Force Marines is usually a part of the defense package on those cruises–Shane and Sam never met. They were on different ships and didn't connect at the ports of call between San Diego and the Persian Gulf, where Shane got off to briefly serve with a marine reconnaissance unit patrolling the border between Kuwait and Iraq, his second tour of duty in the Arabian sands.

Cori Childers was aware of the need to reconcile her husband and Shane, and would often make social efforts to get them together in San Diego. But these attempts were generally a disaster, typical of the missed connections between the two brothers. Shane's madass schedule and exhausting pace took a heavy toll on the relationship.

"If it wasn't so sad I guess you can say it was funny," Cori said. "But it was classic Shane. At four o'clock, when he was already supposed to be at our apartment near the base, Shane would call and tell me that he was on the way. All he had to do before he got there, you know, was get his surfboard waxed, check out new pickup trucks, and stop at the mountain bike store. Then, when he finally rolled in two hours late, it took us forever to pick out videos and buy pizza, because Shane always had to dominate, he had to control what we would buy. Then, when we got back to the house, Shane was so exhausted that he would collapse on the couch or on the floor before the video even got started. That's my most common memory of Shane—watching him snore on the couch in the middle of a video. Obviously, he and Sam never got much of a chance to talk."

Shane had another trait that bothered Cori and Sam. Shane always insisted on paying for everything when they were together. This was typical of Shane's overboard generosity, which showed itself in many other ways. Shane's sports addiction cycled quickly through new pursuits every year—rock and ice climbing, kayaking, surfing, mountain-biking, and Roller-Blading. By the time he was ready for a new interest, his equipment from the old sport was still almost new, so he just gave it away to family and friends—kayaks, rappelling gear, skis, brand-new biking helmets or the piles of T-shirts he had accumulated in a single year as a competitor in marathons or triathlon meets. There was just an incredible haul of great loot to be had from knowing Shane, and he often supplied friends who came along on his junkets with free airline tickets or motel rooms. Jessi and Jonna dubbed him "First National Shane."

But it was grating on Sam. When he volunteered to pay for something, the answer from his older brother was always the same. *No. I'll pay.* The behavior wasn't deliberately clueless on Shane's part. It just wouldn't occur to him that perhaps his younger brother would receive an ego boost from occasionally picking up the check himself.

In other ways, even as he progressed in the navy, Sam just couldn't get away from Shane. The San Diego naval yards occupy a position on the Pacific seaboard almost geographically opposite Charleston and The Citadel, two thousand miles away on the Atlantic coast.

"In the late nineties, when Shane was at The Citadel, I had come along enough in the navy to be teaching a firefighting course in San Diego," Sam said. "Every summer a bunch of midshipmen from the various academies would come out and get my training, and some of them would be MECEP guys from The Citadel. As soon as they heard my name they would say 'Wow, you're the brother of Staff Sergeant Childers? He's really hard core.' I mean, Shane was practically famous back there already. They all knew of him as this amazing marine."

For all of their frustrations dealing with him, however, Sam and Cori did enjoy one particularly fun aspect of knowing Shane, the constant speculation about his girlfriend woes and love life. By now there was a kind of global gossip chain made up of marine wives on the bases where Shane had served, and friends and family, informally called "The Shane Childers Fan Club." Jessi and Jonna Walker, of course, were close enough to Shane to get the back story on most of his relationships, but with everyone else Shane's reticence about sharing details of his romantic life added to his mystique. They knew, vaguely, about the exotic Israeli girlfriend from his Africa days. He'd been involved with a beautiful French college student while in Geneva. There were several false starts in Charleston, intimations of summer flings while he was studying in France and Vermont, and then the very public whirlwind romance and sudden breakup with Leo

Kelly. Women found it impossible to be around him without asking themselves why this supremely attractive and engaging marine wasn't already taken.

Sam and Cori never expected Shane to marry. He was too goal-oriented and was always flying off somewhere for a mountain-climbing trip or a new marine assignment, a moving target that couldn't establish a relationship and make it stick. In early September 2001, when he flew from Washington to San Diego to take over his new platoon at Camp Pendleton, Shane was excited because he'd met a California girl on the plane and talked with her for several hours. They dated briefly on the west coast, but it turned out that the woman disagreed with Shane about politics, and she couldn't keep up physically with his insanely busy days. Shane was upset about it at the time, perhaps still feeling the residual sting of the Leo Kelly rejection. His schedule and need for dominance, in effect, made him incredibly picky about women, because there were so few candidates out there who could keep up.

"Shane was what I would call macho-sensitive, and women really like that a lot," Cori said. "They were instantly attracted because he really made you feel that he cared only about you. But then they got to know him. The day revolved around Shane, period. He wouldn't have been sympathetic to what someone else wanted to do. Like Shane, hello? Maybe if you let her tell *you* what to do sometimes she would find that attractive?"

Jonna Walker didn't agree with the family sense that Shane might be incompatible with marriage. He was probably more flexible than they all thought and knew he still had some maturing left to do. In one of his last e-mails to her, Shane included this goal in a list of things he planned to do after Iraq: "Ask a few dozen girls out on dates."

"Shane knew that he had neglected the relationship side of his life and now it was time to make that happen," Jonna said. "There were signs that he *was* changing. I think he would have come back from Iraq, probably affected a lot by the experience, and analyzed what he was doing with women and realized that it had to do with his enormous need for control. Well, if that was the problem, Shane being Shane, he would have fixed it. He would study the problem and fix it. It's just so sad because I know he would have listened to us and changed. He would have made this amazing husband and father."

Shane's macho-sensitive ways, and his clear desire to develop parenting skills, emerged in his personality as "Uncle Shane." He adored children and teenagers, was excellent around them, and frequently arrived for visits at friends' homes with new sports gear, video games, and a full agenda of afternoon fun that revolved around the kids.

"Shane was really amazing this way," said Cori Childers. "He never forgot a child's birthday or Christmas and was always sending presents and cards. Do you know how unusual that is in a man, remembering birthdays? My sense of Shane was that he was great at wanting to do things with kids but could never imagine taking full responsibility for them as a parent. But, God, did Uncle Shane love spoiling those kids."

Robbin Whitten's three daughters first met Shane in 1994, when he arrived for security guard duty at the American Embassy in Nairobi. They reunited with "Uncle Shane" in the fall of 2002, when he was working up his platoon at the Combined Arms Training Center at Twentynine Palms, California, where the Whittens had settled after Steve Whitten retired from the marines. At night, Robbin and Shane would often sit up late while Robbin sewed up the holes in Shane's camouflage fatigues, talking about his need to settle down after the coming war and find a wife. But first, Shane always wanted to spend time with the Whitten children.

"There was a very real sense of priorities with Shane whenever he arrived at our house, no matter how tired he was after a week of training," Robbin Whitten said. "Shane would basically say, okay, you guys are adults, we can talk later tonight. Let me spend time first with the kids. And he was great with them, even if they were just sitting around the pool. Here was this hugely accomplished and interesting grown-up fellow who wanted to hear about their lives, encourage them, find out what they were studying and all about their history projects, what their problems were. Children just melted in his presence because he was so *there* for them."

By then, Sam Childers had retired from the navy, and he and Cori had settled with the children in La Salle, Illinois. Sam found a promising job as a field engineer for a power supply company, and he and Cori bought a nice Victorian house and fixed it up. Life was good. In February 2003, just before Shane deployed for Kuwait and then the Iraq War, Sam's company scheduled him for advanced training out in southern California. He was excited about it, not simply because he was traveling for his company, doing something that felt like progress in his job. He would also get a chance to visit with Shane. When Sam called out to California, Shane sounded excited about the possibility of getting together, but warned his brother that his unit was on deployment notice and that he could ship at any time. But they scheduled a day, an afternoon together, and they were both looking forward to it.

When Sam arrived on the west coast and attempted to call Shane from his hotel room, he learned from the Pendleton marines that Shane and his unit had departed by air for Kuwait just two hours before.

"I guess you could say that this was the relationship, right there," Sam said. "I was out in California on company business. Shane was shipping off to war. We had a date to meet. But we missed each other again. We didn't connect."

The distance between Billings and Captain Hutchison's hometown on the Pacific coast just south of Los Angeles, Palos Verdes, is a long way over the mountains and rivers of the American West, nearly a thousand miles. But on Saturday night, when Shane Childers arrived at the United Airlines cargo bay at the Billings airport, Hutchison thought that his mind was playing tricks on him about that. The vast terrain between Montana and the far-off, sunny beaches of L.A. seemed inescapably joined.

That night was cold and clear in southern Montana, with the residual effects of the high pressure system from the night before turning the sky a hard black with purple auras on the Beartooths. When Hutchison and Morgan arrived at the airport cargo facility in their government Suburban, funeral director Laura Richardson was already there, her long, black hearse parked near a loading ramp.

Richardson was so self-evidently in charge, so competent at her work, that Hutchison realized that a different moment in his CACO mission had arrived. For now, he wasn't in charge of the details, he wasn't really in command, and only later would he realize that the absence of control made an immense difference for him that night. Instead of thinking and leading he was now freed merely to observe and to feel, which was fortunate, he thought. His emotional response to Shane coming home was so intense he wouldn't have been much good for anything else.

The flight had been late, and then there was mail and cargo to offload first, with only a small weekend crew of cargo handlers around. It was nearly midnight before Shane was lowered from the back hold of the Boeing. The driver of a blue cargo truck with a conveyor belt assembly on its front end pulled up to the plane, and then raised the lift while Hutchison and Morgan watched through an immense overhead door.

Hutchison was surprised when the casket emerged through the hold, because it was wrapped in a reinforced cardboard container, not the flag-draped coffin he expected. But Richardson quickly assured him that this is the way caskets are transported, to avoid shipping scrapes and other damage, and told him that they would remove the container back in Powell. When the cargo truck lowered the container onto the loading ramp, Richardson cheerfully waved away the marines' offer of help and muscled the heavy cargo box into the hearse by herself.

As the container carrying Shane was lowered from the plane, Hutchison's throat tightened and his heart raced. He felt exhausted that night, but strangely alert. He was a captain in the marines, standing on the cold cement floor of an airport cargo bay, with the Montana chill coming through the open space of the overhead door, reaching right through his thin dress blues. He was on CACO duty and was supposed to be disciplined, controlled. But he didn't feel that way at all, and perhaps the pressures of the week had something to do with that. He felt sadness, yes a great deal of sadness as the container with the casket inside was lowered, but he also felt relief, almost wondrously so. Emotions beyond that swirled in as his heart raced.

Oh, Shane, you're home. Semper Fidelis, brother marine. You're back, and I'm taking you home to Powell, to your parents. I've done the best job I could with Judy and Joe. You're back, Shane, and I'm taking you home.

That's what he felt, but mostly relief. Hutchison being Hutchison, of course, there was some guilt mixed in with that. He was certainly entitled to feel relieved about a burden being lifted from his shoulders, now that his obligation to return Shane to his parents in time for the Tuesday funeral was fulfilled. But he felt guilty about feeling relief for himself, when he should have felt only more sadness for Shane and the Childers family. That's the head trip that the CACO was playing on Hutchison now. I feel relieved that Shane is back, but maybe more for myself than for the Childerses, which makes me feel guilty. But he knew that perhaps he was just being too earnest here, too Hutch. The next time he spoke with his mother on the phone, he thought, they would have to debrief this little number that he was pulling on his brain.

Hutchison and Morgan were now good to go on escorting the hearse down to Powell. Shane Childers was back in the snowy bosom of the Bighorns, where he belonged, and now they were anxious to deliver him to his family and the necessary catharsis of a funeral.

Laura Richardson gently pushed the insulated rear door of the hearse shut, so that it settled against its frame with the sound of a soft timpani drum. Then the hearse and the marine Suburban left the grounds of the airport in tandem formation, descended the serpentine road down the rimrock plateau, and headed through Billings for the interstate west. At Laurel they turned south for the hour's drive into Wyoming, down through the black Pryor Mountains void.

In their SUV, following the taillights of the hearse through the mountains, Hutchison and Morgan talked for a while. The CACO mission was going well, they agreed, but they were both still worried about Judy. One of the things that was returned to Billings with the casket was a clear plastic bag containing the "initial personal effects" found on Shane's body. They could see through the plastic what the bag contained: Shane's picture I.D. card, his watch, and a lanyard flashlight that he had worn around his neck as he went over the line into Iraq. The CACO manuals required immediate return of the initial personal effects to the family, and the marine tradition was that they be given to the mother. But Hutchison and Morgan weren't at all sure how Judy would react when she received these possessions. They would just have to see tomorrow. There were other things to discuss, including Morgan's return to Billings on Sunday to continue the drilling of his honor guard team.

But after that they were quiet in the car together, not a glum quiet, just quiet and relieved. They had been through a lot all week, attending to innumerable details and worrying about Shane's body returning on time, and now they both just wanted to be alone with their thoughts as the lights of Rockvale and Bridger went by.

After the Belfry cutoff, the Polecat Bench became a purple-black rim surrounding them in the darkness, and Hutchison couldn't make his mind behave. A strange mind-wander, like an emotional compass, was overwhelming him now. He was crossing the open range country along the Wyo-Montana line, but his mind, uncontrollably, raced southwest over the mountains to California.

Earlier in the week, Joe Childers had told Hutchison that Shane had picked up surfing over the past two years at Pendleton, a weekend pastime that allowed him to escape the pressures of preparing his platoon for Iraq. After college, before joining the marines, Hutchison had spent an aimless year surfing the California beaches, all the way from Malibu to Baja. He knew all those beaches down past Dana Point and San Onofre, the surf Shane had done. And it just felt right to Hutchison now, really good, bringing home to Wyoming the marine who had surfed his own waters in southern California. But now he couldn't prevent his mind from returning there, to his home, too. Palos Verdes. Surfing the big ones on a windy day along Haggerty's Reef, just below the cliffs. If he had been the one to take the bullet in Rumaila, and not Shane, Hutchison thought, well I would want to be taken back to my special place too.

They had reached the canyon badlands now, just above the Wyoming line. The snowy Bighorns were in view, reflecting the moonlight, and the occasional antelope spooked in their lights.

Shane, we're bringing you home, brother. Semp Fi. But, oh, take me home too, take me home. Carry me back to Haggerty's Reef below the cliffs at Palos Verdes and give me back to the surf. Shane, we're almost there, and we're giving you back to the mountains.

Hutchison just couldn't get rid of that mind-wander all the way across the range lands, along the winding road up through the Polecat Bench, and then down into Powell. Geography became spiritual as he followed the hearse carrying Shane.

Oh, take me back to the reef. Shane, we're bringing you in now, Semp Fi. I can see the lights of Powell, and there's Heart Mountain. This will be my last time alone with you Shane so Semp Fi. You're home.

Immense black Wyoming sky with moonlit snowy Bighorns in the middle merging southwest toward aquamarine Palos Verdes.

That was Hutchison's big mind-wander bringing Shane in.

Just past the grain elevators along Highway 14 on the outskirts of Powell, Hutchison pulled out into the passing lane and sped past the hearse, then glided back into the driving lane to lead Laura Richardson in. He knew the way to the funeral home from there and it was just something that he felt he should do as a marine, and for Shane. Don't follow, lead, bring the hearse in from the front. Semp Fi, Shane, and we're here.

Hutchison switched to his high beams and lead the hearse along the highway, parallel to the Burlington Northern Railroad tracks. The big water tower outside town and the grain elevators in the distance were vaguely lit by the moonlight. Then, just before he could make the turn onto North Absaroka Street, something very simple but touching happened.

Four police cruisers–two from the county sheriff and two from the town of Powell–were quietly waiting along the gravel shoulder of the highway just outside of town, their lights dimmed. Oh, Hutchison thought, they knew we were coming. Laura Richardson would have informed the police about our arrival plans. As the government Suburban leading the hearse approached, the cruisers started rolling.

Merging, merging, merging in bumper-to-bumper formation, effortlessly graceful, their lights not coming back on until just the right moment, tires softly whooshing in the Wyoming night, two patrol cruisers pulled onto the highway to form a new lead from the front. Hutchison didn't have to touch his brakes or change his speed. They were just there now, two patrol cruisers in front. The other two cruisers fell in behind the hearse to bring up the rear. No flashing lights, no sirens, no fanfare. Just a quiet early-morning whoosh of the tires merging with the vehicles delivering the dead marine.

It was a local convoy for Shane now and they were bringing him in all together, a six-car formation turning left onto North Absaroka.

At the funeral home parking lot on East Third Street, the patrol cars parked in formation at the edge, thirty yards from the hearse, and dimmed their lights. Four officers emerged from the cruisers, stood beside their doors, and removed their Stetsons and police caps, holding them against their chests. They would keep their distance. They didn't want to be intrusive. But they would wait there until the hearse was emptied. It was more than a display of respect for Shane, a resident of Powell who was the first killed in this new war. The body language of the officers, with their hats on their chests, said: We're here if you need us. Just let us know.

Hutchison was moved by the presence of these policemen and deputy sheriffs because like many California boys, and even many marine officers, he'd never had much use for local cops. He'd spent his youth squealing off from the lights in muscle cars, careening down beaches in VW dune buggies, DWI, stuffing "chickenshit" speeding tickets onto the pile in his glove compartment, a teenage life right out of the scenes in *American Graffiti*. Marines don't like cops on principle. When you're drunk and having fun outside Pendleton or Lejeune, the local law is just a nuisance in your face.

But Hutchison liked these patrolmen and deputy sheriffs that night, and appreciated why they were there. With the help of an assistant waiting at the funeral home, Richardson unloaded the container carrying Shane and his coffin onto a four-wheeled dolly, and then wheeled it through the rear loading doors of the funeral home. Once Shane was safely inside, Hutchison turned and faced the patrol cars and officers, saluting them from his officer's cap. He watched from the parking lot as the patrol cars backed and turned and then whooshed off again into the night, disappearing as quietly as they had first appeared out on the highway.

Inside the funeral home, Richardson and her assistant used box-cutting knives to slice away the cardboard around Shane's casket. Then they removed the nylon straps securing the casket to a plywood "air tray" base that had kept the whole cargo package in place. Hutchison, with his usual curiosity about things, was fascinated by all this. He didn't realize that so much engineering had gone into shipping bodies and caskets around. The cargo container carrying Shane was as lightweight but durable as a marine ammo crate.

When they were done, Richardson and her assistant wheeled the casket into the front of the viewing room "chapel" where Shane would be resting during the reception-wake.

"Presentability of the remains" is a sensitive issue for CACO details, and the marines pay careful attention to it. Most soldiers returning as fatal casualties take as long to return home as Shane did and the consequences of the delay—desert dehydration, emergency medical care, then the flights home in military transports before proper embalming—can shrivel up a face and turn its complexion almost black. That can't be hidden from a family, and CACO officers are generally advised to prepare them beforehand about how the body looks. Also, all branches of the military, but particularly the marines, are meticulous to the point of obsession about a proper uniform and medals rack being presented on a dead soldier.

For these reasons, Hutchison needed to view Shane's body, but the Childerses had also presented another issue, in a way. The normal schedule for a returning fatality is that a private family viewing is held one day, followed by the public wake a day later. That way, the family has some time to recover after initially seeing the body and is more composed about facing the large group of strangers who often show up to pay respects to a fallen soldier. But Joe and Judy hadn't decided about a private family viewing yet. They were waiting for Hutchison to tell them about the shape Shane was in so that they could make a decision about an open or closed casket.

So Hutchison decided to view the body that night, even though it was now after 1 A.M. This would enable him to give Joe and Judy some indication in the morning about Shane's appearance, in case they planned a private viewing tomorrow.

It was difficult for Hutchison and Morgan when Richardson finally opened the lid of the casket. There was Shane, the marine they'd heard so much about by now that they felt they practically knew him. The prominent Roman nose, the slightly protruding ears, the handsome cleft chin and the dark brown hair with natural sandy highlights.

But he did look pretty bad, his face gaunt and emaciated, with the effects of dehydration and the long ride back from a field morgue in Kuwait evident in his skin tone, which was a mottled brown-black. This was not the Shane the family remembered, and Hutchison knew this would be rough to deal with.

Richardson assured him that with a little rouge and other cosmetics, Shane's skin tone and facial look could be improved. She was trained in mortuary cosmetics herself and would personally do the work in the morning. It was her judgment, and also Morgan's, that Shane's appearance was not as bad as they might have expected, and that the Childerses would be realistic about it. It was important for them to confront the face of their son, to accept his death. Closure about that would be harder to achieve if they lived for the rest of their lives with the mystery of what had lay underneath a closed casket.

Reluctantly, Hutchison agreed. Already, he was rehearsing in his head what he would say to Judy in the morning. "Judy, he's not the son you remember, okay?"

Hutchison did feel good about one minor problem concerning Shane's uniform, because he had anticipated it. The green fourragère, a braided cord that marines wear above the ribbons on their chest, was missing from Shane's uniform. But Hutchison expected that the uniform specialists at the national mortuary in Dover, Delaware, might have trouble remembering this final touch, and he had taken precautions. The marine casualty branch at Quantico had already dispatched a fourragère by Federal Express, and it would reach Powell by Monday, in time for the public viewing and wake.

Their work done for the day, and subdued by the viewing of Shane, Hutchison and Morgan left for the Lamplighter Inn over on First Street.

Checking into his room and then carefully hanging up his dress blues, Hutchison collapsed on the bed, exhausted from his day and the late hour. He was mildly frustrated as well. This CACO work just kept presenting new difficulties, new pressures. Two hours ago, he had felt such relief about Shane finally being home. But now he felt pressured all over again about what to tell Judy regarding Shane's appearance. Solve a problem, create a new one. Solve a problem, create a new one. He just seemed trapped in an infinite regress of CACO pressure.

There were other things about the CACO experience and its related emotional toll that were fascinating, except that it was all happening to him. In the space of a single week, his short-term memory had become so degraded that he could only keep track of details that he wrote down on yellow legal pads. His sense of time was vanishing as well. The big mind-wander from Wyoming to Palos Verdes had somehow vastly stretched time, so that he felt that tonight's hearse escort from Billings took place a month ago. He'd heard so many stories about Shane from Joe by now that he felt he'd known the family for years, and not just a week. The drive between Billings and Powell felt like one that he had been making all his life. When he talked to his mother on the phone, he felt that he was a boy again, a rushing sensation inside that he hadn't experienced for years.

It just went on and on like that, all these CACO-connects banging around in his brain. CACO, Shane Childers, snowy Bighorns in spring, Palos Verdes, the Belfry cutoff, the taillights of a hearse, Joe and his piles of farm machinery and his mules, it was a major period in his life now, a matter of years, oh, rediscovering the good sense and love of his mother and maybe the Peruvian girlfriend will come back to the states finally and God I should just marry that beauty. The wind really kicks up here down here at night. You can hear it whistle around the corners of the motel.

Hutchison found this ironic, because learning to manage stress was one of the things he most liked about being a marine. At twenty-two he had given up the surfer boy life to become a marine because he thought that the career would be romantic, but in fact he had learned something else. Running a rifle platoon or a small command like Billings was inherently chaotic and demanding, and the only way to manage the stress was discipline and routine, and then more discipline on top of that. But there was something else that he liked about stress. A fatigued brain working right past the threshold of exhaustion suddenly produced these wonderful insights, particularly about human nature. Being stressed as a marine, somehow, renewed his faith in people and refreshed his love of humanity and life. Stress, get a thought about motivating other men. Stress, get a thought about the impact of family baggage. Stress, get a thought, stress, get an insight. He loved being a marine.

But this CACO stress was very different. It had to do with the supremely conflicting and confusing emotions related to life and death, and not just Shane Childers's life, but Kevin Hutchison's, too. These emotions couldn't be managed by discipline alone, he didn't have a control mechanism to deal with so many new and involuntary sensations. Meanwhile, he was the CACO team commander, and he wasn't allowed to show the stress.

But he knew that he was just tiring himself out by all this. He had to rest up and relax so that he could adequately face Judy Childers in the morning. Before Hutchison finally nodded off, he set out his running shoes and outfit. He was annoyed at himself for breaking marine routine and not getting enough exercise. In the morning, he'd take a long run out into the farm country that spread south to the Shoshone River. The Crown Hill Cemetery, where Shane would be buried, is out that way, and he wanted to inspect the layout to get a sense of what he faced on Tuesday.

Back at the funeral home, Laura Richardson had lingered for forty-five minutes, getting some paperwork out of the way before she faced what she knew would be a difficult few days with the funeral. From the door of her viewing chapel, she switched on the lights and took one last look at Shane's casket up front, and then crossed the vestibule for her front door.

The prospect of Powell at night from her funeral home entrance had always pleased her. The floodlights from the parking lot nearby on North Absaroka Street cast interesting shadows and highlights on the cottonwoods in the front lawn, and there was a nice stretch of well-porched homes that formed a quaint depth of view toward the prairie. She'd come here from New Mexico to finish raising her children and to declare her independence as a single mother. Leaving work late at night like this, often, she felt satisfaction about her success. And church tomorrow. Father Johnson at Saint Barbara's. She needed the refreshment of Mass before she could face burying this marine.

As she was locking her front door, Richardson felt the presence of someone approaching from behind. When she looked over her shoulder, a Powell policeman was crossing First Street from the empty parking lot of the Community First National Bank. She could tell without asking why he was there, because the officer's demeanor made it clear. He had been waiting at a respectful distance for her to close and lock up. He would remain at the entrance to the funeral home all night, occasionally patrolling out back, too. Someone should be there until dawn with the marine.

Richardson didn't know the police officer's name. She didn't know if he had been assigned this job by the police department, or just elected to assume a post outside the funeral home all night on his own. Maybe the officer just wanted to do this for himself, to get closer, somehow. Everyone in Powell had been emotionally needy, on edge, since the news arrived about Lieutenant Childers. She didn't know for sure.

But she knew what she felt when she looked into the officer's face. She felt deep gratitude for him, for Powell, for Captain Kevin Hutchison and how all this had been handled so far. It had been such a demanding week. But she was the funeral director in town and this moment required restraint, not a show of emotion.

The officer spoke first, and then Richardson replied.

"Did you just bring Shane home?"

"Yes, officer, and thank you. He's home. Shane is home."

THE SANDS OF RUMAILA

O n Sunday morning it was sunny but blustery outside, with scattered clusters of pink and gray cumulus beginning to form
out over the Beartooths. Inside the Childers house, the
mood was expectant but calm. Joe, Judy, their children, and guests
were all vaguely aware that Shane had been scheduled to arrive late
the night before. But Laura Richardson and Captain Hutchison inspired such confidence in the way they handled these matters that the
family was content to wait for Hutchison to visit and see what he said.
The atmosphere around the dining-room table, where the family was
dawdling over breakfast, was friendly and warm, with everyone using
second cups of coffee or more helpings of eggs and coffee cake as an
excuse to catch up with in-laws and friends. For the moment, they
were all talked out about Shane. Five grandchildren chasing around
the house and colliding on the stairs contributed to a feeling that was
more like a family gathering for the holidays than for a funeral.

Later, after breakfast was over, Robert Reagan arrived from his
motel and began holding court out on the front patio. Sam Childers
and his brother-in-law, Richard Brown, were there with a few other

men–one of Judy's brothers, and some Shoshone Back Country Horsemen. They all found Robert to be a soothing, entertaining presence, his therapeutic sarcasm quite welcome. Like many of those gathering for the funeral, some of the men continued to be concerned by Judy's stoic reaction to Shane's death.

"Robert, I just don't know what we're going to do here," Richard Brown said. "Judy isn't showing *any* reaction yet. Shouldn't we be worried?"

"Oh Lord, here we go," Reagan said. "What are you? United States Army or something? Figures. I know Judy. When she blows, she blows. And make no mistake about it. She *will* blow."

"Yeah, but, Robert," Brown said, "she's not showing any reaction."

"Oh Christ, do I have to tell you everything, kid?" Reagan said. "If you're based up in the Aleutians and there's volcanoes all around, you don't sit around and watch for eruptions. They blow when they blow and then you do something. You don't watch your freaking grass grow, do you? Judy's going to blow and it will probably be a doozy but let's just chill until then."

"Robert," Brown said, "maybe someone should talk to Judy?"

"Oh, sweet," Reagan said. "Are you volunteering for that job?"

"No, not particularly," Brown said.

"Well good, because neither am I," Reagan said. "Just listen to your Uncle Robert here. Chill your butt until she blows and everything's going to be fine, just fine."

"Okay, okay!" Brown said. "I'll try and relax about it."

Earlier, at the Lamplighter Inn in Powell, Captain Hutchison had woken with a pleasing thought. He suddenly remembered that during a phone call earlier in the CACO drama his mother had told him that he "was chosen" to help the Childerses, as if his selection were divinely inspired, or that there was something inherent in his personality that made him fit for the job.

In fact, he now realized, there was something that made him particularly appropriate for the job. He was the marine captain from the family who had "put the fun back into dysfunction." Growing up in his amusingly blended and sometimes fractious clan had prepared him for many things in life, and that included feeling comfortable in a large, extended family like the Childerses. In some respects, compared to his own family, the Childerses were practically cupcakes.

There had always been one thing that the Hutchisons did particularly well—meltdowns. It was insane what happened sometimes on those blended family vacations, who was melting down for what reason. Still, they always had fun. This was the family baggage, he thought, that had prepared him so well for the marines—after growing up a Hutchison, running some crazyass rifle platoon at Lejeune was a snap. It wasn't that he was hardened or repressed about family relations, in fact he was quite sensitive. But his threshold for people acting out or displaying other personal eccentricities was very high. It was just something about himself that he knew. Hutchison had great proficiency training in managing meltdowns.

So, while he was worried about confronting Judy Childers that morning with the clear plastic bag of Shane's personal effects, he knew there was no way to anticipate her reaction. He might face the same situation when describing the state of Shane's remains. The only way to control his side of the equation was to carefully rehearse what he would say. That's what he knew about managing meltdowns, or preparing for them when one could reasonably be expected. Rehearse your own part, position things as directly and as sympathetically as you can, then go with the flow, embrace and respond to the melt.

It was his old "putting the fun back into dysfunction" proficiency training kicking in, Hutchison realized. That's why he had automatically begun rehearsing his lines for Judy last night.

"Judy, you're going to see your son tomorrow, but he's not the son you remember. Okay? May I explain?"

So as he took his morning run, showered, shaved, put on his uniform and then went over to the Skyline Café for breakfast, Hutchison repeated his line like a mantra. He didn't want to forget it under stress.

"Judy, you're going to see your son tomorrow, but he's not the son you remember."

When Hutchison arrived at the Childerses, a few of the men were still standing outside talking with Robert Reagan. Hutchison said hello and asked them how Judy was doing, and they told him that everyone seemed to be having a relaxed morning, considering the circumstances. When Hutchison went inside, they all had the sense to wait out on the patio because they knew that for the first time Judy would be confronting the news that Shane was home. The issue of finally seeing him could not be put off much longer.

Joe, Judy, and their children were still in the dining room, drinking coffee and discussing their plans for the day. Hutchison decided that it would be deceitful and just prolong Judy's agony to delay handing her the bag containing Shane's picture ID, his watch, and lanyard flashlight.

Biting his lip, Hutchison looked boyish and hurt handing her the small bag of personal effects, presenting it to her as she sat at the table. Judy wasn't surprised to receive the bag, but she wasn't prepared either, at least not when she saw Shane's military ID card.

Her eyes welling with tears, Judy looked first to Hutchison, then to Joe, and finally started to cry.

"He's not coming back, is he?" she moaned, looking up at Hutchison's face. "Up till now, I just thought of Shane as on deployment."

Hutchison knew that it was best to be direct. She was saying it now, "he's not coming back," and it was his job to reinforce what she could now see and was indeed holding in her hands.

"Judy, you know how hard it is for me to say it," Hutchison said. "You know how sorry I am. But Shane's not coming back."

Judy repeated that several more times, sobbing now, the tears running down her face.

"He's not coming back. He's really not coming back."

"He's not coming back, Judy," Joe said. "It's time we all faced that Shane's not coming back."

Joe was crying now too, uncontrollable tears, but mostly in response to Judy's sorrow. He was not sobbing or breaking down. There seemed to be an important emotional equation to the moment. He'd exhausted himself with tears and a monstrous weight of grief all week, and now he was played out and had faced that Shane wasn't returning. So he could be there for Judy now, and he did his best to comfort her, wrapping her in his arms and crying too. In their adjoining chairs at the table they seemed to form together a portrait of desperate coping.

Joe helped Judy open the clear plastic bag, and they shared in their hands Shane's watch and his lanyard flashlight, talking about how these objects reminded them of him. It was just unbearably difficult, yet strangely comforting, too, to hold Shane's watch and his lanyard flashlight.

Sandra Childers was crying now too, and her husband, Richard, had joined her. Soon, other shivers of crying had passed through the rest of the house as some of the Childers relatives who had arrived realized what was happening, and it lasted a long time.

But everyone felt better when it was over. In all the details of bringing the West Virginia relatives to Wyoming, the marines coming in and out, and friends arriving unpredictably, it had been easy to become distracted from what this was really all about. Shane's strong personal force and his aura of invincibility had also contributed to the deferred emotions—they all couldn't believe at first that he was gone. But now the initial personal effects had arrived, and they were all facing it. Shane really, really wasn't coming back.

Hutchison stood at the edge of the family in the dining room and talked quietly with some of the men for a while. He wanted to give Judy some time. He could see that she was really unbending now, allowing herself to cry and to be comforted by Joe. She was Judy Childers and for more than thirty years she had been the quiet force holding the family together, while Joe was away on his Seabee trips. Now it was her turn to be needy and exhausted by sorrow for Shane and she was indulging that. Finally, cried out for the moment, she returned the personal effects to the bag and looked up, her face puffy from weeping.

Hutchison joined Judy and Joe, and, gently, waiting for the right moment, he brought up the difficult subject of the condition of Shane's remains. "Judy, you're going to see your son tomorrow, but he's not the son you remember."

Then he explained everything, about the effects of dehydration on a body, and Shane's long, arduous ride home from a field hospital in Kuwait. Everyone discussed it calmly, and Hutchison felt emotional himself for a bit, because he was so proud of the way the family was handling everything. But there was also something else happening, which was palpable in the room. The emotional center of gravity, authority over decisions, was shifting to Joe. Yes, he was never going to be a great detail man who spent much time filling out CACO forms or filing for insurance. He grieved by telling stories and then hitching up his team. But he was so open and generous, so uncompromisingly honest about his emotions, that the family was ready to follow him as soon as he was ready to lead. Instead of crying now, he was frequently sitting silently, just pondering events and the next decision. Now he was considering what Hutchison had said about the remains, that Shane did not look particularly good but was presentable. Joe spoke up with his eyebrows raised, his chin slightly out, and his eyes clear and earnest.

"I just think we all need to be realistic about this," Joe said. "I don't want to wake up some morning a few months from now and expect to see Shane come diddly-boppin' down the lane to see us. We have to accept that he's gone, and an open casket will help us."

When he spoke the inflection in Joe's voice was not insistent. Instead, he was seeking consensus. But he did feel that it was best that they not have a private family viewing today, because they all needed to recover first from the knowledge that Shane was finally back. Maybe he'd hitch up the team later and take all the grandchildren and visiting aunts for a long hayride. They'd spend time together as a family, visit and have dinner, and gird up for the stress of the wake tomorrow.

Joe easily persuaded them. The other family members didn't want to live the rest of their lives either with the dream of a phantom Shane diddly-boppin' down that lane again. He was just so powerful a figure in their lives, a model that couldn't be forgotten, that they had to confront his remains. They had to see him to accept his death.

Later in the morning, when Laura Richardson called from the funeral home to find out about their plans, Joe informed her that the family would not have a private viewing today. Tomorrow, at the large reception and wake, they would have an open casket.

Judy was markedly changed in her demeanor for the rest of the day. She spent most of her time on the couch in the family room, letting some of the Childers aunts sit with her, or attend to the house, while she quietly talked and coped with her grief. When she felt like crying, she did.

Relieved by the release of emotion, and freed for the day from any real funeral responsibilities, the family went about its activities. One mixed party of Childers cousins and visiting marines headed off for some sightseeing–the Buffalo Bill Dam and Yellowstone National Park. The Childers uncles wanted to get into the Buffalo Bill Museum in Cody, which was known to house an excellent rifle collection, while their wives hit the downtown crafts galleries and outlet shops. Many of the visitors who had hurriedly dropped their lives to travel to Wyoming still needed something to wear to the wake and funeral–a better pair of dress shoes, a tie to go with a new suit–and they scattered too, mostly for Cody. Their place around the house was quickly taken up by newly arriving Childers relatives, old marine friends of Shane, or more Shoshone Back Country Horsemen. The house was never empty and Judy announced plans for a big midafternoon supper, cobbled together from the generous donations of cooked meals that were still arriving from the American Legion women's auxiliary or Judy's Avon friends. But she let the other women in the house do all the work while she remained on the couch.

This was just the excuse that Joe and Robert needed to put together an old act. The two old Seabee pals headed off in Joe's battered pickup for Powell. Robert needed film for his camera and wanted to buy a western-style belt, and Joe wanted to show him around town. They could check out the town, and down at the Big "R" feed and tack store there were some real pretty cashiers who were decent flirts. They just needed a fun goof-off together and so they got lost in town for a few hours, joyful for each other's company.

They'd been doing this for years together, ever since Vietnam was over and, on and off, they were stationed together as Seabees. Chase across the base all day Saturday shoeing horses together, welding someone's flatbed trailer, or making extra money building an extended kitchen deck for a friend. Often they were still out carousing somewhere an hour or two after they had promised Judy they would be home. Over the years a strict protocol had evolved concerning the placement of blame.

"All right, let's just say that I'm out somewhere with Joe and he's the one who's acting out, it's Joe who has screwed the poodle," Reagan said. "Doesn't matter. It's Robert's fault. That's the program and that's my relationship with Judy. 'Robert, this is your fault.' It's automatic. I'm always the one who screwed the poodle."

In the afternoon, when the big supper was prepared and everyone around seemed ready to eat, Joe and Robert weren't back yet. Judy dragged the phone over to her place on the couch and dialed around Powell until she tracked them down. She made it clear that they were expected home posthaste for the meal.

When Joe and Robert finally blew in, Judy got up from the couch and faced them, standing near the dining-room table. Joe got the "I'm pretending my husband doesn't exist" treatment and she didn't even look at him. Instead, Judy squared off for Robert.

"Robert, this is your fault. You kidnapped Joe and you were late."

"Oh, now, c'mon here, woman, let's not argue about it, okay?" Reagan said. "We just went in to town because I needed a belt."

"Robert, it's your fault. You kidnapped Joe and got lost in town. The day before my son's wake."

"Judy, now look here. I wasn't driving the vehicle, okay?"

"Robert, it's your fault. One hundred percent."

"Well, let's just get it back down to fifty percent, Judy, okay? I was just the passenger on this deal."

"It's your fault, Robert. Stop making excuses."

They went back and forth about it for another few minutes, an entertaining family farce. "Oh, this is beautiful," Sandra said. "If Mom and Robert weren't arguing? It just wouldn't feel normal." Judy was miffed at Joe for being late and so she blamed Robert, a classic Judy revert. From the kitchen, a few visitors popped open soda cans and watched the verbal exchange, and then the men who needed one last smoke before supper stepped outside. After Judy was done with him, Reagan stepped out to the patio to join them.

"God, don't you just love a woman who can treat a man like that?" Reagan said to the other men. "Judy is the best."

The cumulus formation was fully developed now and had moved over from the Beartooths, raking low across the prairie. The scattered clouds were intensely white and puffy with a patina of gray underneath. The landscape out to the mountains was a black mosaic of shadows, with the ground in between the clouds, where the sun got through, a rich bright gold.

"Yeah, but, Robert," Richard Brown said, "are you sure that was fair to you? I mean Joe was late, too."

"Oh Christ, kid," Reagan said. "What are you, United States Army or something? Get with the program. Whenever we're together, this is the deal. Joe screws the poodle, and I take the rap."

Laughing and comfortable with each other, forgetting why they were all there, the men crushed their cigarettes out by foot and went inside to join the family dinner. Everyone was relaxed and casual around the table, enjoying the cornucopia of food delivered by the American Legion ladies—turkey tetrazzini and fried chicken, lasagne and country-fried steaks—and Joe's stories were entertaining. He described the day Shane got thrown by the big black mule, and landed on his brand-new cowboy hat. When Shane was home, Joe frequently was leaving for work in his pickup just as Shane was riding off for Belfry on his mountain bike, and they raced the first couple of miles down the farm lane together, until Joe left him in a wake of dust. Joe's stories were long, but relaxing. The house felt moody and reflective now, less stressful, now that Judy was finally having the emotional reaction everyone had wished for her.

It got even better after supper, when the Childers grandchildren were all banished from the house for a while, so Judy could have some peace and quiet. There was some pretty good Childers family mayhem out in the front of the house now. While the men talked and smoked on the patio, Joe dragooned Richard Brown and a couple of visiting marines into helping him move some farm machinery away from the parking space up on the hill. The grandchildren were tear-assing around in the middle of all this. Little Aksel and Aiden were chasing each other with sticks and rolling in the dirt, and Hannah and Marta were playing with the garden hose. Then one of them went plowing straight through the ornamental plaster donkey in the garden, neatly guillotining the head. When Judy came out and saw that, she blew her stack.

"Oh, this is good, this is good," Robert said, watching from over by the toolshed. "She's really piped now."

Joe's suggestion, earlier in the morning, about organizing a hayride had excited the grandchildren. They had been pestering him about it all day. Take us for a hayride, Granddaddy, take us for a hayride. When the West Virginia Childerses got back from Cody, some of the aunts got into the act, too. They wanted to see the country around Joe's ranch.

Joe was ready to do it now. With a coterie of middle-aged men trailing behind him, he headed for the barn, harnessed and hitched up his matched Belgians, and then asked a few of the men to throw some hay bales up onto the wagon bed so he could form some passenger seats. When he got the team up front by the house, a Childers in-law held the horses by their bridles while Joe set up a small stepladder so that everyone could get over the freeboard of his hitch. It was joyful, festive even, as the children and all the West Virginia women piled up the ladder and then found places to sit among the bales of hay.

Once Joe had climbed back up to the front seat, he called back to his grandson.

"Aksel, c'mon up here and help me drive the team."

Aksel brightened and smiled broadly, scrambling up over the bales and all his relatives legs to join Joe. He stood in between his grandfather's knees, and Joe cupped Aksel's hands around the reins, holding them in his callused palms.

"All right now, Aksel, we're horsemen here, do you understand that?" Joe said. "We don't razz our animals. We talk to them."

With that, Joe looked back to make sure that his wheels were free of people and then pushed his USS *Tortuga* ball cap up and spoke to his team.

"Amigo. April. Let's go."

The Belgians smartly picked up their front hooves and jingled off, prancing, shying slightly sideways against their traces, just to show Joe that they were energetic and loved the work. The team pulled hard from their collars and bent their heads against the check lines to get the heavy wagon rolling.

As the wagon rumbled off, the jingle of the harness echoed back against the house. Joe was teaching Aksel how to gently hold the team to the center of his freshly graveled drive. His voice reached back to the men in front of the toolshed with pleasing attenuation.

"Okay, see? Just gently with the reins, Aksel, just guide them. We don't yank our horses around here," Joe said. "This is how I taught your Uncle Shane."

The men back in the driveway were pleased, infinitely pleased for Joe. He needed this, and not simply as a distraction from Shane. Most of the family hadn't seen Wyoming yet, or Joe's dream ranch. It was good for him to be the paterfamilias of them all, and to show them the neighboring prairie, to share with them his stories and running commentary while the team pulled up front.

"Oh, this is so good for Joe, he's in his element," said his brother, Richard Childers, who had arrived the night before from Huntington, West Virginia. "He always told us that he'd settle in the West someday, and we never believed him. Look at him now."

"Yeah, he's a pretty good washed-up old Seabee now," Robert Reagan said. "Freaking Joe. He's got his dream ranch."

And from the prospect of the hill above the house, the team and wagon moving down the Wyoming section road were as pretty and as lyric as a photograph in *National Geographic*. The metallic ringing of the harness was carried back by the wind, the wagon wheels curled up some dust, the children and aunts sitting on the hay were laughing and enjoying themselves as the prairie went by. The big sky was full of gorgeous low cumulus, and where the land was not a black mosaic of shadows from the clouds, it was golden bright from the sun. Joe would take them all the way down past the Van Valins and right up to the edge of the Polecat Bench. Eventually, the team and wagon grew smaller, and then disappeared over the rise. It was a lovely scene, really, just a good Wyoming family and the visiting relatives out for a Sunday drive behind a well-matched team of cream Belgians.

Back in front of the toolshed, the men were glad that Joe was off with his team for another reason. They had all viewed Shane as a hero, and considered him the star of the Childers clan. They were still having difficulty coping with his death, but they were trying to restrain themselves in front of Joe and Judy. Now at least they could talk and some of them were close to tears.

"The last time I saw Shane was in August, and it was pouring rain in Salt Rock," Richard Childers said. "Shane was out on one of his fifteen-mile runs over the hollows to visit all the relatives. He didn't have a shirt on, just shorts and running shoes, and he was real excited about getting back to Pendleton after his leave and training his platoon. It's just hard, hard, accepting the loss of a person like that."

Now that Joe wasn't near, Robert Reagan could let down his guard, too. Every time he thought of Shane, focused on him with a specific memory, his heart would suddenly race and he felt profoundly sad and anxious. He was having "panic attacks for Shane," he said. He knew that Richard Childers and some of the other men around the toolshed were Missionary Baptists, but he didn't let that affect his choice of words.

"Yeah, well, my ass isn't very happy about this either," Reagan said. "The last time *I* saw Shane was in London, and he was diddly-boppin' down that street with a ninety-pound knapsack, headed for the Alps. I told him where to go to find new hiking boots. Jesus, I'm just so sad over this. It's a sonofabitchin' deal. Shane Childers, dead. I still can't believe it."

An hour later, when Joe returned in the hay wagon, Robert, Sam, and Bill Hendry helped him off-load the grandchildren and all the Childers aunts. Then they hopped on board and jingled through the barnyard, opened the gate by the field, and went out with Joe to use the hay to feed the cattle. It was chilly by the time they got back to the barn, almost nightfall, and steam rose off the backs of the team while Joe removed and stowed away the harness, fed his horses and mules, and then tidied up the stable while chatting with Robert and Sam.

That night, Judy finished sewing the hems on Joe's new chief petty officer's pants. Before he had taken the grandchildren out on the hay-ride that afternoon, Judy had stood Joe in the dining room with his old Seabee uniform on, fitting the legs of the trousers with straight pins taken from a glass dish beside her on the floor. Before he went to bed that night, Joe tried them on, pronouncing them "just right," with the proper amount of break. He had new shoes as well, and along with the belt also provided by the Billings marines, he was all set for the funeral Tuesday.

By the end of the weekend, the Childerses had also discovered new information about Shane's death which was upsetting, but helped them accept his loss because now they finally *knew*. Judy and Captain Hutchison had been looking at articles about Shane on the Internet to make sure that the memorial albums they were compiling weren't missing any important clips. Jonna Walker was checking newspaper websites because she thought they might contain an account of Shane's last moments that might help her to understand.

More or less simultaneously—afterward, they all couldn't figure out who made the discovery first—they came across an account of Alpha

Company's encounter with the ragtag Iraqi army units defending Pumping Station Number 2 in Rumaila, written by Gordon Dillow, a reporter with the *Orange County Register* of southern California, who was embedded with Shane's unit. Dillow's articles appeared in the *Register* the weekend after Shane was killed and described a haphazard and essentially pointless firefight that occurred after the pumping station had been taken. These reports confirmed that Shane had lost consciousness and died within a few minutes after being shot on the desert floor, and not after a prolonged death agony at a field hospital in Kuwait, as the first incomplete accounts seemed to indicate. This was something that the family had been worried about, and now they could move on to a funeral at least partially resolved about how Shane died.

They went to bed that night a family preparing to attend their son's wake the next day. The house was quiet and restful now, with the rooms slowly emptying of guests and the grandchildren finally asleep. From the road toward Powell, the Childers place looked lonely, but distinct, on the prairie. Late on Sunday the sky was clear and awesomely black, with just a few clusters of stars. A thin purple line marked the ridge along the Polecat Bench. And, from the way the lights rigged from the house glowed around the half-mast flag, there was a sense that the family's sacrifice could be seen for miles and miles across the Bighorn country.

The reflective, intensely bookish and cultured marine officer who graduated from The Citadel in June 2001–the Shane everyone felt was about to turn a major corner in his life–never really had a chance to emerge. While Shane was at Quantico attending basic officer's and then infantry officer's training, the aftermath of the terrorist attacks on New York and Washington on September 11, 2001, was transforming both the world and the U.S. Marines, making it difficult for anyone in the military to pursue much of a personal agenda. By the time he reached Camp Pendleton in southern California in the late spring of 2002 and took over the leadership of his platoon in Alpha Company, events were already hurtling toward an American invasion of Iraq and Shane was swept up by the frantic preparations for war.

Settling into an apartment in suburban San Clemente that soon filled with his usual athletic accoutrements—surfboards, a kayak, his mountain bike, and mountain-climbing gear—Shane was soon so busy training his platoon that he virtually dispensed with all pretense of a personal life, or at least one that he shared much with others. His reading was now mostly devoted to tactics manuals and the technical specifications for the equipment operated by his unit. The long, meandering late-night phone calls were often spent with the sergeants of his company, discussing training for the next day.

Preparations for the war in Iraq brought out his lonely, brooding side. The effortless sociability of Shane's Nairobi or Charleston years was now a thing of the past, something he didn't have time for anymore. On Sundays, to escape the grinding regimen of marine training, Shane appeased his need for adventuresome physicality by surfing alone, or occasionally hiking in the San Bernardino National Forest. He seemed his old self again only when he could completely escape the performance-mentality of the marine camps and get away for long spells with friends—occasional vacation skiing trips and journeys home to Joe and Judy in Wyoming.

The pack trip on mules up to the snow line along the Jack Creek Trail that Shane and Joe made in May 2002, just after Shane finished infantry officer's school at Quantico, was deeply symbolic for this reason. Shane was on his way to Pendleton to accept command of his platoon, every young marine officer's dream. But he wasn't quite in the frantic marine-mode training environment yet. He was relaxed and fun, calmed by the long pickup drive across the country to the Powell ranch. When they got up to the snow line with the mules, he sat up late with Joe in the campsite, laughing and talking. That night, Shane told his father about the dreams he had for himself after the war in Iraq was over. He was planning on a big adventure. He wanted to use his savings to buy a sailboat and go on an around-the-world cruise. He was also beginning to think about buying a ranch like his father's, right here in Wyoming. All through that pack trip, Shane exclaimed about the beauty of the scenery, and how much he liked the timber spruce up above the Greybull River.

Jack Creek was the last time Joe saw his son that way—the comfortable outdoorsman and horseman he remembered—Shane undistracted by preparing for war. Shane's visits from Pendleton after that were often rushed, made by airline connections into Cody, and it always took him several days to decompress from the training intensity of a marine camp before he was himself again. Then it was almost time for him to return to Pendleton.

The looming war in Iraq, and the events of September 11, altered Shane's outlook in another important way. His most compelling personality feature was his bristling, restless intellectuality. Shane had always been somewhat conservative, pro-military and pro-Republican, but his rejection of evangelical Christianity and right-wing intolerance and gay-bashing also demonstrated a flexibility, an openness toward others that reflected the broad intelligence of a humanist. He was still very much that way, when he had a few moments away from Pendleton to reflect. But now he'd also become a fervent defender of the Bush doctrine of preemptive strikes against perceived enemies like Saddam Hussein, a crusader who believed in the American mission to rid the world of Islamic terrorists. Everyone around Shane now knew that it was pointless to argue with him about American policy or the coming war. He was more than his old insistent self when it came to discussing these matters. He was dogmatic.

In a very real sense, September 11 had brought out a side of Shane that had always been there. The boy along the Little Biloxi River who defended his playmates by killing copperhead snakes, The Citadel cadet who defended gays, now had a new group of people to defend. They were the innocent American civilians threatened by Arab terrorists and the rogue nations alleged to be harboring weapons of mass destruction.

At Pendleton, and later at the Twentynine Palms training area on the edge of the Mojave Desert, Shane was as compulsive as ever and quickly gained a reputation as an officer who asked a lot from his men by his intense example. "He was the kind of officer who didn't have to give many orders," said Captain Matt Ward, an aviation weapon systems officer who knew Shane at Pendleton. "You took one look at him and just followed." With eleven years service as an active-duty marine, five of them as an infantry grunt, Shane was considered an exceptionally valuable officer because he knew and understood the enlisted men who would do most of the fighting during a war. His platoon soon emerged as a front-line unit, one that would probably be positioned to be among the first over the line into Iraq. Under Lieutenant Shane Childers, the Second Platoon of Alpha Company consistently scored high performance grades in training and earned their place at the front.

"During his visits home, Shane wouldn't say much about what his group was specifically training for," Joe Childers said, "but we were all aware from what Shane said that last summer and fall that his unit was training real well and getting all these great performance marks. It just seemed to be expected that he would be right up front."

Shane was focused on high performance for another reason. He told many friends that he lived in fear of being assigned a position as a support or supply officer, and he hadn't worked hard getting through The Citadel and becoming an officer to accept a position like that. "This is not well known, but it's actually pretty rare to get a chance to lead men in battle," said Lieutenant Kerry Quinby, a naval aviator who met Shane at the Basic School at Quantico. "Only about eight out of twenty-four officer positions in the marines are actual combat slots, and Shane wasn't the sort of person who wanted to sit out a war helping with planning or delivering ammunition."

Shane's Alpha Company group at Camp Pendleton in California, even though it would spend the fall of 2002 preparing for desert warfare in Iraq, was called in marine parlance a "boat unit." These forces traveled in twenty-eight-ton amphibious assault vehicles (AAVs), also called "tracks," which carried about twenty marines apiece in a cramped passenger compartment in the rear. Boat units were trained for making mechanized sprints across beaches or short patches of land after being delivered to their destination by ships. They are considered elite units because they are frequently used to make the first assault against primary objectives in a war, and thus face the toughest resistance from well-defended enemy positions. For Iraq, however, these amphibious units had to make drastic adjustments for the conditions they would face—preparing for both a long, marathon run across almost five hundred miles of desert to Baghdad, and urban warfare. It was tough, grueling work, particularly when twenty or more marines had to be jammed into the rear passenger compartment of the AAVs for long practice runs across the Mojave Desert. The vehicles had been designed for short runs and then quick exits as the marines reached their objectives, but now Alpha Company members were riding inside them and making long crossings for a whole day.

When he was training with his unit at Twentynine Palms, Shane often spent weekend nights with Steve and Robbin Whitten, his old marine friends from Nairobi, who had settled with their daughters nearby. After the Whittens picked him up at the marine base, Shane usually came in dog-tired from his training and either took a nap right away or quickly fell asleep after a barbecue. But he also liked sitting up late with Steve, drinking Moosehead beer and probing the retired master sergeant for ideas on how he could improve his platoon. It was clear to Whitten that the intensive training at Pendleton and Twentynine Palms was bringing out Shane's perfectionist nature.

"We had a good time together, but it was very classic Shane, too," said Whitten. "He was just so devoted and focused on the mission. Hey, Steve, how can I fix this problem with a staff sergeant I have? How can I make these improvements to the platoon? He was aware that his commanders rated his platoon highly, but still he could make it even better."

Still, Shane's seeming invincibility, his careful judgment about things, reassured everyone that he would be all right in Iraq. The last time the Whittens saw him in Twentynine Palms, in November 2002, Steve and one of his daughters drove Shane back to the base on Sunday night. They sat in the front seat of their car watching as he trudged across the base with his light pack, and then Shane paused, turned, and faced them.

"He was smiling and looking back at us with that confidence he had," Whitten said. "His face seemed to be saying, 'It will be okay. It will be okay.' We just weren't worried about it. Shane would be all right."

In early February 2003, just before Shane deployed for Kuwait with his platoon, the possibility that Saddam Hussein would use chemical or biological weapons against American troops was receiving a lot of attention in the press. Jonna Walker was worried about this and e-mailed Shane. He responded in his usual way—very methodically. Via return e-mail, he shared with Jonna a Power Point presentation on defensive measures against chemical warfare and reassured her that the threat she was reading about in the news magazines was vastly overrated.

"Shane's basic position was that I shouldn't worry because chemical or biological weapons were too complicated and sensitive to use," Jonna said. "He didn't give the Iraqis credit for having enough sophistication to use them."

Shane's unit arrived in Kuwait during the first week of February and camped for the first two weeks in a rear area in the desert about forty miles south of the border with Iraq. Conditions slightly improved by the end of the month when tents with raised wooden floors and portable latrines were installed, but Shane's letters home to Joe and Judy made it clear that the conditions were grim. The men had no air-conditioning, phones, or Internet access, and the portable shower units were so crowded that Shane rose at 2 A.M. to use one, just one day a week. The marines were mostly subsisting on prepackaged Meals Ready to Eat. The tension and boredom in camp about when the troops were finally going to move north into Iraq were relieved by desert warfare training exercises. At one point Shane's unit was marching with heavy packs and keeping in shape just three miles from the Iraqi border.

On the night of March 17, Shane's unit was finally ordered to stage up by the Iraqi border, and he and other company officers were briefed on their assignment. Alpha Company was to take and then secure an important first objective of the war, the huge oil field facility and pumping station at Rumaila, about eighteen miles north of the border with Kuwait. Securing the complex of industrial buildings and pipelines at Rumaila with a lightning strike was considered vital, because American military planners feared that the Hussein regime would order the oil fields torched and destroyed by retreating Iraqi soldiers, which would impede rebuilding the country once the military battles were over. Intelligence reports indicated that at least one thousand Iraqi soldiers were guarding the facility, most of them holed up in well-defended concrete bunkers.

Alpha Company stormed over the border and headed north over the Iraqi sands in their AAVs just before midnight on March 20. As they approached the massive pumping station at 3 A.M., a barrage by marine artillery units in front of them had just begun. After the artillery fire ceased, Shane and his unit moved closer in their AAVs, with Shane surveying the horizon from a stand-up conning station in the track. The sky was now filled with smoke from the fires set off by the exploding artillery and trench fires around the perimeter that the Iraqis had set. When he was ordered over his radio headset to take the facility, Shane instructed his men to exit the AAVs and to begin surrounding the outlying buildings for attack.

The "attack" on the pumping station at Rumaila, however, proved anticlimactic. In fact, long before the artillery barrage had begun, most of the Iraqi Army units had fled, many of them prompted by propaganda leaflets dropped the night before urging them to surrender. As the marines of Shane's company began coursing through the buildings and mazes of pipes, they found a few Iraqi soldiers injured by the artillery fire, many more voluntarily emerging from their bunkers with white flags, others hurriedly attempting to escape across the desert with civilian robes thrown over their uniforms. The operation, in fact, was a complete rout of the Iraqis, abetted by the notoriously bad supply train of Saddam Hussein's army, which had failed to motivate the defenders by providing adequate food, water, or arms.

But Shane was pleased, and too intelligent an officer to be disappointed by the lack of active fighting. His orders had specifically requested that the pumping station at Rumaila be secured *before* the Iraqis could torch it or sabotage it by destroying equipment. That was the priority, his objective—securing the oil field intact and in running order for the future of the Iraqi people. It didn't matter that the Iraqis had fled, and were probably too inept and frightened to have even considered sabotaging their oil field. Shane Childers and his unit had taken the first objective of the desert campaign, according to orders, with only one injury on their side, a corporal who stepped on a land mine while searching a building. The operation was clearly a success, and perhaps even boded well for the rest of the war.

As the first dawn light reached the murky sky around the oil field complex, there was a feeling of elation and purposeful work. Along with other marine officers now on the scene, Shane ordered his men to dig in around the perimeters in case of a counterattack, which was not really expected. The rounding up and processing of prisoners began, and medical corpsmen were brought forward to attend to the Iraqi wounded and the injured marine corporal.

One event that occurred just after dawn pointed up either a weakness in reconnaissance information or just a failure of the marines to appreciate, this early in the war, a peculiar habit of the Iraqis. The concrete bunkers surrounding the Rumaila works were large enough to drive trucks and cars into, and the Iraqis had positioned vehicles inside for quick escapes. Just after dawn an Iraqi soldier burst out of a bunker on a motorcycle, trying to flee across the desert, and was quickly cut down by marine M-16 rifle fire. But the incident seemed a fluke, unimportant, and as the building searches and the herding up of prisoners continued, no one thought much about the hazards of other Iraqis trying to escape that way.

A couple of hours after dawn, after the complex appeared to be fully secured, Shane ordered his men back to the cluster of AAVs along the perimeter of the oil field. He was planning on debriefing the operation with his marines, breaking for a hasty breakfast of Meals Ready to Eat, and then await further instructions from his battalion commanders. As Shane walked along the perimeter road toward his men, a Toyota pickup raced around the corner of a bunker and accelerated down the road toward his position. Shane crouched onto his knees and peered intently at the approaching truck, switched off the safety on his M-16, being deliberately careful not to overreact. He was just raising his rifle to fire when the pickup reached a few feet from his position on the road.

The pickup was filled with six or seven Iraqis who somehow had eluded the search operation at the complex. As they fled down the road toward Shane's position, they opened up with a "spray and pray" burst of automatic rifle fire, in an attempt to clear the area of Shane and other marines in order to flee across the desert to avoid capture.

Marine Corporal Jesse Odom, who was standing near Shane on the road, saw the ground break into dust storms around him, and orange muzzle fire from the guns in the pickup, as the fleeing Iraqis sped past.

There was more confusion in the area as the marines from back by the AAVs opened up on the truck, finally stopping it a hundred yards down the road. Under the murky skies, with fires burning all around, a few marines ran down the road to surround the pickup and capture the surviving Iraqis on the truck.

In the chaos all around now, no one sensed right away that Shane was hit. He had been kneeling anyway, squinting ahead to the truck on the road, and now he was still kneeling, holding his rifle in his hands, with his Kevlar helmet plunked onto the sandy roadway. He didn't yell out. No one could see a wound. But then he just fell sideways, pivoting on his knees and helmet, into a fetal position by the road.

When Corporal Odom rushed over, Shane had a vacant expression on his face and was staring into the sky. He groaned and tried to say something.

"I'm hit. In the gut."

Shane died rather quickly after that, falling in and out of consciousness a few times and occasionally muttering, "Can't believe I got shot." Before medics could reach him, he stopped breathing once, and Odom revived him with mouth-to-mouth resuscitation. When the medics arrived and stripped off his clothes, they found a small, bloodless entry wound in Shane's abdomen just below the bottom of his body armor. But the AK-47 bullet severed a major artery and caused massive internal bleeding, hit his kidney and other organs before exiting through the back. With his blood pressure plummeting, Shane was moved over to a grove of palm trees and placed on the metal ramp of an AAV. The medics gave him a shot of morphine and delivered fluids through an intravenous line attached to his arm.

But it was no use. Shane's internal bleeding was too massive. He died beneath the palm trees while Corporal Odom gently stroked his face.

The medevac helicopter called in for the marine who had stepped on the land mine carried Shane away. On his third trip to the Middle Eastern sands—four if you count Iran as a boy—Shane was dead at thirty. He had always tried to be first in everything, and now he was the first killed in action in Iraq. Perhaps his fearlessness and his unique fighting style, his caution in a crisis—the boy who never raised his fists against bullies—was fatal, and he should have squeezed off a few early shots against the Toyota. But perhaps it wouldn't have made a difference.

But he was dead now, and speculation was pointless.

Dust was swirling near the edge of the Rumaila oil field now, the helicopter was rising into a sooty sky, and Shane had begun his journey home to Powell.

All weekend, up at the armory in suburban Billings, First Sergeant Barry Morgan had been drilling his men. Morgan is a former boot camp drill sergeant and loves the work, but he was also under pressure because he knew that the arrival and departure of Shane's flag-draped coffin from three locations—the funeral home, the gym at Northwest College, and the cemetery—had to be pulled off flawlessly. The governor of Wyoming, the media, Marine Public Affairs officers from Quantico and probably more than a thousand spectators would be there. Veterans groups, who would be attending in great numbers, are notoriously picky about the ceremonial drilling at military funerals. As they age, the VFW members and Legionnaires become more sentimental, the marching matters a lot to them, and they consider it an important part of the show. But mostly, Morgan just wanted to make sure that the funeral and graveside service were done right for the Childerses.

Among marines, drilling and marching is a passion, and there is a simple truth about it. Performing properly, a formation of dress-blue marines is supposed to look effortlessly graceful, even simple in their movements, but it's actually an enormously complex business to organize. From his small command in Billings, Morgan had to recruit and make travel arrangements for reservists from all over Wyoming and Montana, most of whom would have to travel hundreds of miles in just one direction and give up three days of their regular jobs to practice and perform at the Childers funeral. Authorization forms for paying day rates for extra color guard members had to be filled out and then routed through the proper marine channels. More than a dozen reservists and active-duty marines had to be whipped into shape by the end of Monday and coordinated into thinking alike, marching step-to-step, with perfect shoulder-to-shoulder confirmation. From the outside, it's supposed to look easy. But it's hard to do.

And nothing was being spared for the Childers ceremonies. There were four separate teams—the rifle detail that would fire the twenty-one-gun salute, the coffin pallbearers, a color guard bearing the Marine Corps and United States flag, and then Morgan and Hutchison as joint heads of detail, who would fold the flag draped over Shane's coffin and then hand it to Judy. In addition to all this, Morgan had to find a bugler to play taps and make sure he could get each note perfect.

The various teams were practicing separately and then together all day Sunday and Monday, marching in the parking lot and the indoor motor-pool area of the armory. The pallbearers had a particularly difficult job because they had to look coordinated and graceful while carrying a great deal of weight. Morgan rehearsed them back and forth across the armory floor using a six-foot embarkation crate loaded with two hundred pounds of weights. None of the drilling marines complained about the long days of rehearsing, with just an hour break for lunch. For once, they didn't mind their drill sergeant's perfectionism. It was unspoken but agreed among all of them. The Childers funeral *had* to be perfect.

But Morgan took particular pride in the drilling for the Childers ceremony for another reason. While his California surfer-boy captain was obsessing on all the other details of the CACO, and sensitively negotiating so many emotions, this was the first sergeant's purview, his role to play as noncom and second in command. Morgan's habitual irreverence doesn't simply project the typical cynicism of the enlisted man, a kind of blue-collar flippancy, toward the officer corps. In fact, his attitudes, particularly about drilling, are what make him such a marine's marine.

"Drilling is built into the Marine Corps philosophy, but it's basically an enlisted man's specialty," Morgan said. "Kevin Hutchison doesn't know shit about drilling. He's an officer. What the frig would *he* know about drilling? It's a real job, you know? In twenty-one years in the United States Marine Corps, I've never met an officer who can tell me shit about drilling. So Kevin left me alone to prepare the teams for the Childers funeral. He knew that I would do it right."

That was their drill for the weekend, their CACO division of labor. While Hutchison negotiated the emotional shoals down in Powell, Morgan was drilling his men up in Billings.

On Sunday night, when Morgan was ready to release his teams after a full day of practice, the pallbearers asked if they could work for another hour, slowly marching back and forth across the motor-pool floor with their substitute coffin. They felt that they still weren't getting the complicated turns just right, and they preferred starting their second day of practice with things nearly perfect. Morgan agreed and they worked until after dark.

They were all tired when it was finally time to go. Outside the armory on the asphalt ramp, the sky was black against the distant mountains, with just the lights of a nearby oil refinery and the hum of the interstate intruding on the peace of the night. But the honor guard teams still had work to do. Most of the men were returning to their homes or motel rooms to spit-polish their shoes, shine their brass buckles, and meticulously place their medal racks on their tunics.

It was an unspoken agenda between them all. The Childers funeral *had* to be perfect, right down to the last shiny button on their chests.

SHANE'S LAST SKY

Captain Hutchison arrived at the funeral home at 11 A.M. on Monday, an hour before the wake was scheduled to begin. There were many last-minute details requiring attention. The green fourragère for Shane's uniform had arrived via FedEx and had to be properly placed on the body. With Laura Richardson's help, he opened the casket and did that, and then he inspected Shane's face for skin tone, agreeing with Laura that the new rouge and cosmetics helped, but only a little. Cases of mineral water had been delivered to the funeral home and Hutchison made sure that the chilled bottles and plastic cups were strategically placed around the viewing chapel and reception area. Boxes of tissues were also distributed around both rooms. Hutchison carefully inspected the arrangements of donated flowers up by the casket and the floral displays around the funeral home.

Two public affairs officers from Marine Corps headquarters in Quantico had arrived in Wyoming the night before and were now at the funeral home. Pensively biting his lip while he cupped his hand on his chin, Hutchison discussed with them the possibility of newspaper or television reporters arriving and attempting to conduct interviews during the wake. They agreed that it would be best for the P.A. officers to stand near the front door of the funeral home and discreetly intervene if that happened. They didn't want to discourage the press or make a scene–interviews with members of Shane's family, or visiting marines who had known him, could always be conducted outside on the porch, or in the parking lot. But they didn't want press-shy members of the Childers family, or the hundreds of local residents and veterans who were expected to pay their respects today, to feel intimidated when they came through the door.

To Hutchison, this fastidious stewardship of the Childers CACO seemed natural, just a marine "taking care of his own." Perhaps he was merely displaying in a public role the tasteful attention to detail that also marked his private life–the beige-tone walls of his thoughtfully decorated house, the neat shelves of books, the love of people expressed by curiosity about their lives. But everyone noticed and, by now, the performance of the marine supervising the burial detail seemed as remarkable as the life of the one who had become the first killed in Iraq. Semper Fidelis. Hutchison took this motto so seriously.

"There was no question in my mind that throughout this Childers funeral we would make sure the family knew we would do anything for them, that we would be there for them," Laura Richardson said later. "But it was Kevin Hutchison's dedication that stood out. He was so sensitive and hard working. I walked away from the experience really impressed with the United States Marines."

At noon, a convoy of passenger vans dispatched by the funeral home pulled up to the Childers place, their tires pinging on the fresh gravel. The immediate family and the West Virginia relatives filed out of the house or from their cars parked up on the hill, and they all made the ten-minute ride into Powell together. They were somber but calm in the vans. The decision to have an open casket had not been shared with everyone, so they didn't know what to expect.

When Joe and Judy arrived at the funeral home, Hutchison was pleased that he had prepared Judy for how Shane looked. Biting his lip again and trying to remain composed, he waited with the Childerses in the vestibule of the funeral home for a few moments.

The tension was palpable. Through the wide double doors of the viewing chapel, everyone could see the open casket up front, with Shane's dress blue tunic and medals shining under the overhead lights. Shane was there, right there now, after the long wait for him to return home. The crowd of family members behind Joe and Judy were anxious for them to go in alone to be with their son. They all wanted to break this terrible, expectant feeling of being able to see Shane, and then to be able to approach the casket themselves.

Finally, Hutchison escorted Joe and Judy inside the viewing chapel and then up to the casket. Joe and Judy were very quiet for a moment or two, with Judy looking stunned as she stared down at Shane, and then they both began to cry and to hold each other. They were trying to make the best of this last, uncomfortable sight of their son and stood there crying and holding each other for a couple of more minutes, reluctant to leave. But then Joe lifted his head briskly and decisively, almost as if he'd been signaled to break away, and stepped back with Judy.

When they returned to the main reception area, Judy sat on the couch, and Joe knelt on the floor in front of her, burying his face in her lap and crying uncontrollably. A few times he tried to stop crying, but he couldn't. He was laboring manfully to be good for Judy, to comfort her too, but it was just hard, unbearably hard finally seeing Shane, encountering all at once the love that he had for this standout son. Finally he just gave in to the grief. Even after he stopped crying, Joe remained on his knees in front of Judy, just talking to her, explaining how he felt and sharing her thoughts, too.

After they had calmed down a little, Judy was grateful for the way that Hutchison had prepared her to see Shane. She was ready for the worst, and that's pretty much what she saw.

"Kevin Hutchison was right," Judy said while still in the reception area of the funeral home. "That wasn't really my son in there, and he did look very dehydrated. But I think that this was the right thing to do for everyone."

For the next forty-five minutes, while the rest of the extended Childers family stepped forward to see Shane, Joe and Judy spoke quietly with their relatives in the reception area, thanked the marines who had traveled to Wyoming from Quantico, and greeted a few people from town who had arrived in the early afternoon to pay their respects. And there were small things to notice, too, just briefly looking through the doorway separating the viewing chapel and the reception area. When Richard Brown approached the casket, for example, he stood at attention and saluted his brother-in-law Shane, as he had always promised he would the next time he saw him. He'd come all the way up from Texas, delayed his embarkation for Kuwait, just to do that.

Jessi and Jonna Walker had gone through a personal hell all week, ever since they learned of Shane's death. Judy had called West Virginia shortly after 10 P.M. the Friday night they were informed of Shane's death while they were still in Texas. She had asked Shane's aunt, Mary Bias, to call all the Childerses in Salt Rock. But Jessi and Jonna's mother had not told them until the next morning. Jessi was particularly upset because she had been awakened the night before with an unusual dream about someone being killed in a bathtub, and had then turned on CNN to watch some news to lull herself back to sleep. The crawlers at the bottom of the television screen reported that two marines had already been killed in Iraq, but she comforted herself with the thought that statistically the chances of one of them being Shane was very low. When her mother called her house in Columbus, Ohio, early Saturday morning and said, "Jess, it's Shane," she immediately considered that dream a premonition. She spent the rest of the morning writhing on the floor of her bedroom, devastated, crying and screaming, unable to be comforted by her husband and son.

Jonna had learned about Shane's death directly from her mother, who drove over to her farmhouse in southern Ohio on Saturday morning, shortly after she had talked to Jessi.

"Jonna, it's Shane," her mother said. "Judy called Mary and told her to inform the family that Shane was the first soldier killed in Iraq. But I think it's a mistake. It *has* to be a mistake. Shane wouldn't get killed."

Jonna didn't want to believe it either, but her first reaction was to take out the American flag that she kept in her hall closet for patriotic holidays, and then place it in its holder on the front porch. Then she and her mother drove over to Wilton Childers' farm along Smith Creek Hollow in Salt Rock, where they knew the family would be gathering. They stopped at a Kroger's supermarket on the way to purchase fried chicken and soda, and by the time they got to Salt Rock the Childers farm was filling up with relatives, and the media was calling for interviews, which appeared to confirm the news. But news is funny that way, Jonna learned. She still didn't believe it until she heard Shane's name on a National Public Radio broadcast that afternoon. By then her grandfather's farmhouse in Salt Rock was swirling with relatives, stunned by the loss of the star of the family, and Jonna had tired of trying to comfort her grandparents, or discovering things to say to her uncles and aunts. Her relationship to Shane had always felt individual, just between them, even beyond what she and Jessi and Shane had all together. And it was certainly beyond the niceties shared with the West Virginia relatives. She just needed some time alone to cope with that.

So, walking out through the backyard, Jonna climbed the cobble behind her grandfather's house, with its carpet of wet, velveteen moss slippery underfoot with spring runoff. Then she reached the beech grove halfway up the slope and started to cry. She sat on a log and leaned against the base of the older-growth beech, the Shane Tree, with its marker of him above her head. SHANE CHILDERS 8/8/86. Jesus, Shane. How could this happen? This was the place where we were together as teenagers. I remember the day you carved your name. And your Citadel years. God, we did so much growing together then. You helped Jess and me so much. Oh God, Shane. Everyone down at the farmhouse is so upset. Shane, couldn't you just think about maybe coming back? You could come back, Shane. You could always do everything.

It was more bitterly lonely than she thought she could endure, sitting on a wet log on a cold March day in a West Virginia forest, crying for what seemed like forever without anyone to comfort her there. Oh, and, Shane, this is the worst part. When I've got a problem like this? I would call *you*. Jesus, Shane, couldn't you just think about maybe coming back? They're so upset down below.

It was all just one big memory blur after that. Jessi came down from Columbus just to be with them. Meeting up with the family at the airport in Charleston, West Virginia, changing planes in Denver, getting into Billings and finding the rental car. God, all these mountains and badlands to drive over, and the wind blows so hard here in Wyoming. They all smiled at each other when they finally found the Childers ranch. *Oh my God, this is so Joe. Shane wasn't exaggerating.* There were piles of farm machinery everywhere, swayback mules in the pasture, and in front the house men with cowboy hats were talking with each other.

At the funeral home, Jessi and Jonna crossed the reception area to enter the viewing chapel through the double doors on the east side of the building. They looked lovely together in their dark dresses, models for a Normal Rockwell portrait of two classically pretty and close West Virginia sisters, and they hesitated in the open doorway when they saw the open casket. Neither of them had expected that, they didn't want to see Shane the way he looked now, but they also knew they probably wouldn't accept his death without stepping forward. Jonna rested her arm on Jessi's and slightly dipped her head to her sister. *C'mon, Jess. We gotta do it.*

At the casket, Jessi rested her cheek on Jonna's shoulder and they held each other arm in arm. They were quiet for a while, whispering things to each other about Shane, and how he looked. Jessi reached out and touched Shane's hand, which felt hard. Oh, and those dress blues, God, the dress blues. The only other time I saw him in those was at The Citadel Marine Ball, in the spring of 2000. Doing it up right in Charleston with all those fun marines. Shane had been *so* alive that night.

Then Jonna couldn't hold it in any longer and she started crying loudly, almost wailing, which set Jessi off. They were two lovely and expressive sisters together, crying arm-in-arm, a part of each other really, actually Jessi and Jonna and Shane all together again, riding over the mountains in the pickup truck, doing Fort Sumter and Tommy Condon's Irish Pub, listening all day to one of his ridiculous book reports. *No, Shane, I don't need any more of your advice on this, I've had enough personal growth for one day.* Oh, and what are we going to do now without crazy, madcap, exhausting, brainy, marine-mode, considerate, annoying, argumentative, vulnerable, and strong cousin Shane?

And it was difficult, too, walking back through the viewing chapel, still arm-in-arm and crying, and exiting through the double doors, because they knew it was good-bye forever now, Shane. Oh, Shane. How in the hell did this happen?

Jonna had another strong reaction when she got out into the reception area and saw Captain Hutchison and the other marines. She so rarely saw men in military uniforms, but now every time she saw another marine, it provoked the same response. Sometimes she just thought it, but sometimes she softly spoke it through her tears. *Oh, why couldn't it have been one of them and not Shane?* She felt guilty about this, and didn't want to share the feeling with anyone else, and then she would see another pair of marines. *Oh, why couldn't it have been one of them and not Shane?* The involuntary response lasted for the rest of her stay in Wyoming for the funeral.

Meanwhile, Jessi was going through her own private torture about Shane, because their friendship had fallen apart after he had been commissioned in the spring of 2001 and then left for Quantico and Camp Pendleton in California. There were a lot of reasons for this. Shane had dreamed that Jessi and her son would move out to California and get their own apartment near San Diego somewhere, so they could all be together and be as close as they had been while he was in Charleston. But Jessi knew that this would never work and, besides, she had reconnected with an old high school friend, Ryan Harper, and eventually decided on getting married. Ryan was on his way toward becoming a successful manufacturing engineer in Ohio, but Shane was worried that he'd pull Jessi back into the orbit of West Virginia. Probably Shane and Jessi would have pulled away from each other eventually anyway, because it was unrealistic to expect that they could forever keep alive a period as intense and fun as Shane's Citadel years. But they did lose contact and drifted away from each other. When she finally got married, Jessi was devastated to receive a cold and impersonal card from Shane, with a check for a hundred dollars. It simply read: "Best Wishes, Love Shane." Their relationship had chilled.

So that's what Jessi felt all through the funeral, a lack of resolution about her relationship with Shane, and the loss of contact with him. But when Jessi and Shane had drifted apart, Shane's relationship with Jonna had strengthened. This was difficult for Jessi and had provoked some sisterly jealousy. Jonna could call up on her computer any number of e-mails that she'd received from Shane in California, especially the ones that he'd sent just before he left for the war. Jessi's old letters from Shane were stuck up in her attic somewhere, not as accessible or recent. So that was difficult. Jessi loved her sister dearly, and they were very sweet and supportive together. But Jonna's relationship with Shane had strengthened as Jessi's had waned. Jessi was reminded of this all through the funeral. The star of the family, with whom she had once been so close, had become a casualty of war. But she had not had an opportunity yet to reestablish their old bonds.

There was another frustration for Jessi on Monday. Joe and Judy had never been very social, except with a few very close friends. They didn't want to remain at the funeral home to greet strangers all day. Once the West Virginia Childerses had viewed Shane, Joe made it clear that they were all expected back at the house for a big dinner and visit.

Jessi knew she had to follow her uncle's wishes on the day of Shane's wake, but she was disappointed. She'd had her meltdown for Shane, up before the casket. Now she was feeling better, relieved, in the mood for meeting everyone who had come to the wake. All these marine and ex-marine friends of Shane were now streaming into the funeral home. She couldn't wait to talk with them, compare notes, and maybe even dish Shane a bit, to see if he had harangued all of them about personal growth, too. That was what she most enjoyed about Shane. You couldn't help loving the guy but boy was he fun to dump on too–his intensity, his aspirations for other people, and his earnestness were so lovably ridiculous that everyone had an even better story to tell about him. Dishing with all the marines would have been fun for Jessi and delivered important closure. But, no. Joe said that she had to return to the ranch.

Reluctantly, Jessi and Jonna left in the vans with the rest of the Childerses. They would have to catch up with the marines tomorrow, after the burial service, when a big lunch was being thrown for the Childerses and all their visitors at the American Legion Hall.

Hutchison felt relaxed and began enjoying himself after Joe and Judy left and, for once, didn't blame himself for having a selfish reaction. He considered it his obligation to remain with Shane's body any-way, and to greet visitors as an official representative of the marines, but it was more than that. He was confident that he had done a good job handling Joe and Judy so far, and he adored them, but it had been a stressful week answering their needs and being there for them emo-tionally. Now he just wanted to enjoy a good wake and get to know the people of Powell a little better, and greet some of the marine bud-dies of Shane who were showing up.

Besides, by now he was very intellectually engaged in figuring Shane out, fascinated by this standout marine. But so far, he'd mostly heard just Joe and Judy's stories. From Jessi and Jonna, before they left for the ranch, he'd heard about Shane's devotion to the personal growth of others, his girlfriend issues, and his manic tourist-guide style when they visited him in Charleston. Shane's marine friends described his frantic studying habits at his officer's and infantry training courses at Quantico. The portrait was beginning to fill in and Hutchison was enjoying himself. Gossip, he thought, even about someone who had just died, was a useful social crutch and filled his need to decipher the many riddles of Shane's personality.

The departure of the bulk of the Childers family generated an-other opportunity for some real breakthrough behavior, the sort of heroic day of personal growth that Shane had always championed in those he knew. When Joe requested that all the Childerses return to the ranch for a meal, his son-in-law Richard Brown stayed behind to greet the people of Powell as a representative of the family. Sam Chil-ders had already made the decision about what *he* would do.

"There was no way that I was ever going to leave Shane at that fu-neral home alone, period," Sam later said. "Yeah, Shane and I had a lot of fights, and I had all these regrets about not being closer to him. But I wasn't going to leave my brother unattended at the funeral home, no matter how many new people I would have to meet."

The rest of that afternoon was a virtuoso performance by Sam. He met everyone who came into the funeral home, he shook hundreds of hands, and seemed effortlessly comfortable making conversation. When word of what was going on back at the funeral home reached the Childers ranch, a couple of the West Virginia Childerses waited until Joe was in the barn and then bolted for Powell just to watch Sam acting as the family greeter. Captain Hutchison, who had picked up immediately on how modest and shy Sam was, couldn't help but notice too. It was another big CACO moment, Hutchison thought, an example of the compressed emotions and change that could come over people during a big military funeral. Richard Brown, who is naturally gregarious and enjoyed his role that day at the funeral home, was also stunned and pleased.

"I don't know what we would have done without Sam on Monday," he said a few days later. "There were too many people to meet and I couldn't possibly have made small talk with all of them."

And the people of Powell, and Wyoming, did come. There was never a long line outside the funeral home, but the reception area and viewing chapel were never empty, either. All the big farmers, equipment suppliers, and realtors of Powell were there, and ranchers from all over the Bighorn country–Worland, Greybull, Basin–showed up in their best Stetsons and pointy-toed boots. There were veterans groups from as far away as Thermopolis and Buffalo and every Cody native who had ever served in the military seemed to be there too. School groups and Boy Scout troops came, just to show their respect. Many of these visitors were deeply moved by the accounts of Shane Childers they had read in the papers, but there was curiosity too. Because he was the first killed in Iraq, and so clearly a stellar marine, Shane had assumed national significance, and that sort of fame doesn't come often in northern Wyoming. Because most of these strangers didn't know Shane personally and weren't experiencing a strong emotional reaction, after a few moments of respectful silence before the casket they could then circulate around the room and visit with old friends.

The funeral home felt almost festive, certainly it had a very conversational air. Shane and his story were the draw, and for most of the afternoon it felt like all of Wyoming was there.

And Sam seemed very good at meeting all these visitors, as effective as Shane might have been working the room. Sometimes Sam stood up by the casket and spoke with people, sometimes he crossed the room because Richard Brown or Captain Hutchison had pointed him out as the brother of the marine. The experience did help him a lot, and he left the funeral home feeling more resolved about Shane.

Back at the ranch, the West Virginia uncles, Robert Reagan, and some of Shane's old marine buddies were gathered in their favorite spot now, the front of the toolshed. They talked, sat on the patio chairs, dished about Shane and his manic ways, frequently replenished by the mugs of coffee, soda, and sandwiches working their way out through the adjoining kitchen. There was a good mackerel sky that night, hazy with high scattered cirrus, pink and blue-gray, out toward Yellowstone and Cody. When the sun went down all they could see were a few ranch lights and the vague outline of Heart Mountain.

Robert Reagan told Sam that Joe was proud of the way he had conducted himself at the funeral home all afternoon. At least that's what Joe had said when he was feeding the horses.

Sam had another thought as the night grew darker and more still.

"I still would give anything, anything, to get Shane back. I just wish he could have seen me today."

On Tuesday morning, the first movement of Shane's flag-draped casket went well. It was a simple transport, just from the back of the funeral home to the waiting hearse in the parking lot, but Captain Hutchison and First Sergeant Morgan were pleased. The pallbearers in their dress blues had moved in unison and with dignity, making their slow, coordinated steps, gently shipping the casket to the hearse bed so that it was perfectly level. It was a good sign for the rest of the day. Hutchison and Morgan wanted to be patient and execute every march perfectly. More than a thousand spectators, Governor Dave Freudenthal, and all the media were waiting for the funeral in the gym at Northwest College. But Hutchison and Morgan were also anxious for it all to be over and to have delivered Shane to his grave without a hitch.

Near the entrance to the Northwest College gym, where the marine pallbearers would carry the casket along a cement walk, a group of about forty Northwest students had begun to gather an hour before the funeral. They were mostly young women, with about fifteen male students, dressed the way college students usually are—hooded sweatshirts or faded Carhartt jackets, hip-hugging jeans, and either Nike shoes or work boots. They were holding to their chests small American flags and hand-painted signs that read SUPPORT OUR TROOPS, or GOOD-BYE SHANE. They were the daughters and sons of ranchers and schoolteachers, mostly from small northern Wyoming towns within easy reach of Powell. They didn't seem to know a whole lot about the war in Iraq, and they weren't particularly political. They didn't know the Childers family. But they'd read about this Shane Childers in their local papers and they liked what they saw. He'd come from a small town in Mississippi not unlike Powell, and then he'd joined the marines and hadn't gone to college right away probably because his family couldn't afford it. He'd done well, traveled, and then the military paid his way through a famous school. They just really liked this guy, especially when they looked at his picture in the paper. And now he had been killed on desert terrain that looked a lot like the sandy prairie around Powell. All they wanted to do now, to show some respect, and make themselves feel better, was to stand outside their college gym and hold up American flags and signs that read GOOD-BYE SHANE.

This was the closest that the Powell Police Department would get all day to a demonstration of any kind, and the situation did not require much enforcement of the law. When the marines carried Shane by, most of the college students wept, some uncontrollably. They hugged each other, held their hair back from wet faces, and stared with looks of grief as the flag-draped casket disappeared through the gym doors. "Good-bye Shane." It just seemed so depressing that a person like this from around here had to get killed all the way over there.

The funeral in the gym was dignified and somber. After the casket and color guard came in, the Childers family was seated to the right of Shane and the marine detail sat to the left. The first song was "Wind Beneath My Wings" and then they played "The Marine's Hymn." A few of the Childers women, and a few in the audience, were weeping, but mostly everyone just seemed to be cried out for now.

Retired navy chaplain Paul Moore, the Childerses old friend from Saucier, Mississippi, officiated and delivered the eulogy. He had known Shane, Reverend Moore said, since he was in the fourth grade and his son Scott and Shane were close friends. When Moore was deployed on ships or to distant naval bases, Joe had taken care of Becky Moore and his family. Moore told all the vintage Shane stories–Shane protecting the boys down on the Little Biloxi, the day the playmates watched as Shane killed the copperhead snake. "Dad," Scott Moore had told his father, "I was never afraid of anything when I was out there with Shane." The boy would grow into a man who naturally emanated courage.

The pallbearers' march out of the gym went well, and the only thing that marred the funeral was an unruly race across the bleachers on the side of the gym by newspaper and magazine photographers, who were anxious to get an overhead shot of the flag and coffin going by. But most of the people in the funeral audience didn't notice, and they sat respectfully until the Childers family had been escorted out by Hutchison and a few members of the marine detail.

The idea for a funeral parade did not originate out of any deliberate plan, and instead was more or less inspired by word of mouth. A number of store owners in Powell either couldn't afford or couldn't find extra help on the day of the funeral, and so they would not be able to attend the services over at Northwest College. Other town residents were aware that the capacity of the college gym was limited, and so they elected to stay away to make room for people who perhaps had a better reason to be there. Powell is known throughout northern Wyoming as a great small town for raising children, and many parents and school groups had passed word through to the police department that they would like a parade. The children needed to deal with this, to confront the fact that a local resident had been killed in the Iraq War, but they would fidget and cause trouble at a funeral but not at an outside parade.

Patriotism, too, was a factor—people wanted to show the flag for a fallen marine. But, really, it just came down to a few simple feelings. Residents of Powell felt terrible for the Childers family, they wanted a public venue for expressing condolence and respect, and as the week passed and they read more about Shane Childers, they just couldn't shake off the idea of a funeral parade.

Laura Richardson had originally been opposed to the idea, because she knew better than anyone how complicated this funeral would be, including the hearse route to the graveyard trailing hundreds of cars. But Hutchison's quiet persistence had prevailed. He felt that the town had been open and welcoming to the marines, that people were anxious and upset about Shane's death, and that a parade would help them recover. So he and Richardson informed the police and a route was devised. The hearse carrying Shane and the vans and cars with the Childers family would make a loop on North Absaroka Street to Highway 14A, and then on the main commercial street through town, North Bent. The word was passed, the Chamber of Commerce decorated with lamppost and storefront ribbons, and the Ace Hardware store and the Big "R" placed overnight orders for American flags.

Hutchison led the parade in the passenger seat of the hearse, with Laura Richardson driving. It was an interesting and even heartfelt experience for him. The presence of Shane right behind him, and the flag draped over his casket, was vaguely comforting, and he and Laura had their first real chance to get to know each other.

Hutchison's reassuring manner and natural curiosity about people helped draw her out, and her story was interesting. After she was divorced and moved back to Wyoming, she was aware that many people doubted her ability to successfully manage a funeral home. Northern Wyoming is conservative, with many evangelical and Mormon churches, with a mild but distinct prejudice against single working mothers. A single working mother trying to make it as a funeral director generated considerable, if unspoken, skepticism. But Richardson had done well, and now the Childers funeral, one of the biggest in Wyoming in years, was going off flawlessly. Richardson seemed almost emotional about it, as if the pressures of the week had produced renewed awareness and pride about what she had achieved.

And there was a pleasant and strong mind-wander in there for Hutchison, southwest over the rivers and the mountains to California and Palos Verdes, at the end of a week of many potent mental associations. When he was fifteen or sixteen, his mother had told him once that he should appreciate and develop his natural ability to get people to talk about themselves. People liked him, his mother said, and they trusted him, and that made them comfortable sharing with him. It was a gift to be cultivated, she thought. He was grateful now that she had said that, because perhaps without the encouragement from his mother, moments like this would not come so easily to him.

When the hearse was finally off and the parade started to move through town, Hutchison, and many of the Childerses in the vans behind him, were amazed at how many people Powell had turned out. There were hundreds of people out on the streets–the whole town, it seemed. People with flags on their porches, people with chairs set up on their lawns, kids in trees with more flags, and many more hand-drawn signs reading SUPPORT OUR TROOPS and GOOD-BYE SHANE.

Hutchison lost it far down on North Absoraka, at a corner with a vacant lot just before the hearse reached Highway 14A. A father and two boys had walked across the lot as the hearse approached. At the sidewalk, the older boy stood respectfully holding an American flag. The father stood in the middle, holding his sons' hands. Then the younger boy, maybe a lad of five or six, clicked the heels of his sneakers together, threw his shoulders tall and his chin out, and briskly saluted Shane going by.

Doubtless this was the little boy's first salute, and one of the last for Shane, and it pushed Hutchison past the threshold of catharsis that he needed. All the pressures of this ten-day CACO, his sadness for Shane and his love for the Childerses, came gloriously pouring out as he wailed in the front seat of the hearse.

And he could feel Shane back there now, with him.

Oh Christ, Childers, what have you gotten me into here? Semper Fidelis, Shane. And you know Shane I don't give a rat's ass for all this manufactured patriotism we're seeing on television right now. You can take all the politicians and the anchormen, too, and throw them out the door without chutes. We're the marines who have to go over there and get shot at and they're the ones who just talk. Manufactured patriotic talk. And I don't care either about how many people might be opposed to this war. It's America. We're supposed to differ. So fuck it and Semp Fi, Shane. It's right here, in Powell, that I'm seeing the pure patriotism, something real, something that I can accept. A little boy just made his first salute to you from a vacant lot. You're back in the Bighorns now, Shane, Semp Fi, and there's Heart Mountain. We're going to bury you now because your work is done, but I wish we could have met sometime and discussed this. But Christ, thanks and Semp Fi. I'm glad I saw this, and the parade has been for you, Shane.

After Hutchison had been crying for a few minutes, Laura

Richardson joined him, and they rode the rest of the parade that way, crying together in the front seat of the hearse.

Shane Childers was buried that afternoon with full military honors at Crown Hill Cemetery in Powell. The graveyard stands on a slight rise east of town with expansive views down the valley to the Bighorn massif on one end and west to Yellowstone and Heart Mountain on the other. After the funeral and the parade, it had taken nearly an hour for everyone to get over to the cemetery, and for the marine guard and veterans groups to form their lines. The ranchers wore their Stetsons and western-cut jackets, the veterans had their blue and red caps with pins, and many of the women had placed quilted ski jackets over their church dresses to protect themselves from the chill Wyoming wind. A large stack of baled hay from the farm next door was piled almost thirty feet high near the edge of the cemetery, so that it felt that Shane was being placed to rest right where he belonged, in cattle country, among fields of barley and winter wheat, around the land where his father had dreamed of moving someday. Of course, being a Childers, he had done it.

Now the chaplain was finishing his prayers above Shane's casket. "Comfort thou your servants that are mourning," Chaplain Moore said. But sometimes these are just words that the ministers say. There wasn't much comfort to go around when it was Shane Childers they were mourning.

Civilians jumped and babies wailed as the marines fired their twenty-one-gun salute. Unseen, from behind the trees of the opposite hill, the bugler sounded taps and all the Childers women wept. Captain Hutchison and his detail folded the flag from the casket, tucked in the dog tags, and handed it to Judy Childers, who stood bravely and wept as she received the flag. Richard Brown was saluting his brother-in-law again, and then he comforted his wife, Sandra, who had her hand to her mouth as she wept for Shane. Joe Childers looked firm and proud in his navy Seabee uniform, bearing now, and bearing well, the grievous loss of an achieving son. As the crowd slowly stepped forward, some to greet the family, some just to linger, the brisk Wyoming wind picked up even more.

At that moment, just then, a large bank of puffy cumulus clouds rolled over the Bighorns, blocking the sun for a few minutes and revealing a soft, blue haze down low near the peaks. The more tender light and shadows seemed to evoke other vistas, even meaning.

Shane Childers would never see the Bighorns again. He'd led a marine's life, cut short at thirty. But perhaps it's a mistake to measure in standard units of time such things as service, intensity, and self-improvement. Valor in battle, or even something as simple as just being there for your friends and the younger cousins, can't be toted up according to the calendar and the clock. In twelve years of hard, dense-packed living since he'd left home, he'd fought in one war, served in Europe and Africa, become the first in his family to be college-educated and then he went over the line into Iraq and he took that objective. He didn't need any more years, years piled upon years so that someday he would be celebrated for having grown old. Meteors, pretty much, come and go fast.

And there was something else in the big sky that afternoon. Mount Kilimanjaro was there, and so were the Alps and Mount Shasta, Mount Mansfield in Vermont, the Appalachian Trail, and maybe even Lake Geneva and Captain Hutchison's distant, dreamy cliffs at Palos Verdes. On a clear day from the prospect at the cemetery, there are views to the snow line at Jack Creek and the road that he biked up to Belfry.

After the services were over and the crowd had dispersed, the Childerses left regretfully but deliberately for town, pleased that there was an excuse to pull themselves away. A roast beef dinner awaited them and all their friends and the marines at the American Legion Hall. But it was hard for a few minutes, leaving Shane. Jessi Walker for one felt that the high plains there were desolate and without trees, so that they were placing Shane in too lonely a place. Like everyone else she vowed to come back and visit.

First Sergeant Morgan, too, suddenly and intensely felt the loneliness of the graveyard, which seemed to be swallowed up by the surrounding Wyoming prairie. He was gratified that his pallbearers, color guard, and rifle-salute team had performed without a mistake. He realized that the discipline of drilling his teams all weekend, and worrying all week about the funeral, had shielded him from an emotional response. But now, as most of his men left for their cars parked along the road to the cemetery, he felt intensely sorry for the Childers family. Crown Hill was a lonely place to leave their son, his fellow marine.

As the cumulus clouds rolled free of the peaks again, a few men, perhaps three dozen in all, remained behind in the cemetery and stood in clusters near the gravesite. There were a few ranchers among them, a few members of the marine honor guard, and a lot of veterans. They talked about the weather and the spring planting, about what they had read in the papers about this soldier, and about how brave and composed the family had looked. They were there simply because they didn't feel like leaving yet. They would stay behind and linger with their marine.

Then there was movement near the gravesite. A backhoe came over to move dirt, the artificial-grass tarp over the topsoil was removed, and the low aluminum barriers around the grave were taken apart and carried away. The men waiting behind knew what to do now. They gathered in one large group behind the grave, removed their Stetsons and military caps, faced Heart Mountain, and saluted. That's the tradition, the direction to face, when a good marine is finally "going west."

The clouds were fully parted now and the snowy bosom of the

Bighorns glowed a soft purple-blue in the haze. A marine was being lowered to his prairie grave. And it did seem at that moment that all of it, the values he stood for, the dreams he had lived, all the peaks he had climbed and the many lives he had touched, was evoked in the mountains and the clouds. For his father and then for the marines he had done all that was asked of him, he was always good to go. More, even, was present in that western landscape that moment in the afternoon– that he represented something big, that he gave back to a generous land. All of that was joined now under Shane's last sky.

EPILOGUE

The Childers Recon

T he summer after Shane Childers was buried, Captain Hutchison drove back down over the Pryors several times, enjoying the rugged landscapes and moody sunsets as he traveled back and forth to see Judy and Joe. He was busy with his marine work that year. Hutchison traveled to Texas for training with his Fourth Reconnaissance Battalion, requalified as an underwater demolition diver at a marine scuba course in Hawaii, and ranged far out through Montana and the Dakotas on long "weekend recon" missions with the reservists who reported to the Billings command. But he felt that it was important to remain in close touch with the Childerses. They had all exchanged something quite moving during the intense, ten-day period in late March when they were preparing for Shane's funeral. Hutchison felt very proprietary toward the Childerses now, and he wanted to demonstrate that he wouldn't abandon them simply because his job was done.

Sometimes Hutchison arrived in Powell just to visit, sometimes he was carrying important paperwork that still had to be completed to close Shane's CACO file. The Childerses were still having trouble with a couple of Shane's bank accounts and loans, and they also had to order a military regulation headstone for his grave. But their relationship was growing more personal now, and was no longer based on the shared work of burying Shane. Often, when Judy introduced him to the visiting wives of the Shoshone Back Country Horsemen, or just friends from town, she told them that "Kevin is our adopted son."

Hutchison didn't consider this odd, and he resisted the temptation of concluding that Judy, out of sadness and confusion over losing her son, was transferring her maternal love to another, similar marine. He felt that what Judy said was true, and he was very comfortable about it. Because of his own upbringing, Hutchison had always believed that the concept of family was as big as his heart could make it, as broad as his natural curiosity about people would allow. The marine code of duty, honor, and service to others had delivered him to the Childerses in a way that made them all family now. Hutchison enjoyed the simplicity of that, but also the irony. The marines had taught him to love.

"My feelings were that the Childerses and I had gone through a lot together, and it was natural for us to think of ourselves as family now," Hutchison said. "I have a wonderful father and mother in California, and a stepfather and stepmother, too. But it's possible to have family in a lot of places according to what you've experienced with people. It had just developed, because of Shane's death, that Joe and Judy were now my Wyoming branch of family."

Hutchison was a good listener, and he was able to nurse the Childerses through the aftereffects of Shane's death and the national attention he had received. By the end of the summer of 2003, the occupation of Iraq was not going very well for either the American military or the civilian reconstruction officials working under the Coalition Provisional Authority. Reporters from all over the country and even Europe had begun calling the Childerses, asking how the parents of the first soldier killed felt about the war in Iraq now. Joe and Judy remained steadfast in their support for Bush administration policies and what they felt Shane stood for, but the interviews kept reopening the wounds they had over his death. Hutchison never explicitly suggested that they stop doing interviews, but by talking the problem out with him they eventually decided to make themselves less available to the press.

In the fall, Judy had begun to complain about another problem. She was experiencing annoying memory lapses about the period just after Shane died, and couldn't recall details about the long wait for his body or the funeral. Hutchison went on-line and read up on this, and was able to reassure Judy that this was a normal outcome of grief. The details would probably return after more time had passed and her mind was more comfortable dealing with the pain she had experienced at the time.

There were other responsibilities that Hutchison enjoyed. Jonna Walker traveled to Wyoming the summer after Shane died to visit with her aunt and uncle, but she was leery about spending all day on a lonely Wyoming ranch while Judy and Joe were at work. By this time Hutchison had become friends with other members of the family that he had met at Shane's funeral and was helping out in other ways. So he met Jonna's flight in Billings, showed her the tourist sights, and then drove her down to Powell and remained for the day himself. At a horse sale, Joe had bought a new two-seat driving wagon, and they all spent the day together in the barn, painting the wheels and the wagon bed.

Hutchison also sensed that Joe missed the companionship of military men. He was doing remarkably well that summer, working at his oilfield job and preparing for a covered-wagon trip with a trail-riding group across the Absaroka Range in southern Montana. There were other signs that life was returning to normal for the Childerses. Judy was bugging Joe to install the new cabinets that had arrived for her kitchen, and Joe was pulling his usual act. He kept promising her that he'd "get to the cabinets soon" but he never did. Meanwhile he had gathered on his workbench all the tools and hardware he needed for the job. But he also missed Shane terribly. Hutchison thought that it would be good for Joe to enjoy some play time with the marines, to indulge in a little goofing off around the ranch with platoon types like Shane. Perhaps this would allow Joe to slowly wean himself off his feelings of loss about his son.

The visits by the men of Fourth Recon were arranged in the usual Hutchison style. Paperwork was filed with command certifying that vital reconnaissance training would be occurring that weekend in the vicinity of the Polecat Bench in northern Wyoming. Then Hutchison and seven or eight of his weekend warriors piled into the government Suburbans or their pickup trucks, and Fourth Recon convoyed south over the mountains. Arriving in Powell, the marines helped Joe move his piles of farm machinery around or remove the rubble left over from his various construction projects. Sometimes they just drank beer out behind the barn, or got smashed in the bars on the way home, but they were good marines and this was their work too. They all enjoyed big lunches and dinners together in the ranch house.

Those junkets down into the Bighorn country to see Joe and Judy–at the Billings command, they were called the "Childers Recon"–were wonderful for Hutchison. He loved the way all the reservists grumbled during the ride down about having to move farm machinery around for Joe Childers, and then as soon as they got there how they all fell under Joe's spell. The reservists were mostly Wyoming and Montana men who liked ranching and cattle and horses, and on each visit there was a marine or two who had not yet enjoyed a Childers Recon. Joe would pull the newcomer aside, escort him into the barn, and commence his standard lecture on MacClellan saddles, walking plows, and the fox-trotter filly. All the other marines laughed about it and then began muscling some farm machinery around.

The weather that fall and spring was beautiful and Hutchison no longer thought of these visits as CACO followup for Joe. It was a vacation for Hutchison too, just being there, surrounded by the Childerses' clutter, listening to Joe's incomparable schemes and dreams. The play value for everyone was exceptionally high. Hutch and his marines loved being down there together, clowning around with Joe, getting a few projects done before they harnessed up the team, then enjoying big meals with the views out the windows to the prairie and the Polecat Bench. That was the agenda now, just being together, doing the Childers experience just right. They were all getting past the immediate trauma of losing Shane.

Iraq beckoned another marine, two of them, actually. Over the winter of 2003–2004, while he continued to run the Billings command and junket around the country on training missions, Hutchison felt anxious about Iraq, disappointed that he wasn't serving while so many other marines were fighting in the Middle East. He was still vexed by the riddle of his career with the marines. Could he lead men in combat? Could he keep his head under fire? Had ten years of training and sacrifice in the marines amounted to anything, after all?

Hutchison spent the winter and spring working the bureaucracies of Recon Command and Quantico for assignment to Iraq, but he didn't really have to push that hard. By this time the insurgent stronghold of Fallujah was erupting, and there was fighting in Ramadi, Tikrit, and Samarra, too. Marine rifle platoons and specialized units from Lejeune and Pendleton were being called back to Iraq for a second time. It simply made no sense for the marines to keep a captain with Hutchison's experience and high performance reviews marking time in Billings, Montana. By July, Hutchison was aware that he could be deployed at any time.

While angling for an Iraq assignment for himself, Hutchison was involved in a quiet subterfuge regarding First Sergeant Barry Morgan.

Recon Command was aware of how well Hutchison and Morgan had worked together and wanted to assign the capable and experienced Morgan to Iraq as well. But Hutchison deliberately stalled on the paperwork for Morgan and intervened with command as much as he could. Morgan had a wife and child in Billings now, he had put in his combat time in the Persian Gulf War, and Hutchison was intent on protecting his first sergeant from dangerous duty in Iraq. Meanwhile, Morgan was working all the angles behind Hutchison's back, trying to get an assignment to Iraq.

They both knew what the other was up to, of course, but there's a silent protocol among marines about that. If Hutchison was trying to protect a beloved first sergeant from combat, Morgan would just have to maneuver for the assignment on his own.

Hutchison finally deployed for Iraq in early September 2004, and Morgan secured an assignment to a unit at Camp Pendleton that was also scheduled to leave for Iraq in early 2005. But when Hutchison left just after Labor Day and they said good-bye at the Billings airport, Morgan did not know yet about his orders for Iraq. He hated watching his California surfer-boy captain going off to war alone like that, and felt that he was letting Hutchison down. He wanted to be at Hutchison's side in Iraq and help protect him.

"Sir, goddamnit, this just isn't right," Morgan said, beginning to cry. "I should be going with you."

"Barry, this was out of my hands, you know that," Hutchison said.

"Bull," Morgan said. "I should be going with you, Kevin."

They embraced, and then Hutchison caught his plane out. All the way across the country to Lejeune, and then across the Atlantic to Germany, where he met his flight for Baghdad, Hutchison was preoccupied by his departure from Billings. He'd never seen Morgan emotionally ramped up like that.

In Iraq, Hutchison was sent directly to Fallujah and spent his first two months as an operations planner for the Battalion Reconnaissance and Operations Center, the marine command unit that managed the massive November assault against the insurgents in the rebellious city. He worked sixteen-hour days in a large command tent, helping to plan and then execute the Fallujah operation, sitting with his laptop computer at a long table manned by other reconnaissance officers. The marine camp outside the city was frequently attacked by the insurgents with rocket-propelled grenades and homemade bombs, but otherwise the conditions were good. His work and living areas were air-conditioned and the food was excellent.

Throughout the fall, Hutchison called home to California a few times, speaking with his mother and stepfather at their home in Rolling Hills. He was upbeat and sounded good, but there were long pauses on the line when they asked Hutchison specific questions about conditions in Iraq. He changed the subject a lot, urging his mother and stepfather to get out to their vacation place in Palm Desert to play a little golf and get away from the news broadcasts on television, so they could stop worrying about him so much.

"It's unusual for Kevin to be so reticent, because he's always been so expressive and had an opinion or crack about everything," his stepfather, Donovan Black, said. "I'm speculating here, but I think he wouldn't say much because he didn't want to lie to us and tell us that things weren't really bad."

Kevin's mother, Nancy Black, could sense something else. "I know Kevin and what he's thinking, even when he won't say it. He was itching to get out into the field and lead a real combat operation. But of course he would never tell me that, because I would just become even more fearful."

Then, in late November, the Blacks received a hurried call from Hutchison. He was leaving for the field. He had been assigned as company commander for a special marine unit that was conducting search-and-destroy missions against the insurgent groups, and Hutchison told them he would not be describing anything specific about his work. After that his phone calls dropped off. They assumed that he was either too busy to call, or didn't want to alarm them by calling and then refusing to discuss what was happening on his missions.

Then, on Christmas Day, Hutchison called home. When the phone rang, Hutchison's mother and two sisters were already crying. For Christmas presents, Nancy had given her daughters a picture of Kevin and his two sisters together in California, taken just before he deployed. Now they were all melting down because it was a beautiful Christmas Day in southern California, but Kevin wasn't there. He was fighting the insurgents in Iraq.

When the phone rang and they learned that it was Kevin, they all gulped down water and tried to swallow away their tears, so that Kevin wouldn't sense that they were crying. The phone connection was interrupted a few times, but Kevin called back. They all took turns on the phone with him.

When it was Nancy's turn to talk with her son, she knew that he wouldn't volunteer much information. She would have to phrase her questions so that he could only answer "yes" or "no."

"All right, Kevin, have you been on any missions yet?"

"Yes, Mom. About ten so far. Don't worry, please."

"Have you found any insurgents, Kevin?"

"Mom, stop worrying, please. But, yes. The mission was extremely successful."

Nancy realized that this probably meant lots of fighting, but at least now she knew.

"Okay, but look, Kevin, just one more thing," Hutchison's mother said. "I know that you are seeing terrible things but we're rooting for you, we love you, we think of you, and just be safe, okay?"

"Mom, yes," Hutchison said. "But stop worrying. You and Donovan should just go off somewhere and relax, okay?"

"Okay, Kevin, okay. We love you."

When they had all said good-bye and Kevin was finally off the line, they cried together. It was just awful, so anxious a moment, doing Christmas morning together with Kevin in such a distant place, in harm's way, in Iraq.

To Hutchison they must have seemed very far away too. The Bighorn country that he'd grown to love was just a memory now. The cliffs at Palos Verdes were a dream. He'd be home to see his family and those places again by April, the marines said, which probably meant that he'd really be back by July. But he was leading men in combat now. He was under fire almost every day. He had his answer now to the riddle of a marine's life.

ACKNOWLEDGMENTS

*A*lmost everyone I interviewed for this book had read my long article on Shane Childers, which appeared in the *Hartford Courant* in April 2003, and knew that I would be applying the same level of candor to this narrative. They were unstinting in their help all the same, and the portrait of Shane Childers, his family, and the U.S. Marines that emerged is more convincing and honest as a result. I am grateful for their assistance.

Joe and Judy Childers, as is evident from reading this book, were extremely generous with their time and indeed welcomed me into their ranch house during the funeral for Shane and on many visits thereafter. Joe Childers in particular spent hours with me, out in the barn or while shoeing horses, describing his romantic upbringing of Shane, his navy Seabee trips, and his son's visits back to Wyoming. I'm sure that the Childerses will disagree with a few of my conclusions, but almost all of them were openly discussed while I was preparing this book. I am particularly grateful for Judy Childers' hospitality and tolerance of my early waking times.

Sam and Cori Childers and Sandra and Richard Brown were

also unfailingly helpful and refreshingly blunt with their memories of Shane and their family life.

All of the West Virginia Childerses were open and warm, and I'll never forget my two days touring Smith Creek Hollow and the Huntington area with Jonna Walker. Mary Bias was generous and hospitable, and wise in her observations about Shane. Jessi and Jonna Walker were particularly perceptive about Shane's growth during his Citadel years, and I found myself wishing sometimes that I had cousins as supportive as these two. A number of other family members were quite helpful but preferred not to be quoted by name.

Family friends Robert Reagan and Bill Hendry, Robbin and Steve Whitten, and all the other marines quoted in the book also deserve my thanks. The Public Affairs Offices at Quantico, Camp Lejeune, and Camp Pendleton, and individual marines at the Billings, Montana, command were also universally helpful. Several marine friends and colleagues of Shane Childers who wished to remain anonymous also deserve my thanks.

Laura Richardson of the Miratsky-Easton funeral home in Powell, Wyoming, is every bit the warm and caring person described in my pages. Adi Arad was particularly insightful and a joy to meet. The residents and store owners of Powell were also extremely helpful. Professors Guy Toubiana and Christopher McRae and the administrative staff of The Citadel in Charleston, South Carolina, made my visit to that historic institution a treat. I was also fortunate to have interviewed Barbara Blatchley of Agnes Scott College in Georgia, a professor of psychology, whose insight into Shane Childers was brilliant and useful.

No one who has read *Shane Comes Home* can doubt my debt of gratitude to Captain Kevin Hutchison. Together we visited the bars and restaurants of Billings, argued decorating points in his house, and then hiked and toured Montana, sitting beside the Tongue River on the Northern Cheyenne Indian Reservation, endlessly debriefing the Childers CACO. These extensive interviews allowed the detailed descriptions of his thoughts and reflections as the narrative progressed. When writing about the modern military, too many journalists default to macho stereotypes and pat conclusions about the motivations of soldiers. In fact, officers of Hutchison's sensitivity and depth are quite common in all branches of the armed services today, and I was delighted through him to be able to provide a more subtle and honest portrait of the character type. Hutchison's mother and stepfather, Nancy and Donovan Black, were also wonderfully helpful.

First Sergeant Barry Morgan tolerates reporters in the same way that he tolerates college graduates and motor scooters–they're just something that the world came up with and that he has to endure. Nevertheless, he bluntly answered all of my questions. He is particularly knowledgeable about Marine Corps rules and regulations.

Writer Hampton Sides graciously allowed me to borrow details about Shane Childers' last hours in Iraq from his excellent article in the December 2003 issue of *Men's Journal*. A fuller version of the piece is included in Sides' latest collection of essays, *Americana: Dispatches from the New Frontier*. I would also like to thank my daughter Sara, who accompanied me on portions of my research trip to Montana and Wyoming, including a long trail ride with Joe Childers in his covered wagon. She is quite expert outdoors and a competent cook already, and she always kept our camp running on time while patiently listening to Joe's tales.

Brian Toolan, the editor of the *Hartford Courant*, is a provocative source of story concepts who fiercely protects the need for his writers to tell their stories in their own way. It was his idea that I travel to Wyoming to follow the drama of a family waiting for their son's body to return from Iraq, and he expertly followed up with advice on completing the piece. Managing editor Cliff Teutsch adroitly handled all of my problems on the road, and Jan Spiegel is great at handling details. Candy Araujo and Cathy Leroy always deserve special thanks. News editor Bernie Davidow has been very understanding as I worked to complete this book. All I can say about Barbara Roessner, who edited my final Shane Childers piece with her usual smarts and élan, is that every time I work with her I wish that I was born a girl.

Sloan Harris, my agent at ICM, puts up with me and persisted with a project long after other agents would have given up, and Katharine Cluverius is a joy to work with. Henry Ferris and Peter Hubbard at William Morrow/HarperCollins have been exceptionally cooperative and pleasant. I particularly appreciate Henry's rare blend of patience and sensibility with a manuscript, not to mention his vision of what this story could be. It's rare and quite rewarding to work with an editor with such a refined sense of narrative.

A number of family members and friends need to be thanked as well, because they both draw me out of my isolation and goad me on while I am obsessed with a project. They include all of the members of my family, but especially my perceptive and wise sister, McNamara Buck-Rome. Others who have been attentive during this time include Roger Linscott, Michael Moschen, Sue Geller, Michael Lee, Bill Carmean and Nancy Ross, Judy and Richard Davies, Geoff and Kathy Marchant, Will and Martha Agate, Danielle Mailer, Cathrine de Neergaard, William F. de Neergaard, Daniel Fetterman, Michelle Danoff, Cindy Kirk, Suzanne McAllister, Dorothy Cochrane and Caroline Sheen, George and Cindy Rousseau, and John and Suzanne Stephan and their insane Oshkosh flying group. Patty Wagstaff's insight and support has been particularly welcome.

Diane Blick and Rhonda Bezio of the Business Center of Litchfield keep me honest and running on time. Walt Dethier of the Berkshire Country Store is the world's most lovable redneck.

Words cannot convey how much I appreciate the love and patience of my wife, Amelia. My daughters, Sara and Charlotte, rescue me every day with their sarcasm gene.